FULLY CONNECTED

A Volume of Memoirs

by

Kenneth G. Greet

TO

MARY

The cover photograph was taken at the centenary meetings of the World Methodist Conference in Honolulu in 1981. Speakers were garlanded with flowers by the local Methodists.

© 1997 Methodist Publishing House

ISBN 1 85852 083 5

CONTENTS

Page

Kenneth Greet

PREFACE

The word 'connexion' is one which Methodists have made peculiarly their own. Every year at the Methodist Conference a simple ceremony is enacted involving the men and women who later on the same day are to be ordained by the laying on of hands as ministers in the church of Christ. Their names are called one by one and when they are all standing they are 'received into full connexion with the Conference'. This is done by a standing vote of the Conference: an indication that this is a moment of singular solemnity.

According to the rubric used for this ceremony reception into full connexion means that the ministers being received accept all the responsibilities and enjoy all the privileges attaching to their vocation. The details of these are not spelt out. The responsibilities are to some extent laid down in the church's rule book, though they are even more indicated in the training which precedes ordination and by the exercise of sanctified common sense when doing the job. The privileges are nowhere codified, the chief of them being allowed to minister.

This word 'connexion' has both an historical and a contemporary ring about it. In the 18th century, when John Wesley went up and down the land forming small religious societies they had to conform to the requirement that all such groups should meet 'in connexion' with a clergyman of the Church of England. So it came about that the church which grew out of the societies meeting 'in connexion with Mr Wesley' not only assumed the nickname 'Methodist' applied to his followers (originally in a somewhat derisory fashion because of his very methodical lifestyle) but also described itself as 'the Connexion'. It was a fair description of the form of government which ensured that all parts of the church were closely linked together.

Modern Methodists still refer to their church as 'the Connexion'. The term is a very meaningful one to me. In a ministry that has been rather more mobile than most, I have been given many opportunities of exploring the Connexion not just in Britain but also in the far-flung reaches of Wesley's world parish. My commitment to ecumenism and to the search for peace are extensions of that same search for connectedness.

Some scholars have suggested that the connexional form of church government and organisation is very close to that of the early church and it is certainly possible to draw parallels. But it is more than that. Paul

5

said that in Christ 'everything in heaven and on earth was created' and that 'all things are held together in him' (Colossians 1:16 and 17). In other words connexionalism is written into the very fabric of the universe which God has created. His creation reflects his own trinitarian image: diversity blended in a perfect unity. The Apostle foreshadows the exciting and essential insights of modern science so eloquently stated by the late Barbara Ward:

> Our links of blood and history, our sense of shared culture and achievement, our traditions, our faiths are all precious and enrich the world with the variety of scale and function required for every vital ecosystem. But we have lacked a wider rationale of unity. Our prophets have sought it. Our poets have dreamed of it. But it is only in our own day that astronomers, physicists, geologists, chemists, biologists, anthropologists, ethnologists and archaeologists have combined in a single witness of advanced science to tell us that, in every alphabet of our being, we do indeed belong to a single system, powered by a single energy, manifesting a fundamental unity under all its variations, depending for its survival on the balance and health of the total system.
>
> If this vision of unity – which is not a vision only but a hard and inescapable scientific fact – can become part of the common insight of all the inhabitants of Planet Earth, then we may find that beyond all our inevitable pluralisms, we can achieve just enough unity of purpose to build a human world.
>
> (*Only One Earth*, Barbara Ward and Rene Dubos,
> Pelican Books 1972, p.297.)

To encourage Methodists to be loyal to each other is to invite them to be faithful to their own rich tradition. To assist them to be in meaningful connexion with the other great religious traditions, Christian and non-Christian, and with the world we are called to serve, is a logical extension of the vital principle which has guided them from the start. Only so can they be loyal to John Wesley, that man of catholic spirit who said, 'I look upon the world as my parish', and more importantly to Jesus Christ, the world's Saviour, in whom all things are held together.

A lifetime exploring the connexion between so many things that God has joined together is the backcloth to the personal odyssey which follows. A merely formal account of the work of one who was appointed to rather too many official positions in the church might be about as entertaining as a trip to the Battersea Dogs' Home on a foggy day. So, although I have perforce to say something about committees and what went on in them, it is what happened on the way there, so to speak, that will, I hope, encourage any who take this book in hand to read on. And since what makes committees worthwhile is the sort of people who sit on them, I have included stories about many of those with whom I have worked. Whenever I have been tempted to wander up a side street I have made no attempt to resist the temptation. If this makes the narrative at points a little disjointed, well, that's how life is most of the time.

In the first part of my account events are set down in chronological order but in later chapters I abandon this approach and deal with particular subjects. Chapter Three refers to my time in the Christian Citizenship Department of the Methodist Church where we dealt with a variety of social, moral and international issues. Chapter Four describes my years as Secretary of the Methodist Conference and the events of my Presidential year. Chapter Five deals with ecumenical matters and Chapter Six with peace and war. In Chapter Seven I write about people and places. The final chapter deals with activities during the years quaintly described as retirement. This arrangement of material has necessitated a certain amount of retracing of steps.

I express my gratitude to Mr Brian Thornton of the Methodist Publishing House and to Mr David Ensor, former chairman of MPH, for their encouragement, to Mrs Susan Hibbins for her care in seeing the book through to print and to Mr Michael Taylor, the Editor of the *Methodist Recorder*, for allowing me to quote from articles written for that paper; and to my wife Mary, who is part of the story.

Kenneth G. Greet
March 1997

My parents, Walter and Renée Greet

Chapter One

BEFORE THE DOOR OPENED

My mother believed that her prayer had been answered. She asked God to bring the Great War to an end before her first-born entered the world. The armistice was signed on 11 November 1918 and I arrived six days later. What part the Almighty played in this happy arrangement of dates is a matter on which I prefer to remain agnostic. I am, however, glad to think that my birth was closely associated with the fervent prayers for peace which my parents offered daily during the long years when the nations were tearing one another apart. Their influence played an important part in planting the search for peace at the top of my life's agenda.

The home my parents made in Bristol was a modest establishment but a haven of peace and security. Monday was always washing day. A fire was lit under a built-in wash tub in the corner of what was called the scullery. When the clothes had boiled for an hour or so they were rinsed and wrung out in the hand-operated mangle – a huge machine with wooden rollers which later on, when I took up etching, I used as a printing press.

Both my father and mother were gentle souls. I never heard anything remotely resembling a quarrel between them. During the Great War father had served in the Royal Army Medical Corps. He refused on grounds of conscience to undertake combatant duties. When the war was over he joined the dental business run by two of his uncles. The elder of these owned one of the first motor cars to travel the streets of Bristol. It had a tiller instead of a steering wheel and rubber tyres filled with black treacle. At the sound of the horn my father had to rush out and open the garage door at the top of a slope so steep that the car could only complete the climb if it approached at speed. Father did the mechanical work in the dentistry business and I often visited him in his small laboratory where he was surrounded by plaster casts. Frequently he would grumble because one of the uncles had made a mess of the wax mould of a patient's mouth so that the resulting dentures proved to be a bad fit, necessitating, so to speak, a second bite at the cherry. My father was not treated very fairly by the senior members of the firm who prevented his taking the examinations to obtain a professional qualification. He was paid a poor wage. The fact that food was never in short supply in our home was due to good management, but paying for school books must have placed severe strains on the family exchequer.

At the rear of our home was a greenhouse which, during the summer months, was always full of colourful geraniums. On the doorpost nearby there was a series of pencil marks. Each year my father would invite my two brothers and me to stand in the doorway. He would place a flat board on our heads and mark our height, noting the name and date. He seemed to derive great satisfaction from this record of our annual growth in stature. Maybe it compensated for a bank balance that must have remained permanently stuck on a lower register.

I learned much from my father about the great events of the past for he was deeply interested in history. As a convinced feminist he had soaked up the record of the suffragette movement. He used to regale me with stories like the one about the public meeting held in the Colston Hall in Bristol, when the speaker was the Prime Minister, Henry Campbell-Bannerman. As soon as he rose to his feet there came the dreaded cry of 'Votes for Women!' An intrepid follower of Christabel Pankhurst had allowed herself to be lowered on the end of a rope into the bowels of the big concert organ and from this impregnable vantage point she was able to make use of one of the large bass pipes to magnify her voice. The meeting broke up in disorder and the fire brigade was summoned to remove the offender. She emerged dusty but triumphant. One more tiny victory had been secured in the long hard battle against male arrogance and intransigence. The eventual granting of the female franchise was to come as a strange anti-climax to a nation exhausted by the waste and horror of a savage war.

My father played the piano at the weekly Band of Hope meeting in the down-town Old King Street Methodist Church. This was an extraordinary affair. There were five hundred girls one week and five hundred boys the next. As soon as you entered the packed hall you were nearly knocked backwards by the smell of rank poverty, for the children were recruited from the slums of the city. The boys smelt worse than the girls because they brought 'stink bombs' − small glass phials of evil-smelling chemical which they hurled about the hall.

The main aim of these meetings was to instil in the children, many of whom came from homes wrecked by drunkenness, the virtues of temperance. The presiding genius was a Mr Richards, a man with an unusually red nose. Before the meeting started he would mount the platform, remove a white card from his pocket and slowly raise it until it was high above his head. As if by some inexplicable and potent magic the din would subside and there would be complete quiet. The best meeting of the year was the one at which father played Santa Claus and distributed a small bag of sweets to each child. I knew a few of these deprived youngsters who joined the church and grew up to be fine and responsible citizens. The Band of Hope Movement, of which for some years I was a Vice-President, is only a shadow of its former self, but it exercised a powerful influence in those earlier days.

Holy Week is full of fragrant memories. On Maundy Thursday we all went down to Portishead on the Bristol Channel where we stayed in a ramshackle bungalow. Across the Channel we could see the Welsh Hills. I did not then know that it was among those hills that I would spend some of the most enjoyable years of my early ministry.

In the evening of Good Friday we attended the Portishead Methodist Church to hear the choir sing Stainer's *Crucifixion*. Its closing chorus, 'All for Jesus', remains one of my favourite hymns. But my most vivid memories are of the evening service on Easter Day in the parish church of St Peter. The church was always packed. We sat near the open door from which we could see the spring flowers blooming among the old grave stones. The preacher was a diminutive Welshman. He climbed a flight of stairs and entered the pulpit through a hole in the wall – enough in itself to induce in a small boy a sense of dramatic expectation. When he began to preach the words poured from him in a limpid stream of inspiring eloquence. He made the Easter message live, the daffodils in the churchyard seemed to tremble as if nature, too, sensed the presence of the risen Lord, and when it was over there was a great silence.

Some years ago I was delighted to be asked to preach in St Peter's Church, and I referred to those Easter Day services. One or two of the oldest members of the congregation remembered the little Welsh preacher and came up to tell me how they, too, had been thrilled by his inspiring oratory.

One of the abiding memories of my mother was of a tea trolley laden with cakes. This would be pushed round to the local Methodist Church for a sale, usually in aid of overseas missions. From earliest days I was left in no doubt about the importance of converting the heathen. Each week I went the rounds of long-suffering members of the congregation collecting pennies in a little grey velvet bag and marking off the amounts in a small book. I was egged on by Mr Rich, the aptly-named missionary treasurer. He had a glass eye which gleamed with prophetic fervour. Each year he would announce the amount collected and cry triumphantly, 'It's up again!' My aim was to collect £5 in a single year, and when at length this ambition was achieved I was presented with a DSO medal on a ribbon. In the years since I have been in receipt of a number of gongs – to use the current jargon – from the Pope and sundry other persons of distinction, but none that compares in significance with that first award for hard labour on behalf of the missionary cause.

On several occasions we were asked to entertain for the weekend a visiting preacher who had served the church overseas. I found it disappointing, no doubt because my expectations were pitched unreasonably high. These men seemed on the whole to be rather dull fellows, often slow and hesitant of speech. My father charitably explained that 'after all those years speaking Swahili a man's English is bound to get a bit rusty'. However, on one occasion when my mother said, 'Now, my boy, next weekend we shall be entertaining a real live missionary', I replied irreverently, 'Well, that I suppose will be better than a real dead one.' The day was to come when I would visit some of the areas in which many of these courageous ambassadors for Christ had done their pioneer work. I stood once on the tomb of Mary Slessor in Calabar and surveyed the graves of those who died within weeks of landing on the West Coast of Africa. Most of them were young men and I recalled those dreadful lines:

> Take heed and beware of the Bight of Benin,
> For few come out though many go in.

I remembered also the solemn midnight candle-lit service held every year in Handsworth College to commemorate those from that community who had died on the mission field.

Nothing should be allowed to detract from the honour due to those who laboured so sacrificially and often gave their lives in the service of Christ overseas. If many of them displayed a paternalism which now would be unacceptable, we must remember that, like us, they were children of their time. Some of the theological emphases of their approach we may regard as equally outmoded. For example, my grandfather's brother, Uncle Will, was a freelance missionary who saw his task as that of 'plucking the heathen from the jaws of hell'. Our modern talk of 'inter-faith dialogue' would have sounded strange, even heretical, to his ears. But there can be no doubt about the quality of his devotion. Indeed it is part of the family legend that Uncle Will 'went native'. He adopted the dress of the Indian villagers among whom he lived in comparative poverty. I have seen photographs of this white-bearded prophet wearing garments made of bits of three-cornered cloth ('to symbolise the Trinity'). I like to think that he was a high churchman in disguise!

By way of contrast, another member of the family who spent most of his life abroad was my mother's brother, Hugh. He went to China and became the General Manager of the Shanghai Tramway Company. He came home every few years and regaled us with yarns about the mysterious Orient. He was very much a man of the world but the fact that he was regarded as slightly wicked was an asset as far as my brothers and I were concerned because it made a nice change from the very good people with whom we were constantly surrounded. When, a few years ago, I visited China I was delighted to find that the trams were still running along the streets of Shanghai.

In spite of financial stringency we were never denied our annual holiday. This was usually taken in Ilfracombe. We lodged in a rather shabby house where we were looked after by a lady of faded appearance called Mrs Williams. Her husband was skipper of a small ship which plied its trade along the Bristol Channel. I remember that one morning mother appeared pale and shaken. She had let the lid of the lavatory pan fall heavily on to this rather antiquated though essential piece of equipment, and it had broken in two as cleanly as a sliced apple. Mrs Williams took this small disaster in her stride. She kindly said that there had been a crack there for some time, no doubt as a result of her having entertained a variety of sitting tenants over the years.

My brothers and I rose early on holiday and ran to the top of Capstan Hill. From there we could see the back of Mrs Williams' house and mother would wave a tablecloth out of the window to show that we had been spotted. We enjoyed watching the fleet of Campbell's white-funnelled paddle-steamers entering and leaving the harbour. Another feature of the town was the splendidly arrayed town crier who appeared each day on the back of a white horse. Ringing his bell he would announce the day's attractions, concluding with a stentorian, 'God save the King.' He would then, not being a Band of Hope man, disappear into the nearest public house to whet his whistle before the next verbal assault on the populace.

Religion was not neglected during our holiday. On Sunday mornings we attended the service in the Wilder Road Methodist Church. Many children sat in the gallery and during the hymn before the sermon a kindly steward distributed a peppermint bullseye to each of us. By some miraculous dispensation these confections lasted exactly the length of the preacher's sermon. I have often thought of the aroma of peppermint as the best that Methodists can do in answer to the incense which flavours the atmosphere in some of our sister churches.

It will be apparent that I had the good fortune to be brought up in a staunchly Methodist home. Bristol is a city rich in Methodist history. In the centre stands John Wesley's Chapel, often referred to as 'The New Room'. It is the oldest Methodist preaching house in the world, and probably the most uncomfortable, with its plain wooden forms and entire lack of any decorative embellishments. But there is a wonderful atmosphere there and visitors come from all over the world to see the strange double-decker pulpit from which Wesley often preached, the rooms that were used as an almonry for the poor, a dispensary for the sick and a classroom for the education of poor children. Outside is the stable where the preacher tethered his horse and in the forecourt a fine equestrian statue of John Wesley. I often wandered round this building as a boy and recall the excitement with which I discovered a verse scratched on the landing window by one of Wesley's early followers:

On brittle glass I grave my name,
A follower of the Bleeding Lamb,
But Thou canst show a nobler art
And write Thy name upon my heart.

In later years I have preached on a number of occasions in this old Chapel. Particularly memorable was the great service to mark the 250th anniversary of the Wesleys' conversions. The warden, the Rev A. Raymond George, had asked me to finish preaching two minutes before 'a quarter before nine', the hour which Wesley records in his Journal as being the time when he 'felt (his) heart strangely warmed'. The arrangement was that immediately after my sermon this famous page from the diary would be read. Suddenly, however, as I finished preaching, a bearded fellow appeared from nowhere, entered the pulpit and began to read a diatribe against black immigrants. As soon as his purpose became clear the great congregation with one voice shouted, 'Shame!' Mr George signalled the organist and we rose to sing the last hymn. The intruder disappeared as quickly as he had come. I leaned across to Lord Tonypandy who had been presiding and said, 'When you give the closing prayer, will you invoke the Lord's blessing on black and white alike?' This he did in his mellifluous Welsh voice. The response of the congregation was a thunderous 'Amen.' So an ugly interruption was transformed into an act of witness of which, I think, John Wesley would have heartily approved.

Returning to the subject of religion at home, life revolved around Bishopston Methodist Church. Sunday was a day to which we looked forward. My parents and their three boys attended morning and evening services with unfailing regularity, and there was afternoon Sunday school arranged in several departments for the various age groups. Father played the piano for the Seniors.

For a period the attractiveness of church attendance was much enhanced by the presence in the gallery of a remarkably pretty girl. However, since she never seemed even to notice that I was there, nothing ever came of it. Among the boys whom I knew well was a lad called Max Ware. His home, like ours, was always open-house. He possessed an airgun and one of our favourite pastimes was shooting at old electric light bulbs which we lined up at the end of the garden. In spite of these 'military' exercises we both became pacifists and Max joined the merchant navy. He lost his life when his ship was torpedoed in mid-Atlantic, one among millions of examples of the tragic waste of war.

Early on I developed a nose for a good sermon and awarded points according to the competence of the preachers to whom we listened week by week. In those days the Methodist principle of itinerancy operated with relentless regularity and we welcomed a new minister every third year. From our family pew in the gallery we would wait with bated breath for the first glimpse of the New Man (note the capitals). If he had a large head my expectations mounted because I suffered from the quaint delusion that a big cranium signified a superior brain. My physiological understanding may have been defective but I have never deviated from the view that preaching must satisfy the mind as well as the heart.

Sometimes I was taken to the Horfield Baptist Church further up the Gloucester Road. This church had maintained a great preaching tradition. I remember the sermons of Guy Ramsey and Ithel Jones who, in the language of that day, were 'pulpit giants'. One of those Baptist preachers was a Welshman with a golden tongue. He suddenly disappeared. When I asked my parents what had happened they looked embarrassed but then they told me the truth. He had gone every week to London 'to attend a committee'. But there was no committee, only another woman. So he had to leave the ministry and his marriage was broken. I was shocked. I have come to a more compassionate understanding of the sexual temptations and failures which have toppled many a preacher from the throne of public esteem. It remains a great tragedy, however, when those who are the public face of the church, and who are trusted by many, betray that trust.

We welcomed to the Bishopston pulpit many of the great Methodist preachers of the day. I remember Dr F. Luke Wiseman whose face looked as if it were chiselled from fine marble and who rarely preached for less than fifty minutes, holding his congregation enthralled from first to last. The church anniversary was usually conducted by the Rev Charles Ensor Walters who worked for many years in the East End of London. He had the appearance of an ecclesiastical bulldog. On the Monday evening he lectured on his work. It was more or less the same lecture every year, but none the worse for that. At a certain point he would tell a particularly pathetic story and wipe away a tear. I used to station myself near the front and wait for that tear. If it failed to appear, I was distinctly disappointed! Another dramatic preacher was Dr Leslie F. Church. He had a way of whipping off his spectacles when about to emphasise some important point. On one occasion, having recounted the brave action of a lad who had risked his life to save a fellow, he thundered, 'He needn't have done it.' This remains a catch-phrase in our family to this day.

As a preacher who has poured out millions of words over the years I have often reflected on the fact that most of what we preachers say is promptly forgotten. Not all, however, and the phrases that stick can often be amazingly influential. I also believe that the steady stream of rhetoric digs channels in the minds of the hearers along which the grace of God can flow long after the precise content of our sermons has disappeared from the archives of memory.

Two people whose religious influence upon me was negative rather than positive were Aunt Hettie and Mr Royce. Both were members of the Strict Plymouth Brethren Movement. Aunt Hettie dressed in black from head to toe. Whenever she visited the family home my parents tried to keep her off the subject of religion. She never left, however, without warning us to 'keep well clear of the Roman Catholics'. My suspicion of our Roman friends was further increased by the fact that one of the uncles in the dentistry business was a member of that church. He was the one who extracted my teeth and so I was prejudiced against him and his religion. Happily, those youthful impediments to ecumenical benevolence soon evaporated. As I shall say later on, the week I spent in the Vatican in 1983 at the invitation of the Pope was profoundly rewarding and enjoyable. I hope that in heaven Aunt Hettie was not too disturbed.

Mr Royce ran a weekly Bible class which I was persuaded to join. He was a good man but I found his constant exhortation to us to get converted somewhat oppressive. He was deeply anxious to save us from hell and kept telling us that a great change would come over us and that we would 'know when it happens'. Paul on the Damascus road was his favourite illustration. No such shattering experience ever came to me and for a time this worried me greatly. But I recollect a Sunday morning sermon preached by a student from a nearby college. I do not recall his name nor much of what he said, but as he described the assurance God gives to those who seek I found that he was confirming my own faith in Christ as Saviour. The false anxiety induced by the well-intentioned leader of the Bible class vanished.

I shall refer a little later to my first ministerial appointment and the experience of dealing with the kind of fundamentalism that insists on biblical inerrancy and seeks to put every individual into a religious strait-jacket. I believe that fundamentalism, whether of the Christian kind or of any other religious sort, is both false and dangerous. I am grateful for those early experiences, painful though they were, which enabled me to confront and reject it. Many of its tenets fly in the face of reason and unless a belief is held to be reasonable there is no reason why it should be held.

As I rummage around among the memories of my early years I keep resurrecting recollections of a procession of characters who are well worth remembering. There was the piper who paraded down the road from time-to-time, dressed in a shabby kilt. My mother, who was of Scottish descent, could never resist the sound of the bagpipes, and, though this particular performer had, I imagine, never been further north than Birmingham, she would rush out and give him a sixpence she could ill afford. She did once confide in me that she doubted the wisdom of this charity since the man smelt of drink. (My parents were convinced total-abstainers, a position which I myself was glad to adopt and have seen no sensible reason to abandon.)

Among the other characters whom I recall with pleasure is Miss Cross, a Yorkshire lady who called each week to take the grocery order. She would sit, pencil in hand, prompting my mother about the items needed to replenish the larder, with a lot of inconsequential chatter in between. Later in the day a boy with a bicycle would deliver the order. Supermarkets were still a thing of the future.

Another choice character was the doctor, Harvey by name. Dressed in black and grave of countenance, he might well have been mistaken for an undertaker. But his visits were always life-enhancing for he exuded an air of calm authority which was of more value than a bottle of tonic. I am, of course, recalling a time well before the birth of the National Health Service. I do not recall that we ever had to hang around in the surgery waiting-room. The doctor always came promptly when summoned. I have the distinct impression that, realising that funds were low, Dr Harvey often forgot to send in his bill. He superintended the birth of my two brothers, Brian and Laurence. I accepted their arrival with a remarkable lack of curiosity as to where they had come from. I received no sex education either at home or at school, though the three 'R's of reticence, reverence and respect were observed in the whole approach to the relationships of men and women. Later on, when teenage curiosity was fully aroused, I read widely on the subject. I came to a very critical judgement about many aspects of the Christian sexual tradition and this was to inform a great deal of my writing and speaking in later years.

Brian

Laurie

The two brothers to whom I have referred – always good companions – went on to achieve great things. Brian, with a brilliant academic record, became a Methodist minister and was elected to the chair of the Nottingham and Derby District of the church. Laurence became the head of the history department in a large school in Bristol, much loved by generations of students. His failing health in recent years has been a great grief to the whole family.

For a time my maternal grandmother, affectionately known as 'Bessy', lived under our roof. She had a voracious appetite for paperback novels, some of which had lurid covers. If I occasionally picked up one of these and pretended to disapprove, she would say, 'It's all right, my boy, there's a minister in the story.' Often I would catch her turning to the final page, 'just to make sure everything turns out all right in the end', she would say.

My paternal grandparents were a remarkable couple. Grandpa had lost two fingers of his right hand in an accident with a circular saw. He was the proud possessor of a Dursley Peterson bicycle, the saddle of which was woven out of thick cord and was slung like a miniature hammock between the front and rear of the machine. For many years in retirement he pottered about in his garden shed. He was frequently visited by a man who wore shoulder-length hair and was known as 'the inventor'. With grandfather's help he was busy perfecting a small tool to assist brain surgeons to open up the skulls of their patients. Grandpa's firework party on the 5th November was one of the highlights of the year. The whole family gathered, vying as to who could bring the largest rockets. A life-size Guy was strung up over a mammoth bonfire.

Grandma's Christmas party was the only occasion in the year when we ate chicken. This luxury, oddly, was accompanied by horseradish sauce. The radish was grown in the garden and was so hot that it made your eyes water. A highlight of the party was a singsong round the piano, when the old lady was always persuaded to sing a couple of items. 'Smiling Through' was a favourite of hers and during the performance of this sugary offering she would wipe away a tear. She was a great believer in the value of herbal medicines, and in this regard, as in others, was a true follower of John Wesley. She knew a Mrs Webber who used to wander the countryside in search of therapeutic herbs and who hit upon the brilliant idea of incorporating them in slabs of pleasant-tasting jelly. Mrs Webber's jellies became quite famous and Grandma would treat me to generous helpings. Whether they ever had the slightest effect on my health I am unable to say.

Grandma's brother, Fred Gould, became Labour Member of Parliament for the Frome Division. I recall a great sermon that he preached in the Old King Street Methodist Church. He spoke about the League of Nations and appealed to the large congregation to pledge their support. Several hundred people rose to their feet in response. One of his sons, Ronald, became the much-respected General Secretary of the National Union of Teachers and was knighted by the Queen.

Caleb Palmer was one about whom Charles Dickens would have written many an entertaining page. He was a man of ample girth who always seemed to be in danger of bursting the buttons on his coat and trousers. He had a walrus moustache and spectacles perched at a precarious angle on the end of his nose. Mr Palmer played the harmonium at a little Methodist Chapel attended by my paternal grandmother. She once persuaded me to sing a solo in the service. I chose the hymn, 'I met the Good Shepherd just now on the plain.' And a very painful meeting it turned out to be. The tune selected was full of strange sharps and flats and my performance was excruciating. It was not improved by Mr Palmer. He pedalled away with great gusto and indulged his peculiar habit of bringing down his two hands, as big as joints of ham, on all the keys at once, to mark the end of each verse. This produced a noise like a caged lion in pain.

Caleb Palmer had a son called Percy and thereby hangs a tale, two tales in fact, one of them very mysterious. Percy was the proud possessor of an airgun which discharged small arrows. One day when his father was bending down to feed the chickens in the garden, thus exposing an expansive target, temptation overcame Percy and he let fly with his gun. The small arrow brought the old man to his feet with a shriek that could be heard three streets away.

When Percy was a young man he became a dear friend of my father who invited him to be the best man at his wedding. Percy's wedding gift to my father was a set of hair brushes in an oval-shaped leather case secured by a substantial strap. Not long afterwards my father was puzzled to discover on rising one morning that the thick strap had been cut in two as if with a razor. Neither he nor my mother could offer any explanation. A few minutes after this disturbing discovery a message arrived to say that Percy had died suddenly and unexpectedly during the night. The mystery was never solved.

My first school was the Sefton Park Elementary School. The headmaster, Charles H. Cooper, was a very large man with squeaky boots. These could be heard at a considerable distance and provided a helpful warning of his approach. One of my teachers was a Dickensian character called Joey Clark. He wore pince-nez spectacles attached to a black cord and he sucked peppermint bullseyes all day long. At the sound of the squeaky boots he would hurry to the open window and send the latest peppermint spinning across the playground.

In my daily journeys to school I walked hand-in-hand with a little girl who lived a few doors away. Her name was Margaret and she had a wonderful head of curly hair. One day our two mothers were observed in deep conversation. As a result of this conclave we were informed that it was no longer proper for us to hold hands. This was the first occasion on which I realised that there was some subtle and faintly exciting difference between boys and girls! Holding hands clandestinely suddenly became much more satisfying than doing so openly.

At one stage my life was made a misery by a small gang of juvenile thugs whose chief enjoyment was in bullying others. My route home went past a rubbish tip. Someone had left there a large wire cage in which, of course, I was incarcerated by these delinquents. I have ever since taken a dim view of bullies, dictators and all other agencies of repression in which our world abounds.

Very early on I formed the judgement that the best teachers are those who have the gift of encouraging their pupils. I recall with gratitude some of those who taught me when, having won a scholarship, I moved on to Cotham Grammar School. This school, formerly the Merchant Venturers' Technical college, had a great tradition. Its coat of arms showed a vessel entering Bristol harbour. The School motto was 'mens bona regnum possidet' ('the cultured mind stands possessed of a kingdom'). The headmaster, T. V. T. Baxter, ruled with a rod of iron; fear rather than love was his guiding principle. Mr Skeens, the art master, looked the perfect model for the cartoonist, with his curly hair, bow-tie and trousers several inches too short. He was a man of great kindness and gave me a love of things beautiful and a desire to use my hands creatively which I have never lost.

Mr Phillips ('Flop' because of the lock of hair that fell over his forehead) was another choice character. Some years ago I went to preach at a little chapel in the Cotswolds. On the Saturday evening my host told me that the chapel had been on the verge of closing when a remarkable man had come to spend his retirement in the village. He had devoted himself to the chapel and now it was a thriving community. I was delighted to discover the next morning that this was none other than 'Flop' Phillips. He invited me to tea in his large stone house surrounded by a beautiful garden. On the iron gate was a notice: 'Children are welcome to play at all times, except on Sunday when we like to rest.'

I suppose that the chief value of this early education was the desire it gave me to learn more and to read widely. It certainly revealed the vast extent of my ignorance. My achievements on the sports field were unimpressive. I did receive a certificate for coming third in the long jump, but that was in the year when there were only three entrants in that event. I also performed rather well in the cross-country race, displaying just the kind of stamina which a Methodist minister needs.

I became a voracious reader and by my middle teens had read all the works of Charles Dickens. While I was at Cotham School I underwent what I suppose could be called a literary conversion. While studying the works of Charles Lamb, the gentle Elia, I realised that one could paint pictures with words. In all the years since I have been struggling to master that art. It is disappointing to find that in these days of greatly enhanced educational opportunity so many people can neither speak nor write English well. I find it difficult to forgive the pop singers for their execrable murdering of the language. Of course, in my school days there was no television to deflect people from reading. The cinema was visited only rarely, though I do remember the first 'talkie' film I saw. It was about a mad dentist who chased his patient and eventually had him swinging from a chandelier while he extracted his teeth. The agonised screams of that patient frightened the life out of me.

As the time approached to leave school the question of a career had to be discussed. Although I had achieved very good results in the matriculation examinations, as they were then described, there was never any suggestion that I should go on to university. The financial situation of the family was too finely balanced for that to be a feasible option. Since I had no very clear idea of what I wanted to do with my life my father went to see a pleasant young man who worked as a clerk in the electricity offices of the Bristol Corporation. He saw his boss and I was granted an interview. Subsequently I was offered a job at a starting salary of £1.50 a week (it was later increased to £3). I was set to work alongside a senior colleague called Bob Weare, a kindly fellow who was always trotting along to the boss to complain that we were underpaid. So we were. In fact it was almost slave labour. Our job was to answer the telephone to customers with a complaint. To use a New Testament phrase, their number was legion. The telephone rang ceaselessly. We had to establish the nature of the trouble and issue instructions to the workmen. One incidental advantage of this was that I picked up a great deal of practical knowledge. Electricity holds no dread for me and I can wire a plug with the rest.

The complaints with which we dealt ranged from the serious to the ludicrous. It might be some huge factory where the power had suddenly failed and five hundred workers were standing idle. Or it might be a purely imaginary fault like the complaint regularly brought to the counter by an extraordinary character. He wore shorts, summer and winter, a green jacket and a trilby hat. He would ring the bell on the counter, and remove his hat with a courtly bow. A piece of rubber tyre always fell from the inside of his hat. He kept it there, he solemnly informed us, to prevent his head from being damaged by the shocks from our cables under the pavement. These shocks were evidently very real to him. I used to thank him for his kindness in informing us and say that we would look into the matter. He always departed with expressions of profound gratitude only to reappear a few weeks later to intimate that though our efforts had been successful for a time the trouble was now recurring.

During my short career as an office worker I entered a public speaking contest arranged by the Electricity Department. The competitors were required to make a speech lasting ten minutes on 'The psychological importance of colour in lighting'. I won hands down and was awarded a prize of £5 – almost the equivalent of a month's salary. This significantly increased both my bank balance and my stock among my colleagues. They were on the whole a pleasant bunch of men and women, except at the time of the Christmas party, an occasion which I detested because some of them got drunk and forgot how to behave.

I had already had some experience of public speaking as the convener of one of the committees of the flourishing Wesley Guild at Bishopston Methodist Church. This excellent movement provided a very varied programme of weekly meetings, and on one occasion we had an evening of 'stump speeches'. Those participating had to draw a subject out of a hat and speak 'off the cuff' for three minutes. I recall that my subject was 'Belisha beacons'. Pedestrian crossings had just been introduced by the Secretary of State for Transport, Mr Hore Belisha. I did not then know that years later I should be knocked down by a car on one of these crossings and nearly killed. I felt very nervous as I rose to speak and indeed have never overcome the tense feeling that precedes a public utterance. I do not regret this. I suspect that some of the dullest speakers one ever has to endure are those in whose veins the adrenalin never flows.

Encouraged by these early attempts at public speaking I decided to make a recording of my voice. My curiosity had been excited by an advertisement in the press which said that a shop in the city would make a ten minute gramophone record for seven shillings and sixpence. I saved hard and prepared a careful script. It began, for some reason or other, with the words, 'In some ways the Bible is the saddest book in the world.' I went to the shop – a dimly-lit emporium in an old-fashioned arcade. I was conducted to an inner room and invited to sit in front of a microphone the size of a meat-safe. I delivered my speech at breakneck speed in order to get as much as possible for my money, and went home with the record under my arm. We played it on an ancient gramophone. I was extremely disappointed. I had thought that I sounded like a cross between George Arliss (a popular film star of the day) and Donald Soper (who was making his mark as an open air orator). But I sounded like a West Country waif with a sore throat.

It was, I suppose, almost inevitable that I should begin to entertain the idea of becoming a preacher. Many of my boyhood heroes were preachers, and whilst the experiences of later years have led me to a rather more realistic assessment of those who respond to this holy calling, I still believe that there is no greater privilege than that of preaching the gospel. I conducted my first service on my seventeenth birthday under the tutelage of an elderly lay preacher called Eustace Keevill, who was blind. When I came to read the Old Testament lesson I was embarrassed to discover that in the large pulpit Bible the chapters were numbered in Roman figures. I did not know how to locate Psalm 128 and so had to appeal to my blind friend to help me out. I made sure that I was never trapped in that way again.

I now began to take services in the country chapels around Bristol. Often a carload of lay preachers would set off early on a Sunday morning and we would be dropped off one by one as we proceeded from village to village. Some of the elderly lay preachers (in the Methodist Church called local preachers as distinct from the ordained members of the itinerant ministry) were quaint characters. There was one with a voice like a rasp who used to say to me as he left the car, 'Well, my boy, may you have souls for your hire', an exhortation the precise meaning of which escaped me.

My favourite village was Aust where I was always entertained by a delightful old couple named Spratt. After a magnificent Sunday lunch they would sit by a roaring fire, and Mr Spratt would light his clay pipe with a taper. After a short while they would both fall asleep and I would go off to the quiet of the old parish church to read through my evening sermon. The congregation was always very appreciative though I am sure that some of my early homiletical efforts left much to be desired.

Many of these Sunday preaching excursions were to a group of small country chapels maintained by layfolk of somewhat independent outlook. They took a rather cavalier view of Methodist discipline and displayed a distinctly anti-clerical view of the ordained ministry. Since, however, the local preachers upon whom they relied came from loyal Methodist circuits in Bristol (a circuit is a group of churches) staffed by ordained ministers who supervised their training, they were really trying to have their cake and eat it.

Three of us were prepared for the local preachers' examinations by an elderly lay preacher called Leonard Snook. He was a choice spirit and a competent biblical scholar. He was, however, accident-prone; on one occasion he fell off the back of the horse and trap that was carrying him to his appointment. He once took us to a country chapel to demonstrate how preaching should be done. He was short of stature and a thoughtful steward had placed an orange box in the pulpit so that our little friend could be both seen and heard. Unfortunately, after announcing his text, he stepped backwards and rolled down the pulpit steps. It was not a good sermon.

My two companions in training were John Stacey and George Lockett. When later we were accepted for ministerial training we entered Handsworth College, Birmingham. We formed a 'firm' called 'The West Country Clods'. Mr Snook was very proud of the fact that he had helped to train three ministers. He would have been astonished to know that John Stacey would become the Secretary of the Local Preachers' Department of the Methodist Church. John has one of the acutest minds of any minister of his generation and during his long tenure of office made a significant contribution to the training of the church's lay preachers. On one occasion at Handsworth College when I was umpiring a cricket match I gave him out, caught behind wicket, a verdict which he has always maintained was grossly unfair since he never touched the ball. It only goes to show that even great theologians are not infallible. Our dear friend George Lockett, one of God's saints, died of overwork in his middle years.

The head church in our circuit was in Old King Street, to which I have already referred. Every Sunday afternoon a group of men and women met for fellowship under the leadership of Martin Edbrooke, a man who loved the Methodist Church and was a devoted Christian. He invited me to address the group. My eye was caught by his daughter, Mary, who played the piano. She was a remarkably attractive girl who, astonishingly, appeared to have no close boyfriend. That afternoon she acquired one and there began a lifetime of partnership and a relationship of love and loyalty the value of which is beyond human reckoning.

Shortly after this I was faced with a decision that was to change both our lives dramatically. The small details I have gathered together in this opening chapter paint a picture of a fairly unremarkable beginning to what promised to be a very ordinary life. Nothing in the events and experiences I have described furnished any indication of the kind of future that lay ahead: the journeys that would take us to the ends of the earth, the fascinating encounters with all sorts of people, famous and unknown, and the opportunities to share with the leadership of the British churches in thinking about many of the crucial issues which have filled the headlines during the second half of this tumultuous twentieth century. I shall always be grateful for those early years of preparation, and the for gracious influences that surrounded me before the door opened upon the lifelong vocation which the following chapters describe.

Chapter Two

THE BRIGHT SUCCESSION

When my call-up papers arrived in 1939 I registered as a conscientious objector. I made it clear that I would on no account allow myself to be conscripted into the armed forces and was quite willing to go to prison rather than do so. The reasons for this stand I shall elaborate in Chapter Six. In the event I was granted exemption from military service.

It was about this time that my minister, the Rev W. Siberton Baker, asked me if I would consider becoming a candidate for the ministry. He gave me what at that time I thought to be strange advice, though I later recognised its wisdom. He said, 'Don't come in if you can stay out.' I promised to think and pray about it. One strong deterrent was the fact that after acceptance the Methodist Church required a minister-in-training to serve for seven years before ordination, and marriage during that probationary period was forbidden. Mary and I were deeply in love and I put the position to her. She replied, 'If that is how it has to be, I will wait.' I still marvel at that response.

For two young people eager to be married a wait of nearly ten years, as it was all told, seemed an eternity. The church was wrong to require it. The constant need to keep love-making within carefully marked boundaries over a long period was unnatural and a strain upon both of us. Another couple in the same position as we were failed to do so and when it was discovered that the girl was pregnant the fellow was promptly dismissed as a potential minister.

During the sixth year of probation, by which time I was in college, John Stacey, George Lockett and I got up a petition asking for permission to marry a year early. We obtained the signatures of about two hundred ministers and spent a few pounds that we could ill-afford on a trip to London. We arrived at 1, Central Buildings, the Westminster Headquarters of the Methodist Church, with the modest petition in our pocket. We were received by the head of the Ministerial Training Department, Dr Sydney Diamond, a saintly soul with an aristocratic stoop and silver hair. He welcomed us warmly and rang for a cup of tea. Then, to our dismay, he suggested that we should pray about our problem. We knelt around his desk and Dr Diamond informed the Lord that he had great sympathy with these young men but that, of course, rules were rules and there was no hope of their being changed. We came away with the petition still in our pocket. If ever an army was defeated without a shot being fired, this was surely a case in point.

The health of any church which employs married ministers depends to a considerable degree on the health of those marriages. Methodism owes an enormous debt to wives who identify themselves with the ministry of their husbands as so many do even when, as is the case with increasing numbers, they follow professional careers of their own. A broken marriage can often mean a broken ministry. When I attended the Methodist Conference for the first time as a representative in 1948 I made my maiden speech to that Assembly. I asked that, as the President always left the Conference for a short time to address the ordinands prior to their ordination, he should also address their wives or fiancées separately. This was accepted, Dr Benson Perkins giving a gruff murmur of approval from the chair, and this happy custom continues to this day.

To return, however, to the question put to me by Mr Baker. I was filled with anxiety and uncertainty. Would I be up to the job? Did I really want to do it? Was it fair to the girl I hoped to marry? Above all, was this what God wanted me to do? Eventually I wrote a letter asking that I be accepted as a candidate. I remember the very postbox by which I stood for what seemed an eternity before plucking up the courage to push the letter through the slot. So often in life I have found that certainty comes later rather than earlier.

A candidate for the ministry had to pass a number of examinations and preach several trial sermons. Mary's father was one of the lay examiners when I preached at a special service at the Bishopston Church. He was a great encourager. Not long ago I delved into the Methodist archives and discovered that I was awarded a 'one' – the highest mark – for the sermon. Candidates also had to submit to oral examination at the District Synod and eventually at the 'July Committee' which consisted of 'connexional' representatives and some closely concerned with the training of the ministry.

In order to begin the process of candidature one had to be recommended by the local Circuit Quarterly Meeting. The voting here was not unanimous. Several members who took strong exception to my views on war voted against me. However, I was duly accepted as a candidate for training. Because of the war all six of Methodism's theological colleges had closed for the duration. I therefore wrote to the headquarters of the church asking if I could be stationed somewhere as a pre-collegiate probationer. I was told that I should be sent to Lowestoft, but at the last minute this arrangement was changed. Alas, the young man who went there instead of me was killed by a flying bomb. I was stationed in the Cwm and Kingstone Circuit with the status of a lay pastor. The Order of Lay Pastors was later abolished because the men so appointed were required to undertake virtually the same work as that done by ordained ministers at about half their rate of pay. This was rightly felt to be scandalous.

My initial difficulty was to find the Cwm and Kingstone Circuit on the map. It turned out to be a group of twenty small chapels covering a swathe of country in the shadow of the Black Mountains. I arrived at Hereford railway station with a heavy case. I said to the ticket collector, 'I have to go to Shenmore.' 'Good God,' he replied, 'whatever for?' It sounded a less than promising beginning. I explained that I was the newly-appointed Methodist minister for that part of the world. 'Well, sir,' he replied, 'you've got a problem. The buses only run out there twice a week and there's no public transport today.' Then he added, 'I tell you what. The Mayor of Hereford is a Methodist; why not go and see him?' Off I went to see the Mayor, Alderman Monkley, who lent me his bicycle. I've always been glad to recall that I began my ministry on the mayoral bike.

After cycling some twelve miles with my case in one hand I arrived rather the worse for wear in the tiny hamlet called Shenmore. Lodgings had been obtained for me in 'New House', where my landlady was Mrs Violet Morgan. The necessity to take in a paying guest had been forced upon her by the fact that her family expanded regularly by one each year. She was obviously a little nervous. She showed me into my room and closed the door.

Suddenly I was overcome by a terrible sense of loneliness. Then I remembered my mother's advice which was to put my books and sundry photographs on the shelves to make me feel at home. Unfortunately, however, there were no shelves. I therefore sallied forth in search of the local undertaker, figuring that he would be able to supply some lengths of timber. He was very helpful and with the planks that he supplied and some wooden missionary collecting boxes left by my predecessor I contrived a set of shelves.

Living conditions in this part of rural England were fairly primitive. The lavatory was a hole in the ground covered by a wooden shed at the bottom of the garden. The pump in the yard dried up in the summer so each day I walked a quarter-of-a-mile to a well where I filled a bucket with water. Mr Morgan kept a couple of pigs, and I was asked to assist at the slaughter of one of these animals. It was a gruesome experience. The poor creature was tied to a bench, its throat was slit, and its expiring squeals were heard all over the village. The carcass was then put on a pile of straw which was set alight. It was then scrubbed and came up clean and white, ready to be cured. At the end of this fearsome drama I retired to my room pale and shaken.

Mrs Morgan proved a gem of a landlady. She served three good meals a day and her husband lit the fire each morning in the winter. I paid her £1.50 a week, precisely half my stipend. While I was there a fourth child was born – one of the most beautiful babies I have ever seen. Alas, after a few weeks the little mite fell ill and died. It was my first acquaintance with death. I was deeply moved and, though I had never done so before, wore a clerical collar when I took the funeral, a tiny gesture of respect for the sorrowing parents.

Not long afterwards there was a second tragedy. At Ploughfield, one of my village causes, there was a young girl called Molly Williams, who was vivacious and lovely to look at. She went swimming in the nearby River Wye. A freak current swept her away and she was drowned, and the whole village was plunged into deep sorrow. This time I did not feel that I could face the funeral alone. I telephoned my Superintendent Minister, the Rev Ernest D. Martin. He said, 'I will come over and we will share it together.'

Mr Martin was a father-in-God to me. He lived twelve miles away and we had twenty chapels to care for between us. Each Monday morning I cycled two miles to the nearest telephone box and we held our 'staff meeting' over the phone. Often he would ask me to accompany him to one of the chapels where he was due to give a 'lantern lecture'. The lantern was powered by acetylene gas. I was in imminent danger of being either poisoned or blown up by the capricious machine. Mr Martin's favourite lecture was entitled 'China, my China'. It was very good. After I had heard it the third time I asked him how many years he had spent in China. With a dry chuckle he replied, 'My dear boy, I've never been nearer China than the Isle of Wight, but I've read the books. Perhaps one day you will go to China.' Though it seemed an unlikely suggestion at the time I shall later recount how that prophecy came true.

Mr Martin was a fine preacher but, like many a saint, somewhat absent-minded. His study was a monument to untidiness and when we met to make the quarterly preaching plan the operation took all day. Mrs Martin provided lunch, usually late. She wore a box of matches on a string round her neck because otherwise she could never find them. This unusual couple dabbled in psychic research. They produced photographs of alleged supernatural appearances and one day gave me a demonstration of a seance. I found it all quite unconvincing.

My appointment to this country circuit came as a considerable cultural shock. It was also, so far as theology was concerned, a baptism of fire. I encountered a rigid fundamentalism which was fiercely hostile to any view other than its own. When I had been touring the circuit for a couple of months I decided that my people were rather behind the times. With youthful zeal I wrote to the lay preachers – on whom we heavily relied to fill the pulpits on Sundays – and invited them to a series of weekly talks in my lodgings. I can see them now, a dozen hoary-headed prophets gathered in the light of my oil lamp. My first talk was entitled *A Modern View of the Bible*. It was also my last. I had read an excellent little book with that title written by the great American preacher, Harry Emerson Fosdick. I gave it to them neat. When I had finished there was a long silence. I felt that I must have made a big impression on my audience. Then one of them rose and said, 'Brethren, I fear that this young pastor is not a man of God. It is clear that he does not believe in the Bible cover-to-cover.' At which they all rose to their feet and walked out into the night.

A week or so later I received a peremptory note from a farmer who wished to see me. On arrival I found him standing with his back to a roaring log fire. 'Young man,' he said, 'we do want to ask ye a question. Dost thee believe that hell be like the fire burning in our grate and that sinners do burn in it forever?' 'Certainly not,' I replied. Turning to his wife the farmer said, 'There you are, I told 'ee so: this young man be an heretic.' They informed me that they would not attend Cagebrook Chapel as long as I was the minister there. This was a blow since there were only six in the congregation. The others were named Mrs Mole, Mrs Grubb and Mr and Miss Lamb. I wrote home to say, 'The ark of the Lord is afloat, but only just.'

A young man called Gilbert Walker came to ask if I would train him for the Local Preachers' examinations. He lived in a remote farmstead and once a year he travelled to Hereford to buy Christmas presents. His knowledge of the world, therefore, was rather restricted. I arranged for him to visit me once a week and started him off on one of the prescribed textbooks: Ryder Smith's *What is the Old Testament?* On his second visit Gilbert appeared to be very perturbed. He said, 'This Ryder Smith is a terrible man; he does not believe in the Bible cover-to-cover.' I tried to explain that the Bible only makes sense if we are able to trace the progress of the Hebrew people from primitive to more advanced understandings culminating in the revelation of God in Jesus Christ. 'But,' said my struggling student, 'if we question any word in the Bible, how can we be sure of all the rest?'

Looking back I realise that my pre-collegiate days in Herefordshire were very good for me. My theological perceptions were sharpened and my understanding of the authority of the Bible hammered out on the anvil of experience. Later on I discovered C. H. Dodd's magnificent book *The Authority of the Bible* which confirmed much of what I had already learned. But the going was hard. The unyielding dogmatism I encountered was, I came to feel, a protective shield against truths which are liberating but can be disturbing.

This narrowness of outlook sometimes bordered on the ludicrous. My little church in Madley was one of the livelier ones. Every Thursday evening a Bible class was held for airmen from a nearby RAF camp. It seemed to me that it would be good for them to have some sort of a social evening once a month. The idea was greeted with a degree of disapproval by the stewards but it was discussed at a Leaders' Meeting. The decision was that once a month there should be a spelling bee – not exactly the most exciting form of entertainment. It was laid down, however, that all the words should be taken from the Bible.

From many of my people there was a warm and generous response to my preaching, and pastoral visits to scattered farmsteads were very rewarding. But some of the more conservative members of the band of lay preachers – many of whom, alas, were not Methodists but belonged to various sects – would plant an observer in the congregation to report on any allegedly heretical utterances of mine. The truly closed mind is a formidable obstacle to progress.

However, one of the local preachers was a remarkable young woman called Jess Lloyd. She had been a victim of polio and preached from her wheelchair. I promised that when we were married we would have her for a holiday, and this we did several times. One of the high moments of her life was when I took her to London and we went in the lift to the top of the tall campanile of Westminster Cathedral. There they rang the Sanctus bell for her and she gazed out across the panorama of the metropolitan city.

I covered long distances cycling from one village to another on my pastoral rounds. Mary's mother, always a staunch supporter, gave me a small motor which operated a roller. When this was lowered on to the back wheel it took the strain out of pedalling. When the roads were wet, however, it slipped badly and its effectiveness was much reduced. It also wore out the tyre. So my kind benefactor replaced it with a Francis Barnett two-stroke motor cycle. This was always breaking down, usually on some desolate country road. I vowed that if I ever met Mr Francis Barnett, I would give him a piece of my mind.

Each morning in my lodgings was spent on my probationer's studies. One of the set subjects was the history of the monastic orders. I enjoyed this very much and came to appreciate the virtues of a form of Christian discipline which had safeguarded the treasures of the Faith in these islands for a thousand years.

At the end of two years I was moved to Ogmore Vale in South Wales, one of the smaller coal-mining communities. The contrast between the two centres of work could scarcely have been greater. Many of the miners in my congregations were self-educated to a high degree of excellence. Some of them would have been university lecturers if they had been given the chance. They were as liberal in their outlook as my Herefordshire folk had been conservative. It was a joy to minister to them and learn from them.

I had charge of two churches, Wesley and Bethel, both lively causes with fine musical traditions. They were less than half-a-mile apart and I used to complain that if I ever dropped dead it would be halfway between the two. Wesley Church was ex-Wesleyan and Bethel ex-Primitive Methodist, representing two of the three strands of Methodism that united in 1932 to form one church. The old traditions and loyalties survived, and any talk of uniting these two churches would, in my time there, have been premature. Later on the Methodist Church embarked upon a great effort to eliminate what was quite scandalous and wasteful redundancy. Nowadays the old pre-union loyalties have for the most part been caught up into a wider loyalty in a truly united fellowship.

I came to love and appreciate the close-knit community life of a Welsh mining valley. I went down a pit and walked two miles underground to the coalface where I was appalled at the cramped and dangerous conditions in which the men worked. I watched many of them die of pneumoconiosis – 'the miner's disease'. I held many a theological discussion with a miner as he washed off the coal dust in a tin bath in front of the fire; pit-head baths had not yet been introduced. Some of my visits took me to homes where a man or woman was dying of tuberculosis. Usually funeral services were held in the home of the deceased, and I counted it a great privilege to minister to folk in their times of acute sorrow.

Again I was wonderfully cared for in my lodgings. Len and Doris Evans made me one of the family. They lived in a small terraced house and each morning I was allowed to take over their front parlour as my study. They had two small sons. Tragedy struck them when the younger one fell into a stream and was drowned. Doris Evans never recovered from this dreadful loss and died herself not long afterwards.

Returning home one evening from a sparsely-attended church meeting I passed a long queue outside the cinema. On some sudden impulse I walked in and tapped on the manager's door. I said, 'There are more people in the queue than I get in my congregation.' 'Whose fault is that?' he very reasonably replied, 'you should put on a better show.' I then had the temerity to ask if I might be allowed to give a three minute talk in his cinema between the long film and the short one that preceded it. To my surprise he said, 'I'll try anything once; I'll give you three minutes next Thursday.' Accordingly I prepared a three minute talk and went with some trepidation to the cinema. The manager showed me round to the mysterious area behind the silver screen. It was very dark. Some foolish fellow had left open a trap door and I fell down a flight of steps, badly spraining my ankle. I climbed back up and stood nervously in the wings. The film showing was *Tarzan of the Apes*. When it came to an end I hobbled painfully on to the stage dazzled by a spotlight. I delivered my brief address. What followed was an experience rarely enjoyed by any preacher. There was tumultuous applause from the audience. When I arrived back in the manager's office he was smiling broadly. 'Boy,' he said, rubbing his hands together, 'this is box office stuff. You're on every Thursday.' So for two years I went weekly to the cinema where I saw the last five minutes of innumerable films and gave a brief address. The result was that I became known throughout the Valley and found an entry into the homes of countless folk whom I might never otherwise have known. On the last Sunday of my ministry in the Ogmore Valley I was asked to broadcast the evening service from the Wesley Church. Such events in those days brought a great response from listeners in the form of letters. In the days that followed I set about answering scores of correspondents.

By this time the war was over and the Methodist theological colleges were back in business. I was sent to Handsworth College, Birmingham where my friends John Stacey and George Lockett were already in residence. My large case containing clothes and books was collected and sent on by railway wagon. It never reached the college. I had to appeal to the family for coupons to buy essential clothes, for we were still suffering from wartime restrictions. I have often wondered what the thief did with my Bible and clerical collar.

On arrival at college I was informed that the new men would have to sit an examination to decide in which academic stream they would be placed. The invigilator at this examination wore an ill-fitting clerical collar and appeared to be looking down his nose at us. I took an instant dislike to him. Imagine my delight, however, when I found that the first question on the examination paper was 'Give your views on the value of religious broadcasting.' I wrote expansively in the light of my recent experience and made a modest reference to the avalanche of letters I had received. It was, however, a fake examination arranged by the students already in residence. The invigilator was one of them, John Mountford, who became one of my firmest friends and had a distinguished ministry as a missionary in India. Alas, the best of the answers were read out to the whole college at supper the same evening. I was immediately nicknamed 'the radio padre'.

Handsworth College, Birmingham

I was able to spend only five terms in college, a ridiculously short time. It meant that all the students taken in at the end of the war had to work very hard indeed. I was entered for the Birmingham B.A. in theology. Part way through the course, however, it was decided that the work could never be completed in time. I was, therefore, switched to the London external B.D. course, the idea being that I should take the intermediate examination while in college and study for my finals when I went back into circuit.

The men of my year were an unusually mature and experienced group. Many had served in the forces and lived in various parts of the world. The fellowship was rich and rewarding. The life of the college centred on the chapel. Morning prayers were led by the staff and evening devotions by the students. Very high standards of worship were observed, enhanced by the organ playing of one of the students, Harry Facer, a most gifted musician.

Our Principal, Dr Wilbert Howard, was widely-known for his work on St John's gospel. In chapel he always read from the Greek New Testament, translating freely as he went along. He led a very disciplined life and expected the same standards of others. Often the light in his study would be burning late into the night. When Dr Archibald Harrison died during his year of office as President of the Conference Dr Howard had to take up the burden that he had relinquished only a few months earlier at the end of his own presidential year. He accepted these additional responsibilities with characteristic courage and devotion. The Resident Tutor, Harold Darby, had a great love for the English language and employed his literary gifts in the compilation of the very beautiful prayers that he used in the chapel. In the churches of today, there are, obviously, various styles of worship. I cannot but feel, however, that much of what is offered to God is slipshod and lacking in that sense of awe which should accompany our approach to the throne of the heavenly grace. I am grateful for the memories of the college chapel where order and dignity, beauty and reverence were the hallmarks of the daily devotions.

I became Editor of *The Cassowary*, the college magazine. The title is related to the Handsworth coat of arms which depicts a cassowary bird, the shells associated with John Wesley, and the Latin words 'Quo Monstrat Dominus': 'Whither the Lord leads'. There is a mythical story that the first Handsworth student to be sent overseas as a missionary encountered a cassowary on the beach when he landed. When I became President of the Conference a Methodist lady embroidered the college emblem on the preaching scarf presented to me by my colleagues on the platform.

Most Sundays saw us preaching in churches in the Birmingham area. Once during our term in college we had to preach in the chapel. Following that ordeal our sermons were criticised in a class called together for that purpose. One hapless brother began his sermon with a splendid story about a river that plunged underground and never reappeared. It was felt by the critics that the same could be said of his sermon.

During the final weeks of my last term in Handsworth I was informed that I had been stationed in Smethwick to begin work on 1st September 1947. Mary and I had arranged to be married in that year immediately following my ordination. I invited her up to take a look at the manse which was to be our first home together. It was a rambling building with an extraordinary arrangement of rooms opening off a long corridor. On the landing was a large tin bath to catch the water which came through the leaky roof. It was not exactly a palace. However, undismayed, I arranged for my desk and chair to be transported from the college to the manse. Returning from superintending this operation I met Dr Howard on the steps of the college. He intimated that he had just arrived back from the Stationing Committee in London and that they had been discussing a vacancy at the Central Hall in Tonypandy. 'I consider that you are the man,' said Dr Howard, 'and I have put your name down for that appointment.'

The movements of ministers in the Methodist Church depend upon a system in which freedom and authority are blended. Circuits are permitted to invite a minister when a vacancy occurs and the minister can either accept or decline. The Conference, however, advised by its Stationing Committee, retains the right to overrule any such arrangement and station a minister where it wills. That option is, of course, only exercised in exceptional circumstances and for good reason. If a minister who is due to move on receives no invitations or declines those that are proffered to him, then the Stationing Committee finds an appointment for him or her. When I became Secretary of the Conference one of my most exacting tasks was the guiding of the work of the Stationing Committee and I was always conscious of the fact that we were dealing with the lives and happiness of ministers and their families.

I was ordained in St John's Church, Sunderland in July 1947. In recent years, as a past President of the Conference, I have been privileged either to preside or preach on these great occasions. The churches are always packed to capacity for the ordination services and it is a moving experience to overhear the remarks in the porch of many who have never attended such a service before. The climax comes with the laying-on of hands. In that moment the ordinands join what Charles Wesley calls 'the bright succession'. The phrase comes from the hymn with which the service opens:

> So shall the bright succession run
> Through the last courses of the sun;
> While unborn churches by their care
> Shall rise and flourish large and fair.

It is a hymn which breathes a sublime Christian confidence in what Michael Ramsey, the one hundredth Archbishop of Canterbury, called 'the great Christian centuries to come'. It sees the present church as still the infant church. Ministers going out into today's world with its secular challenge need that confidence if the sacred flame of devotion is to remain alight. The service concludes with another great Charles Wesley hymn which contains the prayer:

> Kindle a flame of sacred love
> On the mean altar of my heart.

The ecumenical movement has compelled Methodists and others to enquire deeply into the meaning of ministry and the significance of ordination. I believe in the ministry of the whole people of God, and therefore in the partnership of ordained and lay folk. Methodism in its early years, following the death of John Wesley, suffered enormously from an overbearing and autocratic concept of ordained ministry. This inevitably evoked a hostile reaction from a laity more and more influenced by the movement towards democracy. But I am wholly persuaded that when men and women are ordained they enter a calling that is distinct from that of the lay person, though clearly complementary to it. Nor is the difference merely functional. A minister is a minister not only because of what he or she does, but because of what he or she is. It is not a question of status, let alone of superior status. The minister is in a special sense the church's representative. The minister is called to 'a principal and directing part' in the work of the church (Methodist Deed of Union). Little wonder that the service of ordination is awe-inspiring, invoking in those who are set aside a feeling of deep humility.

Within a few days of ordination I was married. The long wait was over. The one note of sadness was the absence of Mary's father who had died suddenly a few months earlier. Over the protracted years of courtship Mary and I had kept up an almost daily correspondence. At lunchtime each Friday she would leave her city office in Bristol and repair to the lovely church of St Mary Redcliffe. At precisely the same hour I would go to the parish church of the area where I was living to keep the tryst. It was, therefore, entirely appropriate that our engagement should take place in St Mary Redcliffe – 'the fairest parish church in all England', as it was styled by the first Queen Elizabeth. Just as I was placing the ring on my fiancée's finger the city organist, whom we had not known was in the building, began to play. It was an altogether delightful public accompaniment to a private ceremony. The wedding was held in the plainer but equally significant Methodist Church at Bishopston where I was brought up.

Wedding Day

Our honeymoon was spent in Salcombe and coincided with three weeks of unbroken sunshine. We borrowed my brother-in-law's car. It kept stopping unaccountably *en route*; and the only way in which I could get it going again was to get out and bang the door. It was nearly midnight when we arrived at the farmhouse we had chosen. We were warmly welcomed by the farmer's wife who handed us a lighted candle. In its soft and gentle radiance we climbed the stairs to our room and closed the door.

At the beginning of our second week we were horrified to witness the arrival of the Rev Harold Darby and his wife from Handsworth College. By an incredible coincidence they had booked their holiday in the same place. However, it all turned out well. They kept out of our way and Mr Darby generously produced some petrol coupons which enabled us to travel further around the area than otherwise would have been possible.

We arrived in Tonypandy in time for the first Sunday in September. The larger attendance at the Central Hall was at the evening service, a congregation of about four hundred. To our delight John Mountford and his wife Kathleen turned up and I persuaded him to sing a Caribbean setting of the Lord's Prayer. At the end of the service a young man came into the vestry and introduced himself as George Thomas, the MP for Cardiff West. He made some kind remarks about the sermon, but then, fingering my preaching gown, he said, 'We are plain people down here in Wales; we don't go in for gowns and things.' Many years later when we were his guests at dinner in Speaker's House in the Palace of Westminster, he asked my wife to tie his bands which had become loose. Commenting on his breeches, lace cuffs and other regalia, she reminded him of that encounter in the vestry long years before. He laughed at the memory.

Our friendship with the man whom we now call Lord Tonypandy has meant much to us over the years. The man who presided with such distinction over the House of Commons learned his parliamentary skills in the Men's Parliament run by the Central Hall. We have admired his consistent Christian witness and latterly his courage in the face of serious illness. He has never sought to hide his humble origins. His mother, a faithful member at the Central Hall, was a very remarkable lady. She brought up her children in a little miner's cottage and the early years were a struggle against poverty. I always enjoyed talking with her. She had a very acute political sense and watched George's ascent to positions of great authority with immense pride. When he became Secretary of State for Wales the Prime Minister, Harold Wilson, invited her to lunch at

10, Downing Street. I met her and George afterwards for tea. She told me that she had bought a new hat for the occasion but was distressed to find that she had put it on back-to-front. I buried her second husband, Tom, a kind and gentle soul.

The ministry at Tonypandy made great demands. My first priority was the pulpit. The preparations for the sermons of the following Sunday began on the previous Monday after the morning meeting with the Wesley deaconess. At this meeting we reviewed the programme for the week and arranged our pastoral visiting, especially of the sick and housebound. We finished with prayers.

My first deaconess was a saintly soul called May Warlow, much loved by all the people. Later on she was succeeded by Agnes Johnstone, a vivacious and attractive colleague, always asking deep and searching questions about the Faith. The Wesley Deaconess Order served Methodism well. It has been succeeded by a diaconate open to both women and men. When the door was opened to the ordination of women to the presbyterial ministry many members of the Wesley Deaconess Order offered themselves as candidates and were accepted. This meant that a considerable number of women already experienced in pastoral care were among the first intake of women ministers, which provided an excellent start.

When I was invited to be a Methodist observer at the Lambeth Conference I addressed the bishops on the ordination of women to the priesthood and shared with them the experience of the Methodist Church. The Methodist Conference had delayed its decision to ordain women for fear of damaging the prospect of union between the two churches. In the event, of course, the Anglicans failed to achieve a sufficient majority for the Union Scheme, and in the end, after years of troubled debate, themselves decided to ordain women to the priesthood.

The Tonypandy Central Hall had a great tradition of social work. My predecessor, Dr Cyril Gwyther, had maintained and developed the work done by the Hall's first minister, the Rev R. J. Barker. 'R J', as he was known, was a man of many gifts: preacher, poet, musician, writer, politician. He bought a large house near the manse in the Rhondda Valley which he called Community House, and it became the headquarters of the Community House Fellowship which he founded. At its heart was the little chapel of St Francis where the sanctuary lamp was always burning. There was a boot-repairing department, a toy-making shop and other activities which were a godsend to the men who were unemployed during the dark days of depression. R. J. Barker was a convinced pacifist and a

Christian socialist. He had a formidable intellect and presented his beliefs with great cogency. His own lifestyle was simple, almost Franciscan. I invited him back to preach on many occasions and he would stay over to speak to our Monday night fellowship group. This was held in the manse and attracted about fifty young people. Over the years I have met many of them all over England: 'the Tonypandy diaspora'. It has been a source of great encouragement to find so many of them holding office in the church.

R. J. Barker went to the Huddersfield Mission when he left Tonypandy. While there he resigned from the ministry in order to give himself full-time to the care of the members of the Community House Fellowship, a decision which many of his friends regretted. He spent years pouring out the riches of his heart and mind in devotional writings for the members of the Fellowship, but the ministry would have given him a wider platform. When I was Secretary of the Conference I received a visitor who said, 'I have been visiting a saint. His name is R. J. Barker. He is old now and living in Ludlow, and I think he longs to be back in the ministry before he dies.' I wrote to R J and invited him to apply for reinstatement. This he did. He was welcomed back by the Conference meeting in Harrogate in 1971 and he appeared in the gallery wearing a clerical collar. The President, the Rev Kenneth Waights, with characteristic warmth, saluted him from the platform. It was a joyous moment.

When a few years ago the Community House Fellowship, whose numbers had dwindled, decided to wind up their affairs they generously donated their assets to the Methodist Peace Fellowship, of which I am Chairman. We set up a trust fund and are able to make bursaries available to young people who are attending peace conferences or working on development projects overseas. R J's widow, Margaret, is one of the trustees.

I was happy to continue the social programme at the Central Hall. We served cheap dinners every day for poor people. For a few pence one could buy a hot two-course meal. It was all done by voluntary labour under the energetic leadership of Mrs Gould who was famous throughout the Valley for her meat pies.

There were some thirty meetings a week of one sort and another. We ran a gifted drama group. When my wife and I returned from the Oberammergau Passion play in 1951 I wrote a nativity play. It followed the famous Oberammergau pattern of presentation: a still-life tableau from the Old Testament on an inner stage, followed by a New Testament action scene on the outer stage. The men of the church built special staging and a local clothing factory made choristers' robes modelled on those of the Passion play. It was an immense success and drew large crowds of people.

Incidentally, during our brief visit to Oberammergau we stayed in the home of the Centurion who rode a big black horse in the play. His daughter, Miss Freisenneger, was in the choir. She was very beautiful and one evening we saw her in the embrace of her lover, standing beneath an apple tree in the garden, a romantic sight which remained in our memory. In 1990 I went as one of the four chaplains at the Ecumenical Centre in Oberammergau. We were there for two weeks and decided to try to track down the girl whom we had seen forty years before. After many adventures and false trails we succeeded. She was delighted to be remembered and now sends us a Christmas card each year with a picture of that beautiful village in the snow.

Two of the big events for the young people of the Tonypandy Central Hall were the Whitsuntide Weekend and the Annual Camp. The former was held in a beautiful country house in Llangynidr made available to us by those generous friends of Methodism, the late John and Sheila Gibbs of Penarth. The Sunday morning open-air Communion service was always an occasion of great inspiration. The Camp was held in the schoolroom of the Tenby Methodist Church. The conditions were primitive but the week full of enjoyment. One day I played the part of the *News Chronicle* mystery man, 'Lobby Lud', who toured the seaside resorts and parted with £5 to anyone who successfully challenged him. I was apprehended (for half-a-crown!) by a vivacious little girl called Gill, now the wife of Stuart Randall, MP.

We were often invited by the BBC to broadcast from the Central Hall and so my experience of radio broadened. Particularly rewarding were two series of 'People's Service' broadcasts. Many of the responses which followed these broadcasts were full of interest. A letter came from the captain of a ship which had been caught in a bad storm in mid-Atlantic, who wrote that the hymns had meant a lot to him. Another letter came from a man in Holland asking for a 'Methodist hymnary book'. He and his wife later came to spend Christmas with us, but we were not able to pay the return visit for which we were invited because their home was destroyed in disastrous floods. They emigrated to South America.

The standard of worship at the Central Hall was high and helped by a number of simple devices. For example, I came down from the pulpit for the intercessory prayers which I led from a lectern placed in the body of the church. This symbolised the fact that we were coming together to the throne of grace. I also had installed a large lantern over the pulpit at the front of which was an illuminated red cross. Late comers were escorted to their seats after the singing of the first hymn while the organ played quietly. When I introduced this practice the number of late comers decreased dramatically.

We were privileged to welcome many distinguished preachers to the Hall and to our home. One of these was Pastor Martin Niemöller, the famous German Church leader. I met him on a number of subsequent occasions when attending the Conference of European churches in the little Danish town of Nyborg. Dr Donald (now Lord) Soper was an early visitor as also was Dr Wilbert Howard, my old college principal.

I suppose that the style of worship which I conducted each Sunday in Tonypandy would today be described as 'traditional'. It was, I believe, acceptable and satisfying to people of all ages, and, I hope, also to God. In more recent times the churches have sought to satisfy the needs of those with a thirst for so-called 'informal services' with a generous use of repetitive choruses. Whatever the style of worship I believe strongly that we must be concerned with its quality – liturgically, musically and theologically. I have sympathy with ministers who find their congregations actually divided because some (usually older folk) want 'traditional' services and others want a free-wheeling style of worship. The holding together of such diverse views presents a great challenge and requires wisdom and pastoral sensitivity of a high order.

On top of the demanding schedule of the Central Hall, which included a weekly class for those who wished to study New Testament Greek, for the first two years of my ministry in Tonypandy I rose at 5.30am and studied for two hours to complete the London B.D. course. I sat the examination at the end of the first year and passed in seven of the eight subjects, so I sat again the following year. To my intense disappointment I again failed one of the papers – in a different subject this time. The University rules required all eight subjects to be passed at one sitting. I felt unable to continue the strain of early rising for a third attempt. It was a pleasant recompense in 1968 to be awarded an honorary doctorate by Ohio Northern University in the USA in recognition of services to World Methodism.

As the church at the centre of the Rhondda community we served the neighbourhood in all kinds of ways. Many came to be married and this involved meeting the couple several times for preparation sessions. I also conducted hundreds of funerals in the windswept cemetery on the hillside. One of these was of a little girl who was killed by a passing car as she ran out of our Sunday School. I went to tell the parents that she was dead. They were sitting in the sunshine on the wall of their front garden. I still recall how the welcoming smile on their faces froze as I gently broke the terrible news.

On one occasion I was summoned by a frantic telephone call to a home where a woman had been found in the bathroom with a gas pipe in her mouth. She was still alive. I rushed next door and enlisted help from a neighbour. Together we lifted the unconscious woman into my car and I drove at 70 mph through built-up areas to the hospital. We arrived in time and her life was saved. I was able to help her sort out the worries that had driven her to such extreme action.

In 1949 our first child, Susan, was born. Mary had been in hospital for the last seven weeks of the pregnancy suffering from toxaemia, a dangerous condition of high blood pressure. The hospital staff kept issuing dire warnings to me that she probably would not survive. But all ended happily. Our little girl arrived five weeks early and weighed only four-and-a-half pounds. She brought great joy into our lives. A couple of years later we were expecting a second child. This time, however, the baby, a girl, was stillborn. The matron of the hospital telephoned me and asked me to go to see her. She handed me a small parcel, about the size of a shoe-box. I was no stranger to funerals but was quite unprepared for this experience. She instructed me to take the tiny coffin to the cemetery and hand it to the sexton. 'There's sure to be an open grave into which he can put it,' she said. So, carrying the little box, I boarded a bus and proceeded on my strange errand. My mind was full of unanswerable questions: what would God do with a little life that had hardly begun? Would we ever know? And so on. I went home to my study to pray but could offer up only my tears. Then I went to the hospital to comfort my wife.

We were strongly advised by the doctors to avoid a third pregnancy. So later on, with the help of the National Children's Home, we adopted a boy whom we called John and then, later still, a girl whom we called Elizabeth. From all three of our children and their partners in marriage we have received unfailing love and support. That support was to be of particular value when the church appointed me to offices that required me to be away from home a great deal, often travelling in distant parts of the world.

At the end of seven happy years we had to leave Tonypandy. Parting from a community we had come greatly to love was like a multiple bereavement. Mary and I had inherited the old car in which we had journeyed to Devon for our honeymoon. Now we motored past the cemetery out of the Rhondda Valley and took the road to London and to a very different kind of ministry. The children were being cared for by our parents during the move. Neither of us spoke a word until we had passed Reading.

Chapter Three

A PROPHETIC CHARGE

Towards the end of our time in Tonypandy the Rev Henry Carter came to preach at the Central Hall. I first set eyes on this outstanding Methodist leader when I was a small boy. My father said, 'I am taking you to hear one of our great men. His name is Carter and I want you to take special notice of his mouth. When he opens it you will think that he will never close it again, and when he closes it you will think that he will never open it again.' I went off to the crowded meeting in the Bristol Victoria Rooms with a sense of great expectation. On the way my father said, 'This is the man the brewers fear.' I was not disappointed. Henry Carter, the great temperance reformer, delivered a mighty speech and held his audience spellbound. It was not so much his mouth – he had a very firm jaw – as what came out of it that filled me with excitement.

By the time of his Tonypandy visit Mr Carter was an old man. On arrival he seemed frail and unwell, and we put him straight to bed. He rose on the Sunday morning like a lion refreshed and gave our people a wonderful day. When it was over he sat in front of the fire in the manse like some fisherman dangling the line of memory into the swiftly-flowing stream of time. He told us about his life's work. He described how, during the First World War, drunkenness became such a national problem that the King took a public pledge of total abstinence as an example. The Methodist Church set up a Temperance Department and Henry Carter was appointed its Secretary. But the drink problem does not stand in isolation from all other social ills. Where people drink to excess they often gamble recklessly. This often leads to crime, the breakup of family life, mental instability and associated problems. So the agendas of Mr Carter's Department began to broaden and they have done so ever since. This widening of the horizons of concern is reflected in changes of nomenclature. 'Temperance' became 'Temperance and Social Welfare'. This in turn was changed to 'Christian Citizenship' and later to 'Social Responsibility'.

Inevitably these expanded agendas involved the Department in wordy battles on highly controversial issues. It fell to my lot to turn out some of Mr Carter's files. There was much evidence of his ability as a doughty fighter. On one or two occasions when the going was particularly rough he wrote a letter resigning from the Secretaryship of the Department, but I don't think that those letters were ever sent. A man who is a pacifist, who opposes great vested interests like the drink trade and the gambling industry, who pioneers new thinking, and would never allow the Methodist people the luxury of a Christian experience divorced from involvement with worldly concerns, is not likely to have a smooth ride.

On the Monday morning I took our visiting preacher to the station. As the train began to move he leaned out of the carriage window and said, 'Kenneth, I could die happy if I could believe that our Methodist people were becoming socially minded.' Not long after that Henry Carter died. I have always regarded that farewell remark as a prophetic charge. Behind the old warrior's words was a lifetime of distinguished service to church and nation (he was made CBE in recognition of this), undergirded by a theology which stressed the wholeness of the gospel. Personal salvation and social redemption were, for Henry Carter, obverse and reverse of the same coin. One cannot help but feel that the Conference was remiss in not electing this great man to the presidential chair.

The growth of the Department necessitated the appointment of a second Secretary. Mr Carter was joined by the Rev E. Clifford Urwin. He, too, had been to preach in Tonypandy and had stayed with us in the manse. He was a man of encyclopaedic knowledge and was always asking questions such as, 'What is the derivation of the name of the District in which you live?' He served Methodism well but never acquired that indefinable gift which enables some men and women to gain the ear of Conference while others fail. In all his labours he was wonderfully supported by his wife, Maude. She lived to be over 100 years old and I paid tributes at the funerals of both of them. Whenever we called on her during her final years she would enquire eagerly about our children and then about the state of the world. 'How is Gorbachev doing?' would be a typical question.

When Mr Carter retired Mr Urwin was joined by the Rev Noel Hutchcroft. His energetic term of service was cut short by his tragically early death. He was followed by Dr Maldwyn Edwards who, with his knowledge of Methodist history and his fluency in communication, built on the fine foundations already laid. He felt inhibited, however, by the restrictions of office routine and after three years moved to the chairmanship of the Cardiff and Swansea District of the Methodist Church.

The Rev Edward Rogers was Dr Edwards' successor. It was he who wrote to me in 1953 to say that the Department wanted to nominate me as the second Secretary when in 1954 he succeeded Mr Urwin. The letter came as a bolt from the blue and shattered the peace of the breakfast table. We had no desire to leave Tonypandy and the generous-hearted folk at the Central Hall wanted us to stay. I had cherished a hope that when the time came to move I might be appointed to one of the Central Halls in England. I wrote to Ted Rogers setting out my hesitations: in particular I expressed some anxiety that my deeply-held pacifist views might be an embarrassment to him. He sent a long and careful reply demolishing all my arguments.

After much prayer and thought we decided that I must obey the will of the Conference. It accepted the nomination and so in 1954, as already recorded, we set out for London. My intention was to serve the Department for five years and then move on. In the event my ministry as its Secretary lasted for seventeen years during which I enjoyed an unusual partnership with one of Methodism's most gifted ministers.

Ted Rogers has a razor-sharp mind and a superb ability to master a complex brief and present it with crystal clarity. Soon after I joined him at Westminster I confessed to him that I found the task of understanding some of the complex issues with which we were dealing somewhat daunting. His typically laconic response was, 'If you don't know, look as if you do.' He added, 'An expert is one who knows just a little bit more than the next chap.' Again and again his mastery of Conference was demonstrated. Indeed I do not recall any occasion on which we were defeated in debate. This was noteworthy in view of the highly controversial issues on which we often had to test the judgement of the Conference. Much of the Department's effectiveness depended on the careful work done by a series of standing committees. By the time we brought a resolution to Conference we had mastered not only the arguments for but were familiar with those that might be used against the proposition.

To say that Ted Rogers had little small talk would be, in the judgement of many who had entertained him for a weekend, a gross understatement. As I travelled around the Methodist Connexion I picked up all sorts of stories about attempts made by genial hosts to engage their visitor in conversation. More often than not the only response was a puff on his pipe and something resembling a grunt. Yet there were great rewards if one could get him launched on some favourite subject, like science fiction. He devoured huge quantities of this kind of literature and has always had a deep interest in the fascinating world of the advanced sciences. Once when I said that I could not understand the technical jargon employed by many writers on the subject his response was, 'I've had to learn it.'

In Ted Rogers I was fortunate to have a colleague who left me free to do my job in my own way and whose loyalty was always complete and reliable. Once when I was involved in a tremendous national argument following the publication of a Report entitled 'Sex and Morality', of which more anon, a Methodist lady who had not read the document wrote to Ted demanding my instant dismissal from the ministry. I happened by accident to come across his reply. It put the correspondent firmly in her place.

With Rev Edward Rogers at the Department of Christian Citizenship

Underlying and undergirding Ted Rogers' work in the field of social responsibility is a remarkably uncomplicated acceptance of the fundamentals of the Christian faith. This shines through his writings. He has a lucid style and in books and through his weekly *Methodist Recorder* commentaries on contemporary events he has made an immensely valuable contribution to an intelligent understanding of the social implications of the gospel.

When his first wife, Edith, died he showed great courage. I went to see him as soon as I heard the news and offered to take him home for the night. 'No,' he said, 'I must write my column for the *Methodist Recorder*.'

It was my privilege to conduct his wedding to his second wife, Lucy. In the vestry before the service he said, 'Now Ken, I want the word obey included in the service.' The bride said, with an equal lack of seriousness, 'In that case I'm leaving.' I concluded this happy exchange of banter by remarking, 'Now you young people, it's a bit early to be calling in the marriage guidance counsellor.' Their marriage has been one of great mutual enrichment.

On arrival at the Westminster Headquarters of the Methodist Church I went to the room which was to be my office for the next seventeen years. I sat down before the desk which was entirely empty save for a telephone, and waited for something to happen. It soon did. A keen Christian Citizenship Secretary from the north of England wanted me to go to conduct a weekend conference in his church. Very soon my diary was bristling with engagements all over the land. Thus began an itinerant ministry which meant constant absences from home, especially at weekends. It was a requirement of the work which I heartily disliked and it made great demands on my wife and the children. There were times when the inner tension between duty to the church and to the family became almost unbearable.

My first task was to read myself into the Department's agendas. It is interesting, looking back, to see what social issues were engaging the attention of Methodism in the mid-fifties. Temperance concerns featured prominently and churches were urged to keep an abstainers' roll. A Citizen's Guide to Licensing Procedures was sent to every minister in the active work. The connection between drinking and road accidents was increasingly highlighted. There was deepening concern about the increase in gambling and the Department opposed moves in Parliament to extend the facilities for running lotteries. The General Secretary went to see Mr Morgan Phillips, the Secretary of the Labour Party, to express the Department's views about the raising of money for political purposes by means of gambling. The Department was also in close correspondence with some of the overseas Methodist Districts where similar problems were being faced. When in November 1956 the Government introduced Premium Bonds there was strong opposition from the Methodist

Conference and from the British Council of Churches. The Department sought and secured safeguards for employees of banks and post offices who had conscientious objections to handling the Bonds.

Many of the matters dealt with, like those just mentioned, were the subjects of parliamentary debate and legislative action. We were greatly helped by Methodist MPs and kept them regularly briefed on the Department's work and judgements. George Thomas became the Department's Treasurer, a post earlier held by Mr Isaac Foot. When Mr Thomas became Speaker of the House of Commons he instituted an annual dinner in Speaker's House at which the guest of honour was the President of the Conference. These occasions enhanced the contacts between Methodist Headquarters and the Palace of Westminster. When Mr Henry Brooke was Home Secretary he set up a committee on juvenile delinquency. He invited me to serve on it and I sat next to Mr Frankie Vaughan, the singer. He was always anxious to cut the talking and get something done, but it was a singularly ineffective committee and was soon disbanded.

During the early years of my Westminster ministry there was a great deal of public agitation about horror comics. These publications exploited violence and the macabre in ways that were offensive to many adults and deemed to be harmful to children. The Department supported the Children and Young Persons (Harmful Publications) Bill which became an Act of Parliament and which imposed penalties for infringements of the code laid down to cover publications for young people.

There were times when I felt rather like King Canute trying to turn back the incoming tide. London has in pre-eminent degree both the virtues and the vices of a great metropolitan city. We were constantly engaged in the battle against pornography and the attempts to produce a clearer definition of obscenity and a more effective law to deal with it. In 1954 Ted Rogers joined a deputation led by the Bishop of London to protest to the Lord Chamberlain about nudity on the stage.

In 1955 the Department discussed the question of capital punishment. At that time there were very divided views on the issue of abolition, and so no resolution on the subject was brought to the Conference. It took time to marshall the facts on which an informed judgement could be based. In the end, of course, we were able to present a coherent case for the abolition of hanging and this was given overwhelming support in the Conference.

This particular bit of history reflects a number of points about the Department's work and *modus operandi*. We believed that there could be no Christian judgement on any subject in default of the facts, and so all the relevant evidence was assembled and analysed. We tried always to listen to the other side of the case and respect differing points of view; in our own committees where the detailed work was done we enjoyed 'the fellowship of controversy', to quote a phrase coined by Donald Soper. I have always believed that Christians should be able to discuss controversial issues within the bonds of secure and unbroken friendship.

Whilst our committees were well-served by knowledgeable and well-qualified Methodists we did not hesitate to call in expert help when we needed specialist advice. The Department's views did not remain static. The movement of thought on the matter of capital punishment is only one example of the way in which judgement changed and developed as a result of careful research and study.

Other issues on which we sought to inform the thought and action of the Methodist people included smoking and lung cancer; mental health and public attitudes to mental illness; the ethics of boxing; vivisection; penal reform and the after-care of discharged prisoners; the law relating to suicide; the relationship between economics and theology, ethics and industrial practice.

One of the most complex and extensive areas of our work was the field of international relations. The Standing Committee which handled this part of the agenda was presided over by the Rev R. Douglas Moore. His knowledge of the world was extraordinarily comprehensive. There seemed to be no place on earth, from the remotest island to the biggest city, on which he could not make an authoritative pronouncement. His handling of our affairs could be distinctly autocratic, but though at first I thought he was infallible I later discovered, to my relief, that he could sometimes be wrong.

It was in dealing with international affairs that Ted Rogers displayed most impressively his ability to talk clearly and concisely about a complex subject. He would arrive at a committee with an armful of papers, rise to his feet to explain the latest developments in, say, the perpetual crisis of the Middle East, riffle through the papers for a moment or two, and then, brushing them aside, launch into a detailed analysis of every aspect of the subject in such a way that we could all see precisely what the main issues were.

One of the matters that fell within the remit of Mr Moore's Committee was defence and disarmament. The Department's Annual

Report for 1954-55 expressed deep concern about nuclear weapons and said, 'For the first time in our history, to speak of "the death of civilisation" is no longer rhetoric but sober judgement. Is "just war" possible with nuclear weapons?' I shall give my answer to that question when I speak of my own involvement in the quest for peace in Chapter Six.

The developing situation in South Africa following the introduction of the apartheid system by the Nationalist government was a recurring item on the Department's agendas. The President of the South African Methodist Conference, Dr J. B. Webb, came to talk with us. We did all that we could to support the opponents of that evil system. Ted Rogers visited South Africa in 1956 for the celebration of the 150th anniversary of the founding of the Methodist Church there. As a result of his advocacy it was decided to create a Department of Christian Citizenship responsible to the South African Methodist Conference. It was ostensibly to celebrate the 30th anniversary of the founding of that Department that I was invited to undertake a month-long tour of the Republic in 1986. In fact the main purpose of that visit was to try to strengthen the hands of those who were still struggling to overthrow the apartheid regime. I give some account of that traumatic experience in Chapter Seven.

The crises and conflicts of a turbulent world were always providing new issues for discussion and action. The seizure by Colonel Nasser of the Suez Canal and the subsequent Anglo-French and Israeli invasion of Egypt blew up while my colleague was out of the country. I did my best to deal with the battery of requests for comment and judgement that came from the press and from anxious Methodists. The carefully considered judgement of the Department was conveyed in the following statement:

> The Department of Christian Citizenship affirms that the essential elements of a directive policy designed to deal effectively with the fundamental causes of tension in the Middle East must include:
>
> 1. Treaty agreements between Israel and the Arab States to end hostilities and to secure recognised frontiers.
> 2. International action in co-operation with the Arab States and Israel to repatriate or resettle Arab refugees.
> 3. International co-operation in plans to improve economic conditions in Egypt.

4. With due regard for the sovereignty of Egypt, recognition of the Suez Canal as an international waterway open to the shipping of all nations.
5. Loyalty to the Charter of the United Nations on the part of all nations, and more generous support of the UN agencies through which the above policies should be implemented.

One of the frustrations of the work was the unnecessary duplication of effort arising from the denominational divisions in the church. On so many of the issues which we studied there was no such thing as a distinctively Methodist point of view; rather there was broad agreement across the denominational spectrum. Yet individual churches would spend precious time considering an issue and putting out statements almost identical with the material produced by a sister communion. We were constantly trying to overcome this problem. We set up joint working parties with other churches and through the British Council of churches we tried to work and act together, applying the 'Lund Dictum' – 'never do separately what in conscience you can do together.' We merged most of our international work with that of the Council's Department of International Affairs. The problem will never be entirely eliminated so long as the divisions in the churches persist. The Church of England often seemed to forget the declared intention of us all to work together, apparently in the belief that as the State Church its view was bound to be different from and more authoritative than that of the other denominations.

There was one area of our international work where we were sometimes accused of acting unilaterally, however, and that was in the field of relief. The Methodist Relief Fund had been established to assist those who had been made refugees by the Second World War. Some felt that all Methodist giving for such purposes should be channelled through Christian Aid, the ecumenical agency. The maintenance of the Methodist Fund, however, was justified by the fact that when urgent needs arose in areas where the Methodist Church existed we were able to act promptly through our own trusted people on the spot. This saved our having to create expensive means of administering the funds and our administrative costs were minimal. Through the generosity of the Methodist people we were able to extend the range of the work and respond to a great variety of human needs. Grants were made to assist development projects as well as to help the victims of natural disasters. Ted Rogers took great delight in this practical expression of Christian compassion and travelled to many parts of the world to examine situations in which we might be able to help.

In addition to our close association with our sister churches and with the British Council of Churches we relied also on our involvement with other ecumenical and secular agencies. The World Council of Churches fed us with a constant stream of reports produced by expert groups. Inevitably much of this excellent material was couched in the rather opaque style all too often adopted by ecumenical bodies. The problem of communicating the findings of ecumenical enquiry to the people in the pew is formidable.

One of the organisations which I served was the Public Morality Council. It had a distinctly Victorian flavour. Its General Secretary was a greatly respected Methodist lay preacher called George Tomlinson. I was Chairman of one of the subcommittees with the intriguing title 'Parliamentary, Patrol and Propaganda'. This was concerned in the main with pornography and prostitution and at our meetings we were asked to examine photographs and pictures which had been submitted by outraged citizens. The members, who included a lady-in-waiting to the Queen and sundry other persons of aristocratic appearance, would say, 'Tut-tut' or words to that effect and Mr Tomlinson would usually sum up by saying, 'I think that we are agreed that this material is vulgar but not actionable.' I got the impression that several of the aristocratic members rather enjoyed the exercise. On one occasion I was given £5 from the petty cash and asked to purchase some photographs from a dubious emporium in Soho which was alleged to have been trading in pornography. I only hoped that none of my friends would see me emerging from this establishment.

Ted Rogers and I both had to be able to answer for the whole area of our Department's work but we divided the major responsibilities between us. I dealt with the committees handling questions relating to temperance, gambling and, in particular, sex, marriage and the family. I was also responsible for publicity, for editing the magazine called *The Christian Citizen* and for promoting the Order of Christian Citizenship.

On gambling we worked very closely with the Churches' Council on Gambling. Its Secretary, the Rev Gordon Moody, was an ebullient character. He became an acknowledged expert and was greatly respected by government officials and in the churches. He founded the British branch of Gamblers Anonymous and spent a lot of time helping those who had become addicted to gambling, often bringing great distress upon themselves and their families.

It was in the broad field of human sexuality that I encountered some of the most fascinating issues and experienced the fiercest controversy. I was invited to join the national executive committee of the Family Planning Association. The members of this body, founded in 1939, were mainly middle-aged and elderly ladies. Their very competent chairperson was Mrs Margaret Pyke. Some of the older members had been supporters of the suffragette movement and had fought to secure the female franchise. There was a campaigning atmosphere in this committee, for the use of contraceptives had not yet become respectable. On one occasion I attended a dinner at which Dr Marie Stopes was present. She was among the pioneers of birth control. When she took her travelling surgery to the Rhondda Valley it was burnt to the ground by her opponents. One morning the committee was interrupted by a member who came rushing in waving a copy of the *Times* dated 30 November 1955. It contained a leading article praising the work of the Association. We had arrived! It was a great moment for these ardent campaigners, though among some of them I thought I detected a certain regret that, as it seemed to them, there were no more battles left to be fought.

Any such judgement was, of course, entirely wrong. The struggle to secure a sane and responsible approach to parenting and to human sexuality generally continues and in recent years has assumed even greater prominence both within the churches and in the nation at large.

Soon after joining the Executive Committee of the Family Planning Association I was challenged by the Rev R. Douglas Moore to whom I have already referred. He alleged that a London factory where contraceptives were manufactured was a sink of iniquity and that the morals of the workers were disreputable. I knew the Anglican vicar of the parish within which this factory was situated and I asked him if we could tour the factory together. He arranged this with the manager and it turned out to be a very pleasant experience. The workers were mainly middle-aged women of eminently respectable appearance. Several of them hailed the vicar with delight; they were members of his Mothers' Union. I reported back to the Committee of which Mr Moore was a member. For once he was lost for words.

The British Council of Churches ran an Advisory Group on Sex, Marriage and the Family. Its Chairman was the Rev Leslie Tizard, the minister of Carrs Lane Congregational Church in Birmingham. When I was a student I often went to hear him preach, and I can still remember the opening words of some of his impressive sermons. He always developed his theme like a lawyer marshalling his evidence. His effectiveness was increased by his cadaverous appearance and his beautifully modulated voice. When Leslie Tizard died, far too early, of cancer, I was asked to succeed him in the chair of the Group over which he had presided with great distinction. During my tenure of that office I chaired two working parties which produced two reports, both of which were of profound significance.

The first of these, published in 1962, was entitled 'Human Reproduction: a study of some emergent problems and questions in the light of Christian faith'. We gathered together a most interesting and diverse group of people which included Dr W. R. Matthews, the Dean of St Pauls; Dr D. Sherwin Bailey, the Chancellor of Wells Cathedral; Dr Kenneth Slack, the General Secretary of the British Council of Churches; Dr Percy Backus, a consultant psychologist and Dr Roger Pilkington, a biologist. We also had the benefit of the knowledge of Mr John Hodges, the Chief Executive Officer of the Milk Marketing Board. Our first task was to assemble a large mass of information about the techniques being used in the field of animal husbandry. It was for most of us an eye-opener. We became familiar with terms like 'artificial insemination', 'host wombs', 'ovarian transfers', and 'sex selection'. We then asked whether any of these techniques were likely to become capable of human application, and, if so, what theological, ethical and legal questions would arise.

I must confess that at times I wondered whether the whole exercise, whilst fascinating in itself, was not entirely academic. It is, however, an indication of how rapidly scientific inventiveness affects human life that with regard to a number of the techniques which we studied there has been a breakthrough from animal to human use. Both church and state have had to look carefully at the issues raised by the use of artificial methods of human insemination. We have entered a whole new world in which men and women are interfering with processes which formerly were left to nature. The newspapers carry reports of the latest developments in the treatment of infertility. We read stories of multiple births induced by the use of fertility drugs. *In vitro* fertilisation, resulting in so-called 'test tube babies' is quite common. Fertilised ova can be stored in a deep-freeze for years and then implanted in the womb. Some women have offered to carry an embryo for someone else up to the point of birth. Experiments are proceeding to enable parents to choose the sex of their offspring. 'Genetic engineering' is a familiar term which carries imponderable implications for the future.

Whereas much of this scientific development has brought great benefits, it has also raised very difficult questions and evoked fears that men and women may be 'playing God' and making disastrous mistakes. Improved methods of contraception are of immense value and must surely be regarded as among the most beneficial gifts of modern science to the human race. Some of the other techniques, however, are not so obviously welcome. The Group which produced the Report on Human Reproduction tried to articulate some of the basic questions that must be faced. The churches can, I think, be grateful that for once they were well ahead of the times and demonstrated the need for an inter-disciplinary approach to a subject which touches the very springs of life.

Our study led to the clear judgement that wise discrimination is essential. Because a technique is available it does not follow that it should be used. We emphasised the very personal nature of the coming together of a man and woman that produces a child. When technical procedures interfere to an inordinate degree with natural processes so that human beings become mere breeding machines it is time to cry 'halt'. In preparing our advice to the churches we tried to present the facts clearly and to bring to bear upon them the insights of the Bible, of theology, ethics and psychology, of the law and of the other relevant scientific disciplines. It is a method that does not produce answers which are either quick or infallible. It is, however, the only wise way to proceed in endeavouring to reach conclusions that Christians can defend.

The second Report to which I referred earlier was entitled 'Sex and Morality'. Its publication in 1966 after two years of very hard work caused a tremendous rumpus and I entered upon perhaps the most astonishing and hectic month in my whole life. The weekend before the Report was due to be presented to the Assembly of the British Council of Churches a copy was obtained by the press. The Sunday papers, having nothing much to write about that week, made it the main item of news. Almost inevitably the content of the Report was distorted. Wild allegations were made that the churches were abandoning their teaching about chastity and flinging all their traditional views overboard. I was besieged by newspaper reporters and badgered to give interviews on radio and television. The Canadian Broadcasting Company flew me to Montreal to take part in a discussion programme on the issues raised by the Report. Incidentally that was my first appearance on colour television. The SCM Press had to go hastily into a second printing. Thousands of copies of the Report were sold and it was eventually published in no less than ten overseas languages.

The debate on the Report took place in Lambeth Palace and lasted for five hours. The Archbishop of Canterbury, Dr Michael Ramsey, presided and when it was over he was heard to say, 'I wouldn't have missed a moment of it.' As the discussion was about to begin a moving incident occurred. The Methodist members of the meeting, led by Eric Baker, rose from their seats and came to range themselves on either side of me: a gesture of support which I greatly appreciated. The discussion spilled over on to a second day. Several representatives of the Church of Scotland made speeches that seemed to indicate that they really did not understand the central issues with which we were seeking to deal.

As we were preparing for the final phase of the debate we received the terrible news of the disaster in Aberfan. A slag heap had slid downhill and buried a school, suffocating scores of children. Suddenly my mind and heart seemed to go dead and I lost all interest in the outcome of the wordy conflict which had absorbed every ounce of my energy for several days.

The Council was not prepared to do more than 'receive' the Report, though at a later meeting it passed a resolution of warm appreciation.

Why was it that this modest document created such a widespread storm of public interest? At its meeting in April 1964 the Council had appointed a working party with the following term of reference (I had, in fact, drafted the wording myself):

> To prepare a Statement of the Christian case for abstinence from sexual intercourse before marriage and faithfulness within marriage, taking full account of responsible criticisms, and to suggest means whereby the Christian position may be effectively presented to the various sections of the community.

We encountered an unexpected difficulty in setting up the working party. Several distinguished Christians who were invited to serve refused to do so. One of them wrote: 'I could not personally subscribe to the terms of reference which imply that it has already been decided in advance that all sexual intercourse outside marriage is wrong and that the only question is how to substantiate this view and to present it effectively.'

As soon as we began our enquiries we met with a number of different views among Christians regarding the place and significance of sex in human life. We noted the very negative attitude of those who early in the Christian era formulated the teaching of the church on the subject, a matter which I examined in some detail in my book *The Mutual Society* (The Beckly Lecture of 1962). We considered some of the reasons for the development of diverse attitudes, notably the advent of contraceptive methods which enable men and women virtually to separate the relational and procreative aspects of sexual intercourse. The response of Christian theology has been, on the whole, to take a much more positive attitude to sex.

One of the reasons why the Report created such a storm of controversy was that we tried honestly to examine the basis of moral judgement. In doing so we questioned some of the easy assumptions that are often made, such as the idea that every moral problem in the broad field of human sexuality can be solved by finding the right biblical text. It can't.

Towards the end of my term of service in the Christian Citizenship Department I wrote a book entitled *The Art of Moral Judgement* (Epworth Press 1970). It was a sustained reflection on the nature of morality. The sort of questions to which I sought an answer were: Is morality static or revisable? Is it best embodied in rules or ideals? Does it bear mainly on actions or dispositions? I went back to the great thinkers of Greece who first articulated the basic questions of moral philosophy. Interestingly, their questions arose out of their experience of moral diversity. When the Greeks began to explore the big world which lay beyond the frontiers of their city states they found that some of the things which they believed to be right were judged wrong by others and the opposite was also the case. Was morality, then, merely a matter of personal choice or preference? Whence came the often vehement use of the word 'ought'? Often those involved in moral argument seemed to be appealing to some external court of appeal. Does that court exist and, if so, what is its nature? It was out of this debate that the concept of 'natural law' was evolved.

The book which I wrote arose out of my own experience of trying to help the Methodist people to reach the right judgement on a large range of moral and social issues. Precisely the same questions have arisen in the more recent debates within the churches on human sexuality. The Methodist Conference has wrestled with a working party Report on 'Human Sexuality' which reflects a wide diversity of views among Christians, especially on the question of homosexuality. It devoted a whole day of debate to it in 1995 and called on the Methodist people to engage in open discussion of our differences and hold one another in a spirit of love.

61

Speaking to the 1996 Conference the President, the Rev Nigel Collinson, reiterated this appeal and stated: 'We cannot proclaim our belief in the inclusiveness of Methodism if our actions push others who are offended, or threatened by what we do, out of the church.'

It was in the last year of my service with the Department of Christian Citizenship that I began to urge the need for an honest facing of the issues raised by the fact that many people are homosexual. When I asked why such folk should be denied all physical expression of their sexuality I was exhorted by several of the 'elder statesmen' of the church to keep quiet or I should get hurt. Now, of course, the church itself cannot keep quiet and must live with the divisions and unresolved perplexities of the issue until they are resolved.

How does it come about that some Christians with the Bible open in front of them reach one view about homosexual orientation and practice while others with similar respect for the Bible reach quite different conclusions? Inevitably one cannot ask that question without inquiring into another: what is the nature of the authority of the Bible and how is it to be properly used in seeking to establish what is right and what is wrong? The Methodist Conference, aware of the importance of this, again very divisive, issue has called for an in-depth study and report. It is bound to prove controversial but will be of great educational value, if sensitively handled.

The questions about homosexuality which are agitating the churches today were raised in 1957 when a Report produced under the chairmanship of Sir John Wolfenden considered the state of the law regarding both homosexuality and prostitution. This was a well-written document of profound social significance. Its major recommendation was that 'homosexual behaviour between consenting adults in private be no longer a criminal offence'. It took ten years for public opinion to reach the point where Parliament felt able to incorporate this proposal in law. The discussion of the Report was an educational exercise of great value. It led to a much more open attitude and to the removal of much, though by no means all, prejudice against homosexuals, and to the elimination of offensive intrusions by the police into the private lives of individuals. The Methodist Conference supported the general approach of the Wolfenden Report.

That Report has a valuable section which deals with the function of the criminal law. It is not, in the wise judgement of the writers, to interfere with the private lives of citizens, or to seek to enforce any particular pattern of behaviour, further than is necessary to preserve public decency and order, and to safeguard the young.

Many of the subjects with which I have been dealing in this chapter were expounded at the training courses for ministers which were held annually at either Grange-over-Sands or Weston-Super-Mare. These gatherings afforded an opportunity for my colleague and me to inform some fifty ministers about the work of the Department and the issues of the day.

I turn now to my diaries which cover the period under review in order to pick out a few of the more interesting events which I have not so far mentioned. Those diaries reflect a saga of ceaseless activity, travel and adventure. At the end of one year I noted that I had been out of my own bed for 113 nights and had travelled over 40,000 miles. That was a typical year.

The first ABC Television Religious Training Scheme

In 1959 I attended the first television training course for parsons. It was organised by ABC Television and held in Manchester. On the Sunday morning we attended an outside broadcast from a Baptist Church in a nearby town. The occasion was historical in that it was the first televised service of a believer's baptism in this country. We watched the nervous young minister pulling on his waterproof leggings: 'pants for the waterbrooks', as one member of our group quipped. Those of us who were on the training course gathered in the church vestry. A monitor screen had been installed so that we could watch the service, and a sound line from the producer's cabin outside, enabling us to hear the instructions being issued to the three cameramen. As the first hymn was being sung we heard the following comment: 'This is an ugly building. What can we shoot during the parson's prayer? Cameras two and three, pan around. Oh yes, that will do, shoot the flowers on the altar.' When the service was over we were lectured on the televisual inadequacy of many of our plain Free church buildings in which there is no imagery, no stained glass, or any object that the cameras can use as a focus of devout attention.

This course stood me in good stead later on when I was invited to become the Free Church Adviser to Thames Television. Together with the Rev Austin Williams (Anglican) and the Rev Michael Hollings (Roman Catholic) I sat down regularly with the religious production team to discuss the shape and content of the programmes in what was popularly known as 'the God slot'. It was a fascinating exercise though often our plans were thwarted by the limited budget we were allowed. However, we did produce some very worthwhile programmes. One of the best series was entitled *Men of Vision*. Dr John Foster, Professor of Ecclesiastical History in the University of Glasgow and a Methodist minister, introduced in telling words and pictures potted biographies of some of the great Christian saints and leaders down the centuries.

In the early days of television I was asked to take part in a Sunday evening programme called 'Sunday Break', specially designed to appeal to young people. One evening we tackled the subject of love, sex and marriage. This created quite a stir. The three of us who had formed the panel to answer questions, Dr Faith Spicer (a psychiatrist), and a medical doctor whose name escapes me and myself were invited to give an interview to the *News of the World*. The journalist who conducted the interview (which later filled their front page) began, 'I should like to offer you £25 each for this interview.' I thought this very generous. To my astonishment, however, the doctor reached for his hat, said, 'Good day to you' and made for the door. The journalist recalled him and said, 'I imagine that I should have offered you more.' 'Look here,' the doctor replied, 'we are professional people. Our fee is at least £100 each.' 'Very well,' came the reply, '£100 it is.' I gasped and later telephoned my wife to say that we had come into a fortune.

In 1965 I was working one day in my office when Eric Baker, the Secretary of the Methodist Conference, rang through, as he often did, to ask if I would step along the corridor to see him. He said, 'I have two ladies with me who wish to discuss a matter that really falls within your bailiwick.' I found him somewhat ill-at-ease in conversation with Mrs Mary Whitehouse and a companion of hers called Mrs Norah Buckland. They had come to enlist the support of the Methodist Church for their 'Clean up Television Campaign'. Dr Baker let me in for attending an inaugural meeting in a lush London hotel.

The meeting left me in a rather critical state of mind. I thought that the attack on the programme makers was too indiscriminate. Moreover the meeting seemed to be sprinkled with strange characters. One man of military appearance said, 'I don't mind a dirty joke or two among men, but these wretched programmes invade our withdrawing rooms when there are ladies present.' I made a rather critical report of all this to the Methodist Conference meeting in Plymouth. On leaving the Conference hall my wife and I were both knocked down on a pedestrian crossing by an elderly driver who failed to stop. One colleague said jokingly, 'That's what comes of attacking Mrs Whitehouse.'

As the years went by Mrs Whitehouse, through the Viewers and Listeners' Association which she founded, brought a more reasonable and better-informed critical judgement to bear on television output. She became, in fact, almost a national institution.

The year 1965-66 was a disastrous one. The accident to which I have referred was a nasty one. As we were placed in the ambulance I looked down at my wife in the lower bunk and said, 'And are we yet alive?' (the hymn with which the Conference always begins). She replied, 'Only just.' I was in excruciating pain; my acetabulum was fractured in five places. She was lacerated from head to toe having been dragged thirty yards up the road by the car that hit us. It took many weeks for us fully to recover.

There is humour in most situations. In the hospital to which I was taken I was put next to a lorry driver. 'What do you do for a living, guv?' he enquired. 'I'm a parson,' I replied. 'Good God, you're not!' was his response. I don't know whether his surprise was due to wonderment that the Almighty should have allowed one of his special agents to suffer in this way, or whether it sprang from the fact that he had never been quite so close to the church before. He was a decent fellow, though. Every time the BBC broadcast a hymn or a prayer on his radio headphones he would whip them off and say, 'Something here for you, padre.' It happened so frequently that I got the impression that the airwaves were saturated with religion. His kindness was only exceeded by that of the hospital staff though there was one exception to this. One day Ted Rogers came to see me. 'Hallo, Ken,' he said. At that moment a consultant in a white coat strode by and said irritably, 'How can I do my work with all this chatter going on?' 'Better go, Ken,' said Ted, and left.

During that same year Ted himself was taken seriously ill and was unable to work for many weeks. With the help of our small but devoted office staff headed by Mrs Wright who exercised a firm but kindly discipline over us all, and with the loyal support of three members of our Standing Committees, we kept the ship afloat.

In 1960 I paid the first of many visits to Africa. I spent the month of February touring Nigeria. It was an unforgettable experience, and especially during the early part of the tour I lay awake at night, my body shining with perspiration, trying to absorb the details of a world so different from my own. My constant companion and guide was a wonderful Methodist minister named Robinson Mba. He and his wife had many children and one day I ventured to speak to him about contraception. His response was peal upon peal of laughter. I shared my puzzlement at this reaction with a wise and experienced white missionary. He said, 'It was not that you said anything amusing. It was a typically African response. Robinson knows that in fact the issue of family planning is one with which the whole of Africa will have to come to terms.'

On behalf of the Methodist Relief Fund I visited Uzuakoli where the Rev and Mrs Alan Roberts had, almost by accident, started a home for motherless babies. Because of the superstition that twins bring bad luck hapless infants were often abandoned in the bush. Mr and Mrs Roberts could not refuse to take such little ones under their wing but the numbers were growing, a proper home needed to be established and this required money. I immediately pledged the support of the Relief Fund. The first child to be cared for was named Obinali, meaning 'the heart endures'. I held this tiny scrap of humanity in my arms. Alas, he died shortly afterwards, but his memory endures. On my return I informed the National Children's Home of this vital piece of work and they sent out Sister Nona Bell to superintend it. They also brought over to England Bella Teite who had been in charge of the work before Nona Bell's arrival. Bella was given a course of professional training in child care. As the story of the Home became known the Methodist response was generous and the Relief Fund was able to pay for the installation of piped water. Before that three workers had spent all day carrying jars of water from a distant stream.

The Home suffered dreadfully during the tragic Biafran war. Bella Teite had to fly into the bush with the children during a raid. When the war ended a great benefactor, Mr Okeke, lent his bungalow, free of charge, while the Home was being repaired.

During the 1960s I travelled to many European countries, occasionally on behalf of the Methodist Relief Fund but more often as Chairman of the World Christian Temperance Federation. This gave me opportunities to observe the temperance work on the Continent and I met some choice characters. One who impressed me was an education expert in the American army in Vienna. He had lost both arms but wore a special slipper on his right foot, which enabled him to hold a cup of tea or extract a note from his wallet. It was all done so naturally that after a while one scarcely noticed his disability.

In 1966 Southlands College in Wimbledon became coeducational. The Principal, Miss Myra Johnson, thought that her students should receive regular lectures on sex. She asked me to undertake this responsibility and there thus began a very happy association with the college which, as I shall later tell, continues to this day. Miss Johnson was a gracious lady with a charming presence. I recall the day when Dr Harold Roberts, a great friend and former Principal of Richmond College, came to my office to tell me rather shyly that he and Myra were to be married. It so happened that on the day after the conclusion of the honeymoon I met Harold Roberts at a function in Cambridge attended by the Queen Mother. He looked very fit and bronzed. I overheard a very elderly lady say to him, 'Oh, Dr Roberts, you do look well.' 'Yes,' he replied, leaning back on his heels in a characteristic stance, 'I've had a little sun.' 'Oh, how wonderful,' replied the old lady, 'when did he arrive?' The Doctor seemed lost for words.

In 1968 I spent an interesting time in America. I trudged round the slums of Harlem when the temperatures were in the nineties. I spent some time with Dr Seymour Fiddle, a specialist in the treatment of drug addiction. We sat talking on a broken-down couch in a shabby shop-front therapy room. He spoke about the vast underworld of pushers and addicts and I noted some of his more striking sayings: 'People must fill their lives with something'; 'the stress on consumption encourages the philosophy that you are only living when you are buying and consuming'; 'with addicts you do not preach, you exemplify'; 'hellfire religion has driven some people to drugs'. I came away from this encounter with an unusual man humbled by his devotion. When I asked him about his success rate he smiled gently and said, 'It's mostly failure, you know. But the successes are wonderful.'

As I returned to the red-hot pavements of central New York the atmosphere was tense. Hundreds were praying in the dim interior of St Patrick's Cathedral; every other passerby had a transistor radio held to his ear. Robert Kennedy had been shot. Yet another little man with a gun had emerged to leave his Judas-mark on history.

One day in 1969 I received a telephone call from the President of the Methodist Conference in Fiji. He asked if I would give some assistance to the Banaban people, the majority of whom were Methodists. About two thousand in number, they inhabit Rambi Island in the Pacific. Their original home was Ocean Island, part of the Gilbert and Ellice Islands Colony, which was annexed by Britain in 1900 when a passing ship discovered that it was virtually a solid lump of phosphate. In partnership with Australia and New Zealand the British Phosphates Commission was founded. The Banaban people were offered a meagre royalty of six pence a ton on the phosphate mined, though this was later increased.

During the Second World War the Japanese invaded Ocean Island and the Banabans were dispersed around the Pacific. After the war Britain sent a ship to collect this scattered people but their island home was no longer habitable because of the extensive mining operations. So they were persuaded to live on Rambi Island 1200 miles away. This island had been bought for them out of the accumulated phosphate royalties. Life on Rambi was hard for the Banabans. Their accumulated capital was totally inadequate for the kind of development project their new island needed. The British had left them with two months' supply of food, some tents, and little else. Since the income from Ocean Island was likely soon to dry up they decided to bring a case for compensation from the British Government.

This was where I came in. The Rev Tebuki Rotan, a Methodist and the Island manager, came to England with his father, the Chief Rotan Tito. We entertained them in our home and we still have the shell lamp they brought us as a gift. I undertook to go with them to the discussions with the Foreign and Commonwealth Office at Lancaster House. The Government laid on a sleek limousine to collect me each day.

The Banabans made a number of demands. They wanted independence so that they would be entitled to the full phosphate revenue for the remainder of the life of the mining operation – about eight years.

They asked for a slowing-down of the rate of extraction to give them longer to work out their future. They requested a grant of £40,000,000 to develop Rambi Island. H. M. Government offered £80,000. Tebuki Rotan and Rotan Tito were outraged. They had always believed in the sense of justice among 'the men at the top' in Britain. After hours of discussion Lord Shepherd, the Minister of State, and his colleagues came to me and said, 'Can you talk to these people and show them that nothing is to be gained by pressing preposterous claims? We are not responsible for what our fathers did. We haven't got the kind of money they are demanding, and if we had, we wouldn't be spending it on the development of Rambi Island.'

I did my best. I tried patiently to explain that politics is the art of the possible and that negotiation and compromise are part of the game. If they were willing to accept that we might make some progress. They said that their demand was absolute and that they would take the matter to the Queen. Poor Tebuki never got further than the railings of Buckingham Palace and expressed grave disappointment that I, 'a man of God' should recommend compromise.

I began to enquire about the possibility of our sending out a development expert to help the Banabans. The Relief Fund made money available and we commissioned Mr Frank Field to undertake this enterprise. His reports were astonishing and conveyed the picture of a primitive people entirely out of touch with the way the world works. For example, a national day of prayer was announced on the Island on the day when it was rumoured that Tebuke Rotan was seeing the Queen. He was, in fact, comfortably ensconced in an expensive London hotel and had merely been to see the Changing of the Guard at the Palace. After a few months Mr Field felt that he had done all that he could and returned to this country. The Banabans employed expensive lawyers to continue their fight but there was nothing more that I could do for them. I was left with the unhappy feeling that it is one thing to build an empire; it is another to deal fairly with the casualties of imperial exploitation.

At the end of this brief survey of seventeen years at the cutting-edge of the social witness of the Methodist Church, and surveying the years since, I ask if the Methodist people, in the words of Henry Carter, 'are becoming socially-minded'. There is certainly no room for complacency. The danger of parochialism is ever present. It is possible for churches to become inward-looking, busy with the task of maintaining the immediate local ministry and with little interest in or any energy for involvement in the affairs of the wider world. There is, too, the temptation to shun controversy and a suspicion that political issues are an alien intrusion into a Bible-based fellowship. This reflects an anaemic and inadequate theology. I do not, myself, feel happy with the apparently increasing popularity of the type of religion that seems almost entirely preoccupied with the inner spiritual life of the believer. I fear that it can become a form of escapism. In some areas where in my time we fought hard to hold the line in such areas as curbing the sale of drink, limiting the volume of gambling and keeping Sunday special, our hedonistic, consumer-oriented society has moved in the opposite direction.

In spite of these negative indications, however, there is much to encourage. The willingness of the Methodist Connexion to take on the big and potentially divisive questions relating to human sexuality is praiseworthy. Throughout the land Methodist congregations, in co-operation with others, are using their premises and resources in the service of the community in all sorts of ways. Individual Methodists carry their religious convictions into their places of work, and some serve politics both locally and nationally, though one could wish for a larger Methodist representation in the Mother of Parliaments.

All in all we can be grateful for a church which seeks to keep in touch with the world and responsive to its needs. Yet there are battles that have to be fought anew in each generation. The work of my old Department is needed as much as ever, and not least its theological emphasis on the wholeness of the gospel which addresses both the personal and the social needs of humanity.

The call to the Secretaryship of the Methodist Conference was unexpected. My ministry from the start had been untypical and almost entirely determined by what the Conference decided I ought to do. When Dr Eric Baker brought me the news that the selection committee wanted to nominate me I asked for two days to think and pray about it before responding, a hesitation which seemed to surprise him. My wife and I talked and we prayed and I said, 'Yes.'

The move meant in one sense a short step along the corridor to the Secretary's office. In another sense it was a long step into a world of still further expanding opportunities: journeys all over the world, meetings with famous people, happy colleagueship with the leaders both of my own church and of our sister denominations, and a pastoral relationship with the ministry without which I should not have cared to do the job at all.

70

Chapter Four

PASTOR AND PEOPLE

No-one could have been more fortunate in his predecessor than I was when I followed Dr Eric Baker as Secretary of the Methodist Conference. During the months prior to my taking up the office he invited me to sit in on all the committees for which he had responsibility. This was an invaluable preparation.

Eric Baker had become a Methodist institution. He was a master of procedure and in Conference successive Presidents leaned heavily on him, especially when the going was rough and points of order started flying around like bats in a belfry. He had a mind like quicksilver which enabled him to make instant decisions, perhaps just occasionally and particularly in relation to people, a little too rapidly. He was always concerned to preserve the prerogatives of the President of the Conference. If, as sometimes happened, the incumbent of Wesley's chair found himself at sea in the middle of some complicated procedural wrangle, Eric Baker would rise and with a gentle smile would say, 'If I read your mind correctly, Mr President, you were about to suggest . . .'; then would follow a perfect solution to the verbal dilemma.

There were those who thought Eric Baker a rather austere person. We who knew him best, however, recognised in him a man with a deep pastoral concern, especially for his fellow-ministers, and a kindness which warmed the hearts of many of those who turned to him for help. His sometimes brusque manner cloaked an essential shyness. Although in Conference he appeared to be the master of all he surveyed, in fact he faced his responsibilities as Secretary with a very real degree of nervousness. His ministry was wonderfully supported and supplemented by his wife, Winifred, a bubbling fountain of inspiration, warmth and friendliness. In 1959 Eric was elected President of the Conference and moved easily from his familiar seat on the platform to the one next to it, and at the end of the year back again.

Eric Baker was occasionally, and quite unfairly, compared with the most famous of his predecessors as Secretary of the Conference, Dr Jabez Bunting (1779-1858), a most formidable character. I turn aside for a moment to comment on the remarkable ministry of the man who perhaps more than any other changed Methodism from a Society within the

Church of England to a church. Bunting became Secretary of the Conference and was President four times. Connexional responsibilities were heaped upon him. He helped to found the first Methodist theological college and became its President. He headed the work of the Overseas Missions Department. He was Connexional Editor. Such an accumulation of power in the hands of one man was dangerous, and some of his growing number of critics called him 'the Methodist Pope' – an epithet earlier attached to John Wesley himself. At his funeral service Dr Leifchild said that Jabez Bunting was 'born to rule'. Dr John Kent asserts that he had 'an ungovernable urge to govern' (*Jabez Bunting: the Last Wesleyan*, London 1955, p.52). Bunting failed to recognise the inflowing tide of democracy which was to change the face of society and its institutions, a fact to which I briefly referred in Chapter Two. The result was a series of disastrous rebellions and secessions and a sad end to the ministry of a gifted man who reached the point where he seemed to be indispensable and reacted badly to any attempt to put forward views that differed from his own. Those who talked of Baker and Bunting in the same breath only showed their ignorance of both men.

On his retirement Eric Baker took a back seat. That is never easy for a man who has been at the heart of affairs. I was glad to turn to him for advice but he never in any way interfered with my work. He went off with his wife for a protracted period to lecture in an American University, 'so that I shan't get under your feet, my dear boy'. One day he telephoned me to say that he was going into hospital. I said, 'I hope that you will make a good recovery and soon be home.' 'I think not,' was his quick and calm reply, 'I have set my affairs in order, so that will be all right.' He died a few days later, leaving me and so many others with a sense of irreparable loss.

In these latter days the Methodist system has become far more democratic than it was in Bunting's time. The ultimate authority in the governance of the church remains the annual Conference, but its powers are delegated to a number of bodies and individuals. Among the latter is the central triumvirate of President, Vice-President and Secretary. The President is elected for one year and must be a minister in the active work. There has so far been only one woman President – the Rev Dr Kathleen Richardson (1993-4).

The office of President is highly regarded by the Methodist people but the person who holds the office has very little executive power. He or she can use the opportunities of the presidential year to talk about particular issues and emphases as I did. It is the office rather than the particular holder of it that is important. That does not mean, of course, that the gifts and personality of the President are unimportant. The value of the office would quickly lessen if the Conference chose its leaders irresponsibly. In fact the Conference and the church have been well-served by a succession of gifted ministers who have adorned the office, though inevitably some have made a greater impact than others.

From time to time there is pressure to increase the term of the Presidency to three or even five years. This would, it is claimed, enhance its significance. It is usually pointed out that the Archbishop of Canterbury remains in office over a period of years and thus becomes known, particularly to the media, which has great advantages (though the scurrilous treatment meted out on occasion to archbishops by the press might lead some to question this assertion). I do not believe that our existing system should be changed. The position of the Archbishop is in a number of ways different from that of the Methodist President, not least in that the former is the clerical head of the state church. All the other non-Roman Churches in Britain have an annual change of President or Moderator. The disadvantages of the short-term incumbency can, so far as the media are concerned, be overcome, at least to some degree, with the help of a good Press Officer who keeps the President in the picture and is also able to direct the attention of press, radio and television to others within the church who are able to speak with authority. During my Westminster years I was well-served by the Methodist Press Office and established a good relationship with the press, especially with the religious correspondents of the major newspapers. For many years, both because of his stature and his superb ability to answer questions on virtually any subject, the representatives of the media have turned to Lord Soper whom they seem to have regarded as the permanent head of the Methodist Church. (He was President in 1953.)

Some overseas churches have a longer term presidency, an arrangement partly dictated by the fact that in smaller churches the field of choice is more limited and it would be difficult to find a different person each year. In the very large United Methodist Church in the USA there are annual conferences for the various jurisdictions and a quadrennial General Conference responsible for the governance of the whole church. There is no office which corresponds exactly with that of the President of the British Methodist Conference. American Methodists sometimes say, 'Ah, your President is the equivalent of one of our bishops.' That is inaccurate. The American General Conference is presided over by the bishops in turn on a daily rota basis, and they meet as a group in the Council of Bishops.

The office of Vice-President in the British Conference is also an annual appointment and it is held by a lay person. It is intended to symbolise the important place of the laity in the life of the church. Like the President, the Vice-President travels up and down the land, and often to overseas churches, speaking and preaching at a great variety of meetings and functions. In recent years more women have been elected to this position than in earlier times. The first woman Vice-President was Mrs Mildred Lewis (1948). She brought grace and charm to the platform as she sat alongside Dr Benson Perkins who sometimes sounded a trifle gruff.

The third member of the triumvirate which exists at the heart of the life of the Methodist Connexion is the Secretary of the Conference. The constitution requires that this office be held by a minister in the active work. Usually the person elected serves for some years. Unlike the office of President the Secretaryship carries a number of executive responsibilities, and for that reason, as well as that of continuity, it is a position of considerable power.

Asquith once said that the office of Prime Minister is 'what its holder chooses and is able to make of it'. During Eric Baker's long period of service the Secretaryship became a much more widely recognised and influential office both within Methodism and beyond. Whereas his immediate predecessor, the Rev Edwin Finch, had been content to work largely in his Westminster office running the Connexional machine, Dr Baker travelled widely, visiting churches at home and abroad and playing a leading part in the field of ecumenical relations. I, therefore, inherited not only a well-oiled administrative setup but a job of infinite fascination and with great potential for further development. I will describe some of the major issues with which I had to deal during my term of service as Secretary of the Conference and then give some account of my year as President.

I had the good fortune to inherit as my secretary Miss Winnie Price, a woman of outstanding competence and discretion. She was a most loyal colleague who dealt with a large number of visitors to the office with skill and friendliness. Among those visitors was a fair sprinkling of American Methodist tourists from whose time-consuming attentions I could not always escape. Winnie's head would appear round the door and with an expression of despair she would announce, 'Mr Elmer T. Boltinghorse, Junior, of Texas to see you', or some similarly frustrating intimation.

However, we remembered John Wesley's assertion about the world being his parish and made them all welcome, even when the day's timetable was seriously disrupted.

I recall that one of my visitors was an elderly retired minister. He looked around my office and at the picture of John Wesley on the wall and then, with a sniff of disdain, said, 'We used to have big men in Methodism; they told others what to do and they did it.' I found myself describing to this caller my own conception of collaborative leadership. My immediate colleagues were the Secretaries of the seven Divisions: Home Missions, Overseas, Finance, Property, Education and Youth, Ministries, and Social Responsibility. With every one of them without exception I enjoyed a relationship of mutual trust and affection. They encouraged me to think of myself as the leader of the team. My office door was always open and I greatly appreciated the privilege of sharing their thinking about the opportunities and difficulties of their work. When I had hard decisions to make it was both a help and a comfort to be able to draw on their willing assistance and counsel.

My ministerial assistant was the Rev Norman Wooldridge. He was the soul of loyalty and relieved me of much of the routine administrative work of the office, freeing me to develop the kind of wider ministry to which I felt I was called. He exercised a most valuable pastoral ministry among the Westminster staff. I have one great regret about Norman: he had gifts which were not fully exploited as my assistant. Though I should have been loath to see him go I was disappointed when his nomination to the chair of the Birmingham District was overturned by the District Synod. I think he never quite recovered from that rebuff.

The nomination for the Chairmanship of a District was made by a committee composed of District and Connexional representatives, the former constituting the majority. I always held the view that the office of Chairman was significant both in District and Connexional terms. I did my best to stress the Connexional role of the District Chairman. I, therefore, regretted when, after careful consideration by the representative group to which I have referred and their reaching a unanimous conclusion, their judgement was overturned by a Synod anxious to see its own favourite appointed from within the District. Such occasions were comparatively rare and the church has been fortunate in those elected to lead the Districts. All the same, there is considerable uneasiness about the middle layer of oversight within the Methodist structures. The District machinery lies between that of the Conference and the Circuits. The District Synod is in my experience the least effective part of our administration. Its role will, I believe, be given careful scrutiny in the coming years.

There is a growing body of opinion in Methodism that our District Chairmen should be called bishops. I have for a number of years argued the case for a change of nomenclature. The word 'chairman' is applied to those holding secular positions and is an inappropriate designation for someone who is the chief pastor of an area. The word bishop comes from the New Testament 'episcopos', signifying oversight. The greater part of world Methodism already has bishops, the term having been adopted almost from the start by the Methodists of the USA.

During the period when the Anglican/Methodist Unity Scheme was under discussion a Commission was appointed by the Conference to consider the question of Methodist bishops. Since one of the requirements of the Scheme was that the Methodist Church should take episcopacy into its system, it was important for us to consider what kind of bishops we would have, and the number and method of their appointment. One reason for the reluctance of many British Methodists to contemplate the acceptance of the term 'bishop' is that they have preconceived ideas about episcopal status and function. When the Methodist Conference met in Norwich the diocesan Bishop came to express his welcome. With great kindness he invited members to take a stroll through the gardens of his palace. It occurred to me that such an exercise might well confirm the worst fears of those who associate the word 'bishop' with prelacy, pomp and circumstance.

In fact, of course, the external trappings of episcopacy, such as elaborate vestments, jewelled mitres, chauffeur-driven cars and large palaces, are in no way essential and certainly do not reflect the pastoral heart of the episcopal office. In the Church of England the appurtenances of episcopacy have been slimmed down and in other parts of the worldwide Anglican communion some bishops live in very humble circumstances. When I attended the Lambeth Conference as an observer I sat next to a delightful little man from somewhere in Asia who told me that he spent a lot of his time canoeing from one part of his huge diocese to another. The idea of a canoeing bishop seemed to me to put the episcopal office into a fresh perspective!

There are those who have argued that the Circuit Superintendent in Methodism comes nearest to the New Testament bishop in terms of pastoral care and oversight. Of course, those whose image of a bishop is limited to that of the Anglican diocesan in England will regard the notion of some 700 bishops as absurd. For the sake of effective inter-church co-operation at the regional level we must have some regard to the way oversight works in other churches and my own view is that our District chairmen should assume the episcopal title. They already work closely with Anglican Bishops up and down the country though, of course, Methodist District boundaries do not coincide precisely with those of the Anglican dioceses. When the Scheme to unite the two churches was under discussion a study was made of the geographical relationship between the Districts and Dioceses. Some interesting maps were produced by Dr Edmund Marshall, then a Member of Parliament. It was felt that some redrawing of boundaries would facilitate closer co-operation between church leaders in the various areas. The collapse of the Unity Scheme put an end to that discussion as to much else concerning the future relationship of the churches.

The Secretary of the Methodist Conference is an ex officio member of all Connexional Committees. I made it clear to my colleagues that I had no intention of attending them all though I would always come if there was some particular reason for their wanting me to be present. There were several Committees of which I was convener, the most significant of these being the President's Council. This came into being when a big programme of restructuring was undertaken at the beginning of the 1970s. Once again in 1996 the church's headquarters assumed a different shape. The seven Divisions have been replaced by a central core team of four officers plus the Secretary of Conference and their support staffs. A newly-created Methodist Council will act as the Executive of the Conference between the annual meetings of the latter. It will take some time for the Methodist membership to understand the new arrangements and there are those who express anxiety about what they see as the concentration of too much power at the centre. The test of the new structures will be the degree of their effectiveness in assisting the Connexion to perform its mission.

I do not for a moment pretend that constitutional change is always a waste of time, but I do believe that Methodism has spent far too much vital energy tinkering with the machine. The book which contains the foundation documents of the Methodist Church and its Standing Orders, *The Constitutional Practice and Discipline of the Methodist Church* (CPD) has grown ridiculously large. The Standing Orders are meticulously drafted and all the parts of the constitution are fitted together with legal precision. For many years the Conference has been guided in all these matters by Mr John Hicks, now a Circuit Judge, and a lawyer of outstanding competence and intellectual brilliance. I think, however, that there is a danger that the spirit of an organisation can be stifled by an excessive weight of rules and regulations. In Eric Baker's time, if sometimes the rules seemed to get in the way of what needed to be done rather than facilitating it, he would say, 'The Conference is master in its own house and the rules are meant to be our guide and not our chain.' It is a sound dictum.

The President's Council was intended to be a think-tank to guide the church in the shaping of policy and the assessment of priorities in the life of the Connexion. The key members of this newly-created body were the General Secretaries of the seven Divisions. The very word 'division' has unfortunate overtones, but the contributions of my colleagues enabled us to see the wholeness of what together we were trying to do. There was the constant danger that the Council would be swamped by all sorts of issues referred to it by the Conference. I did my best to ensure that there was sufficient leisure for creative thinking. This process was greatly helped by holding our meetings residentially at the Luton Industrial College, the scene of the Rev William Gowland's unique ministry which did so much to develop a Christian approach to industry.

The President's Council in session at Luton Industrial College

There were many occasions when one or other of my Divisional colleagues was able to bring to the Council for its judgement proposals on some important issue later to be submitted to the Conference. On other occasions the Council considered matters hammered out in working parties which had been set up by it or on the direction of the Conference.

One of the early concerns of the Council as it began to find its feet was the question of Methodism's headquarters buildings. My own office and those of four of the Divisions were in the Westminster Central Hall complex known as 1, Central Buildings. This location, on one side of Parliament Square immediately opposite Westminster Abbey, had a certain value in terms of prestige, but there were disadvantages. The original idea at the turn of the century of creating a 'monumental building' to be both a great preaching centre and a home for the church's central offices was not a good one. I was for many years a Trustee of the Central Hall whilst at the same time concerned to uphold the interests of the Divisions who were its tenants. The relationship of the Central Hall as church and the offices was never an easy one.

A succession of gifted ministers struggled with the immensely difficult task of maintaining a meaningful ministry in that huge edifice. Dr William Sangster drew an enormous congregation Sunday by Sunday by his powerful preaching. He was a larger-than-life character. On one occasion he happened to sail through the lower hall when I was on a ladder blowing up balloons in anticipation of a temperance bazaar. 'Ah, my dear friend,' he boomed, 'inflating air balls, I see.' It was a typical Sangster utterance. His preaching was always dramatic, sometimes electrifying. But his departure from the Central Hall marked the end of an era. Congregations slumped as they did at the City Temple when Leslie Weatherhead retired, and at Kingsway Hall during the last years of Donald Soper's ministry there.

I admired the courageous ministries of Derrick Greeves, who used to drive round London in an old taxi that he had bought, of Maurice Barnett and John Tudor. These men had to shoulder much of the burden of overseeing the management of the premises. The Central Hall relies on the letting of its premises for a large part of the income necessary to maintain them. In order to make this commercially viable large sums have had to be spent on substantial repairs and interior reconstruction work. Some of the Divisions have moved out of the building making way for secular lettings at more realistic rents.

Much thought and effort in recent years has gone into the question of how this great building can continue to be a focus of Christian witness.

It has maintained a fine musical tradition but that in itself does not attract large numbers of people. During Dr Tudor's ministry ecumenical relations between the Hall, Westminster Abbey and Westminster Cathedral were strengthened. Although the Central Hall attracts many visitors it cannot compete in this regard with the Abbey, with its great historic associations, nor with the Cathedral which is the Mecca for huge numbers of Roman Catholics. On one occasion, after I had preached at Westminster Abbey, a member of the staff there, who has since left, said, 'What you need at the Central Hall is a scholar in the pulpit.' Quite apart from the slur on the distinguished preachers who have ministered at the Central Hall over the last fifty years and before, this bit of Anglican superiority seemed to me wildly unrealistic. It is doubtful whether the Archangel Gabriel could fill the Central Hall in these days, not after the first Sunday at any rate, and not even if he went to the trouble of equipping himself with a couple of Oxford degrees.

In 1994 the Conference appointed a new Management Committee for the Central Hall. It will oversee further refurbishments costing many millions of pounds. The raising of money for this kind of project is no easy matter when churches throughout the country are often stretched to maintain their own work. The Management Committee is charged with seeking ways in which the resources of this great central building can be made available for the mission of the wider church. Dr Peter Graves, who began his ministry at the Central Hall in September 1995, will face the challenge of all that this implies with vigour and courage.

A couple of years before I became Secretary of the Conference I was asked to convene a Commission on the future of Methodism's theological colleges. When I entered the ministry there were six of these. The number had been reduced to four: Wesley House, Cambridge; Richmond College, London; Wesley College, Bristol; and Hartley Victoria College, Manchester. My own college at Handsworth in Birmingham had united with the Queen's Anglican College in that city – a fine example of ecumenical co-operation unhappily not as yet followed up elsewhere in the country. The Commission included two non-Methodists: the Rev Paul Rowntree Clifford, the distinguished Baptist, and the Rev Sydney Evans, later Dean of Salisbury. They proved most valuable in bringing an outside and completely unbiased judgement to our proceedings.

Our task was a difficult one. It had become clear that Methodism neither needed nor could afford to run four independent theological colleges. It was recommended that Richmond College should be sold or leased; that Hartley Victoria College should be improved and become the training centre for about eighty students; and that students not trained elsewhere should be trained at Wesley College, Bristol provided that by 1972 a viable scheme for training, ministerial and otherwise, at that college was produced. The Conference appointed another Commission with my old friend John Stacey as convener to consider the future of Wesley College, Bristol.

John Stacey's Commission worked hard. It examined a number of possible schemes but in the end concluded that none of these would be effective or financially viable. This conclusion was reached with real regret. The Bristol College was a new building well equipped for catering, teaching, and with a residential block housing sixty students. It had a modern worship centre and enjoyed a close relationship with Bristol University where a Methodist, the Rev Kenneth Grayston, was Professor of Theology.

My own Commission had been made fully aware of all these facts and we visited the colleges to examine the situation on the ground. I well recall our visit to Hartley Victoria College. I could understand why some critics nicknamed the sprawling buildings 'the jam factory'. Dr Percy Scott, the Principal, showed us round with characteristic gusto. I commented behind his back, 'This man could sell us the *Titanic* without letting on that it had sunk.' In spite of all this, however, we came to the conclusion that Hartley Victoria should be retained. The excellence of the Theological Faculty at Manchester University weighed heavily in the scales of judgement as did also the conviction that the environment provided by a vast urban connurbation was more suitable for ministers in training than the pleasant green-belt location of the college in Bristol. When Dr Scott read our report his characteristic comment was, 'I like the colour of your writing.'

This difficult and contentious matter came on to the agenda of the President's Council because the Conference of 1971 approved a motion requesting the Council to look again at the financial cost of concentrating ministerial training at Hartley Victoria. If it felt that the cost was too high it should advise the Conference of 1972 what steps to take. The Council went over all the ground again. It confirmed the view that ministerial training should cease at Richmond and at Bristol and that provision should be made at Hartley Victoria for 90 students. The Conference debated these recommendations. College loyalties run deep and there were hard-hitting speeches on all sides. The actual vote, which was taken by a show of hands, produced a moment of high drama. The Conference was precisely divided, half voting for the retention of Hartley Victoria and half for Wesley, Bristol. It seemed to me that it would be unfair on so emotive and partisan an issue to land the President, the Rev Harry Morton, with the unenviable task of giving a casting vote. I therefore suggested that when the Conference reconvened after the tea break it should take a vote by ballot. This was agreed and when the subsequent vote was taken it showed a narrow majority in favour of the Bristol option. This decision inevitably caused great hurt and dismay to the staff and students of Hartley Victoria. That hurt was to a large extent healed, however, by the invitation of the Principal of the Northern Baptist College, the Rev Michael Taylor, to make his college a joint Baptist/Methodist enterprise. This happy partnership has continued. Michael Taylor, now the Director of Christian Aid, is a man with broad and liberal views who combines grace and vision with a great gift for leadership and the establishment of good personal relationships. He was the right man in the right place at the right time – as he still is.

A question that figured largely on the agenda of the President's Council in the early 1970s was that of securing a more equitable representation of women on the major committees of the church. There were several reasons for this concern. One was that it seemed grossly unfair that in a church where the membership is predominantly female the decision-making offices should be largely filled by men. But this, of course, was only part of a wider recognition that the churches generally had shared in the age-long subjugation of women and must now seek to overcome their prejudices.

One obvious difficulty for those who wrestled with this problem was the frequent conflict between the need to find the best person for a particular task and the scarcity of suitable women candidates. Such scarcity is the direct result of the failure of the church to train women for leadership roles. The position is improving rapidly but it requires a definite resolve as a matter of policy to search for women with the gifts and competence for the work in hand and encourage them to come forward. Some distinguished women tend to be grossly overworked by being asked to serve on too many committees and some complain that they are selected to fill the role of 'the statutory women'.

On the advice of the President's Council the Conference approved amended Standing Orders laying down precise figures and percentages governing the inclusion of women in Connexional Committees. These constitutional arrangements signify and give effect to the church's desire to encourage the full partnership of women and men in church and society, and its abhorrence of discrimination based on sex.

The development of an ordained ministry open equally to women and men has greatly assisted the correction of the distorted ideas of the past regarding the relationship of the sexes. This does not mean, however, that there is any room for complacency. It is significant that many women ministers have found ground for complaint that they are not fully accepted as equal partners by their male colleagues. Within the church generally one sometimes hears complaints, from both men and women, that some feminists are harsh and strident in their attitudes and public utterances. That is a pity, for a good case can be ruined by a bad presentation. But even the most aggressive defenders of women's rights can scarcely rival the appalling arrogance that some men have displayed in their contemptuous denial of those rights. Extremist views tend to provoke extremist reactions.

The President's Council was involved in the discussion of other forms of discrimination. In 1969 the World Council of Churches had launched its Programme to Combat Racism. The aim was to conduct research into the nature of this great evil, to sponsor projects such as consultations on theology and racism, racism in education, and so on. A Special Fund was created to help organisations of racially oppressed people and their supporters. It was the activities of this Fund which stirred up a great deal of controversy, fanned by much hostile misrepresentation in the press. In Methodism there was concern that money given to the Special Fund was being used to help liberation movements involved in armed conflict. I am bound to say that much of the criticism seemed to me to be a bit rich coming from people who had enthusiastically supported our own country in its resort to war. When I was President of the Conference I deliberately made an early official visit to the Ecumenical Centre in Geneva to express Methodism's support for the PCR.

The argument about the Special Fund reached a climax when the officers of the WCC decided to make a grant to the Patriotic Front in Zimbabwe. This organisation was engaged in widespread guerrilla warfare and was accused of atrocities against innocent civilians. Members of the Methodist Conference expressed opposition to the making of grants by the Overseas Division and the Division of Social Responsibility. They felt that if money were to be sent at all it should be given by private individuals. The two Divisions concerned presented a very full statement to the Conference. They pointed out that the Special Fund grant was an attempt to raise a non-violent voice on behalf of the oppressed in a conflict that was becoming increasingly violent; that the WCC had made clear its condemnation of atrocities whoever had committed them; that the grant was political in that it expressed opposition to political 'solutions' based on racism; and, very importantly, that the grant was given specifically for humanitarian relief. The Conference registered its firm support for the PCR and the work of its Special Fund, and authorised the two Divisions to continue their existing policy. The President's Council then reported that it had asked Pauline Webb (Methodist representative on the WCC's Executive Committee) to convey to the Officers of the WCC its concern that they had failed to send to the member churches adequate advance explanation of their intentions and had shown insensitivity to public reactions, and had thereby contributed to the widespread misunderstanding of the operation of the PCR.

In the mid-1970s the Methodist Church was advised that it would have to introduce a parliamentary private member's bill. The main purpose of this was to enable the business of leaders and trustees in the local churches to be combined under a new body known as the Church Council. Formerly the Leader's Meeting, with the minister, had been responsible for the spiritual oversight of the church while the Trustees took care of matters relating to the property. Obviously it is not possible rigidly to separate these two areas of responsibility and occasionally disagreements arose between the two bodies. The Conference, therefore, decided to abolish this system of dual control.

Our legal advisers asked whether, since it was an expensive operation, there was any other matter requiring parliamentary action which we would like to incorporate in the bill. I thought that it would be a good thing to remove from the existing legislation the restriction on the church's freedom which prevented it from altering its statement of doctrine contained in Clause 30 of the Deed of Union, the document that sets out the basis upon which the three major branches of British Methodism – Wesleyan, United and Primitive – came together in one church in 1932. There was apparently a certain lack of trust between the three uniting churches on matters of doctrine and it was decided at the time that they should ask Parliament to 'entrench' Clause 30, that is to enact that no changes could be made to it without parliamentary permission.

My own view, shared by others, was that this rather shameful anachronism should be removed on the ground that in this matter, above all others, the church should be free to state or restate its fundamental

84

beliefs entirely as it wishes without any externally imposed restrictions. The Methodist Church Bill was accordingly drafted to secure this end. Although it was only a small section of a fairly complex measure it attracted opposition from a group of Methodist members, some of whom were active members of an organisation called the Voice of Methodism set up to oppose the Anglican/Methodist Unity Scheme. Their decision to oppose the bill added greatly to the cost of getting the measure through Parliament. There were hearings in committees of both the Lords and the Commons. I represented the Methodist Conference and was subject to cross-examination both by our own 'parliamentary leader', a distinguished Queen's Counsel, and by the lawyer leading for the opponents. Altogether I spent the best part of two weeks in the Palace of Westminster attending these hearings.

I was distressed by the fact that the opponents of the bill refused absolutely to believe me when I told them that, so far as the doctrinal clause was concerned, the action was being taken purely on grounds of principle – a principle with which I should have expected them wholeheartedly to agree. I assured them that there was no intention of altering our doctrinal statement but that we believed it was quite unacceptable that our freedom to do so should be restricted by an earlier Act of Parliament. They nevertheless asserted before the Parliamentary Committees that there was a plot by 'the men at Westminster' to change our doctrine. In my opinion they made themselves look ridiculous. I never questioned their democratic right to oppose, only their motives and wisdom in doing so.

During the second reading of the bill in the House of Commons I was invited to occupy a special seat on the floor of the House so that honourable members could consult me during the debate, as several did. Part way through the discussion the Speaker (the Rt Hon George Thomas) arrived to take his seat. 'Ah,' cried one Methodist MP, 'here come reinforcements.' 'Not today,' responded Mr Speaker, 'Strictly neutral.' This sally was greeted with laughter.

The bill was passed by Parliament and received the Royal Assent on 26 October 1976. One curious feature of the second reading debate was that the Liberal members of Parliament voted against it though most of them were not present during the discussions and could have known little about the measure. When I taxed one of them with this strange, and as I thought very undemocratic, behaviour, he said, 'Ah well, Richard Wainwright is one of our boys so we had to support him.' Mr Wainwright was one of the leading opponents of the bill and the spokesman in Parliament of the dissident group to which I have referred.

During the 1970s the affairs of the Methodist Publishing House ran into difficulties. In 1980 the President's Council learned that a number of creditors were pressing strongly for the payment of accounts long overdue. It was clear that urgent action should be taken to safeguard the good name of the church and to overhaul the management of the Publishing House. The Council acted promptly and appointed the Rev Derek Farrow, the General Secretary of the Division of Finance, and Mr David Ensor, a layman with long experience in publishing, to carry out the necessary reorganisation in consultation with the President of the Conference. The Council authorised the Division of Finance to provide £210,000 (including £50,000 which had been earmarked for the publication of a new hymn book) to meet the demands of creditors and to finance essential supplies of hymn books and service books.

A further important decision was made. Successful negotiations were completed to allow the Student Christian Movement Press Limited to market and distribute titles bearing the Epworth Press imprint. The Editorial Committee of the Epworth Press was made directly responsible to Conference and was authorised to publish books only after the SCM Press had carefully costed both production and distribution.

Inevitably the whole exercise caused pain to some of the people most closely involved. In February 1981 Mr Sydney Clark, a gracious and loyal servant of the church, resigned his position as Chairman of the Board of the Publishing House and two of his colleagues also resigned. Mr Albert Jakeway, the Manager, continued loyally to serve under the new arrangements. He was succeeded by Mr Brian Thornton. Under his energetic leadership Methodist publishing has prospered and he has played an important part in establishing profitable links with Methodist publishing interests in other parts of the world. The Conference of 1995 endorsed proposals to bring the Methodist Publishing House and the Epworth Press back into closer relationship again.

I referred briefly to a new Methodist hymn book. This was published in 1983 under the title *Hymns & Psalms: a Methodist and Ecumenical Hymn Book*. The previous hymn book had served the church well but it was fifty years old. It was felt that a new book would be able to include some of the work of writers and composers of the previous half-century, like Dr Fred Pratt Green who has made an outstanding contribution to modern hymnology. The Conference of 1979 authorised such a publication and entrusted the work to the Faith and Order

Committee, one of the most fascinating of our Connexional Committees the meetings of which I always enjoyed.

The new book was not brought to birth without some pain and the period of gestation produced some difficulties. The main contributors to the truly monumental labours involved were the two scholarly Jones's of the Connexion – Dr Ivor Jones who chaired the production committee and its convener, Dr Richard Jones. They consulted widely within Methodism and beyond. The Conference considered various drafts and the *Methodist Recorder* rendered most valuable service, as it has done so often, by publishing periodic progress reports.

It had been hoped that the new book would be published jointly by the Methodist Church and the United Reformed Church. However, in November 1980, during my year as President of the Conference, the General Secretary of the URC, the Rev Bernard Thorogood, wrote to me to say that there were difficulties for his church. The URC Executive Committee had decided that it was no longer appropriate for their church to continue as a formal participant in the project. I took immediate steps to call together a small group representing both churches. The URC representatives undertook to have their decision reconsidered. They had difficulties over the proposed title for the new book, about the Wesley content of it and about the amount of capital which it was suggested they should invest in the project (£50,000 out of £200,000). In the end the URC decided regretfully not to proceed with the partnership arrangement which would have produced a hymn book bearing the imprimatur of both churches. It was a pity.

The crucial debate on the shape of the new book took place in the 1980 Conference when I was in the chair. It was a lively occasion. Methodists who can sit calmly through discussion of such crucial issues as peace and war suddenly spring to life when the subject is hymnology. Long queues formed at both tribunes in the Conference Hall. As so often happens, many came with prepared speeches and took no account of what other speakers had said, which always results in a certain amount of vain repetition. Some questioned the need for a new book. 'We haven't yet sung all the hymns in the old book', they said. I wondered whether, if they had not done so in fifty years, they ever would! There was much individual concern about favourite hymns omitted and some criticism of the balance of Wesley hymns included in the draft. When all the speeches seemed to be going in the same direction – that of warm approval – I asked any who might be of a contrary view to come forward, and some did. It was a good debate.

I had myself hoped that the whole of John Wesley's Preface to *A Collection of Hymns for the Use of the People called Methodists* published in 1770 might be included, as it was in the 1933 hymn book, for it is a gem of literary artistry. However, Ivor and Richard Jones quoted from it in their own Preface. They say:

> As the music of this book has been selected to encourage congregational singing, so too the words have been chosen because they are representative of the best of ancient and modern hymn writing. All of them, in Wesley's words, 'talk common sense'; the greatest of them demonstrate, as he finely put it 'the purity, the strength, and the elegance of the English language; and, at the same time, the utmost simplicity and plainness, suited to every capacity'. Wesley desired his readers to judge 'whether there be not in some of the following hymns the true Spirit of Poetry, such as cannot be acquired by art or labour, but must be the gift of nature'; but he considered that the needs of the religious life were of paramount importance. 'That which is of infinitely more moment than the Spirit of Poetry, is the spirit of piety. And I trust that all persons of real judgement will find this breathing through the whole Collection.'

Hymns & Psalms is serving the church well. It would be a great pity if its place in our liturgy were usurped by the plethora of inferior collections which seem to have proliferated across the Connexion. Some of them contain much that is scarcely expressive of Wesley's 'true Spirit of Poetry', nor indeed of the 'spirit of piety'.

I have dwelt at some length on a few of the issues with which I was involved as the Convener of the President's Council. There were, of course, many others. I was also responsible for the work of two of the other major Connexional Committees: the General Purposes Committee and the Committee on Law and Polity. Some of the legal issues raised in the latter I found fascinating, others somewhat tedious.

It will be apparent that the job of Secretary of the Conference involves a fair amount of administration, but so, of course, does the work of a circuit minister, especially if he or she is the Superintendent. I tried to administer fairly and efficiently, believing that organisation is essential to the effective ordering of the life of the church. However, I could never have done the job if that had been all that there was to it. I was ordained to the holy ministry and my ordination vows as well as my own sense of vocation were kept intact by two facts. One was the pastoral dimension of the work; the other was the preaching ministry I continued to exercise.

I have already referred to my happy relationships with colleagues at Westminster and in all the Headquarters offices. Eric Baker had convened a periodic meeting of them all and had presided over it with grace and humour. We were able to talk about our work, our problems and our hopes. Our proceedings were confidential though, of course, we had no authority in that meeting to make decisions on business that fell to be considered elsewhere. We accepted Eric as our unelected leader. I was very grateful when I was encouraged to take his place and the meetings I convened were a source of enjoyment and mutual refreshment.

Such meetings were discontinued in the end for an interesting reason. The church had begun to appoint lay persons as Divisional Secretaries. Formerly all such posts had been held by ministers on the ground that the Conference had more direct control over those who had been ordained than it could properly exercise over layfolk. The latter had by law to have contracts of employment. No such contracts exist with ministers; they are bound by their solemn vows when they are received into full connexion with the Conference and at their ordination. Some of our lay colleagues objected to a meeting that was exclusively ministerial. They felt, understandably, that they were being shut out. We therefore invited them to join us: a decision that was entirely right and just. The fact is, however, that the meeting subtly changed and enthusiasm waned. The loss of this valuable means of fellowship was, perhaps, part of the price that had to be paid for learning what the full partnership of ordained and lay people should mean. Behind our fraternal gatherings lay a long tradition of meetings for ministers only. In Wesley's day, and for some time afterwards, the Methodist Conference itself consisted of ministers only. The Conference still meets in two sessions. The Representative Session consists of an equal number of ministers and layfolk and meets for a week. The Ministerial Session lasts only a couple of days and its powers are severely limited. But there has been, and to some extent still is, a distinctive if undefinable ethos about meetings of ministers only. This is understandable and I see no reason to apologise for it. But great sensitivity is needed in these days of shared ministry if we are to preserve and enhance the relationship between the ordained ministry and the laity.

One aspect of my ministry as pastor was often the cause of great pain. The Secretary of the Conference is, by our constitution, involved in the administering of ministerial discipline. Inevitably there are from time to time sad cases of ministerial breakdown. These are sometimes caused by illness, sometimes by loss of faith or sense of call, and sometimes by behaviour unbecoming a minister, more often than not of a sexual kind. Whenever a minister submitted his or her resignation to the President of the Conference I had to convene a President's Advisory Committee. Occasionally there would be a situation where, although a minister had not resigned, there was evidence of impending scandal. On a few occasions I had to urge Chairmen of Districts to take disciplinary action. Their reluctance to do so was understandable but my experience was that unless prompt action was taken an even worse crisis could develop.

The proceedings of the President's Advisory Committee were often extremely distressing. To talk with a minister who has lost his way, who is in despair, whose marriage, perhaps, is in ruins, is hard. The Committee, operating in strict confidentiality, was always compassionate. It had also to preserve the integrity of the church and its ministry. At the end of the interview it would decide what advice to proffer to the President. Even in the most serious cases where a minister had to resign 'under charges' the hope was expressed that at some future date he might return to the ministry. Some have done so. In such cases there is no question of 'reordination'. The person concerned may have resumed the status of a layman or woman and the form of address appropriate to that status, yet our practice asserts the view that the orders conferred by ordination are indelible.

I have called this Chapter 'Pastor and People' because during my Westminster years I travelled ceaselessly up and down the land as well as overseas. Almost every weekend I was preaching somewhere. When I was a circuit minister I loved the pastoral work, the caring for people in their homes, the sharing of their joys and sorrows. When the church pulled me out of this work among a settled community I had to come to terms with the limitations and opportunities of a travelling ministry. I decided that there was some value in a wandering ambassador who could bring direct news and insights from the wider world beyond the parish boundaries. I find this conviction reflected in my sermon register.

There was also the privilege of staying in the homes of our people. Week after week I enjoyed the hospitality of choice folk. I found this rewarding but also demanding. Often I was required to minister to people who were passing through a time of great sorrow or distress, sometimes deeply anxious about their children. I found the constant talking within the home as well as preaching two or three times on the Sunday very wearing. I have been grateful that in recent years when I have gone to

90

preach over a weekend my wife has been able to come with me to share the burden of constant conversation. There is a reward in heaven for the occasional host or hostess who after Sunday lunch shuts the preacher off in a quiet room. These weekend forays gave me a wonderful opportunity to 'take the pulse of the Connexion' and to hear about local situations. It was always encouraging to hear people talk appreciatively about their minister. Occasionally I was distressed to hear about inexcusable pastoral neglect by ministers who never seemed to call on their people in their homes.

Not infrequently I was invited to preach in churches of other denominations, sometimes on great occasions. I preached in many of the Anglican Cathedrals. On one occasion when I preached in St Paul's Cathedral the Dean said to me at the conclusion of the service, 'I want you to come with me to the vestry.' On arrival there he said, 'Now this is no charge on the Cathedral funds. It is the practice of the City Fathers to present a bottle of the best sherry to visiting preachers.' He handed me a large bottle. I accepted it with gratitude whilst at the same time hoping that any fellow-abstainers in the congregation wouldn't spot it under my cassock. It lasted my wife for several years as a modest additive to certain culinary dishes.

A particularly memorable occasion was the Three Hour Service on Good Friday in Canterbury Cathedral when I was asked to give the addresses. On arrival I was surprised to find that no-one else was playing any part. I went to the pulpit and remained there alone for three hours. I read a scriptural passage, gave an address, said a prayer and announced a hymn. This pattern continued through the service. The Cathedral organist played for a couple of minutes after each address. The congregation grew until it was very large; few left but more were arriving all the time. As the service proceeded I had a strange experience. Time seemed to be suspended. Although we finished on the dot I was astonished that three hours had passed since we began.

One unwelcome intrusion into our lives during my years as Secretary of the Conference was a series of sinister telephone calls. They came at all hours of the day and night and sometimes several times in the small hours of the morning. They began on the day when the IRA committed a terrible outrage in Hyde Park, killing a number of soldiers and their horses. I picked up the telephone and a cultured voice said, 'We know that you are behind these killings. We will get you for it, have no doubt.' This nuisance continued over many months and in the end we had to have the telephone disconnected. The calls always came from a public kiosk. The police were unable to help us and we never discovered the perpetrator. He was obviously a very sick man. It was all the more worrying for my wife and family because the caller gave evidence that he was following my movements from newspaper references. Eventually the calls ceased.

In 1980 I was elected President of the Conference which met that year in the Victoria Hall, Sheffield. My duties as Secretary were taken over by the Assistant Secretary, the Rev Frank Smith. He, along with my other colleagues, were immensely helpful during a taxing year.

With the family at the opening of the Sheffield Conference, 1980:
L to R Susan and Bill, Elizabeth, John and Cheryl, Kenneth and Mary

Whenever Britain gets a heatwave it seems to coincide with the date of the Methodist Conference. As the Sheffield Conference opened I waited in the vestry for the summons to enter. This rather nerve-racking vigil was shared by Mrs Elsie Moult who had been designated as Vice-

President – a gracious lady with a reassuring serenity. When the moment came to enter the crowded hall I was almost knocked backwards by a huge draught of hot air. I thought, 'Shadrach, Meshach and Abednego had nothing on me.' But more importantly I was conscious of a wave of affection and loyal support from the members.

The simple but not unimpressive service of induction took only a few minutes. My predecessor, the Rev William Gowland, handed me John Wesley's Field Bible (so called because it was published by a firm called Field), John Stacey put on my gown and Winnie Price the preaching scarf which my platform colleagues had had embroidered with the Handsworth College coat of arms. I thanked Bill Gowland for his year of service. I said, 'You have turned up in all the usual places, like the Manchester Mission, and the Vatican. You have travelled ceaselessly but have always emerged from your engagements as bright as a ball-bearing, to coin a phrase.'

The theme of my Presidential address to the Conference was 'The Servant Church'. I pursued this biblical theme under the headings of ministry, unity and mission. I concluded with these words:

> Our agenda reveals a church prepared to say and do unpopular things. If we had wanted a quiet life and a placid church we could have avoided saying anything about homosexuality. We did not and we will not. We could have declined to involve ourselves in the fierce struggle for racial justice. We did not and we will not. We could have been content to bind up the wounds of humanity without seeking to influence the political systems that inflict those wounds. We did not and we will not. We could have been content to concentrate on the salubrious suburbs where we seem to do well and retreated from the forbidding wilderness of the inner city. We did not and we will not. In thus prosecuting the many-sided mission of Christ's church there is great joy – the joy of creative action. But read between the lines and there is revealed also a suffering, vulnerable church: sorrowing because it does none of these things as well as it should; agonising over the pain of the world; weeping because of hopes deferred and battles lost. Which church we offer up to him who for our sakes made himself nothing, assuming the nature of a slave, and whom God

raised to the heights, bestowing on him the name above all names, that at the name of Jesus every knee should bow.

Following the tea interval after my speech we had to transact a little business before the arrival of the leader of the City Council, Mr David Blunkett and his guide dog, Ted, at 7.00 pm. By 6.50pm we had reached the end of the business scheduled so I called my old friend Ted Rogers to present the report of a body called the Beckly Trust. This usually takes about thirty seconds. I invited Ted to take his time. He obliged with a wonderfully witty speech delivered with his familiar deadpan expression. It contained such remarks as 'members of Conference will find the report on page 45 of the Agenda; this comes before page 46 and after page 44'. On this showing Ted Rogers would have made a fine politician: he spoke for ten minutes without saying a thing. Then Mr Blunkett arrived. His speech warmed our hearts. He obviously felt completely at home among us, and the other Ted – the dog – looked on, also with a deadpan expression. Thus began a very enjoyable and good-humoured Conference.

One afternoon the hall got so hot that I called for the Superintendent of the Mission, the Rev Frank Thewliss, to ask what had happened to the air-conditioning. He came down the aisle waving his hands in characteristic fashion. I said, 'Keep doing that; it will help to shift the air around.' In response to my enquiry he indicated that when the air conditioning system was switched on it made a humming noise. 'Well,' I replied, 'it would seem that in this Conference we either hum one way or another.'

Again and again the tedium of routine business was relieved by refreshing bursts of laughter. During a discussion of a report on human sexuality Mrs Norma Cradock appeared in the tribune looking extremely attractive. She said, 'Mr President, many years ago in a meeting of young people you told us that sex was a gift of God to be enjoyed, but when I look around this Conference . . .' She paused and I leaned forward to say, 'Some look sexier than others, Mrs Cradock?' The Rev Gordon Barritt, presenting the Report of the National Children's Home, began, 'The other day I received a telephone call from Buckingham Palace.' 'Don't we all?' I intervened. In the laughter which ensued I said, 'Pray continue, Sir Gordon', after which the dear brother had some difficulty in resuming his speech. On the last morning of the Conference it was announced that the Rev Norman Wallwork, a dear friend and the largest man in the hall, had left a pair of his trousers on the bed in the house where he had been staying. 'We will have a station wagon go to fetch them,' I said. Well, if we have to have conferences, we might as well enjoy them.

Of course, there were the solemn moments. The reception of ordinands into full connexion with the Conference is always, as I said in my Preface, a moving occasion. In order to accommodate the crowds of parents and friends who attend that ceremony we moved to the Top Rank Suite in the centre of Sheffield where there were big coloured lights and all the accoutrements for discos and dances. I briefly addressed the ordinands who were to be ordained later in the day. Earlier I had met and spoken to their wives and fiancées.

I was very fortunate in that I had more than thirty years' of experience of the Conference. As Secretary I had been responsible for making the Conference Agenda (in my year a volume of 476 pages; by 1995 it had increased to 1024!). I had also sat next to successive Presidents, most of whom were good masters of assembly. I had noted, however, that if the President did not exercise firm control and direct proceedings in accordance with the Rules of Debate, the Conference could become restive and even a little unruly. The Sheffield Conference was an orderly assembly. There was a long-established tradition that the Conference did not clap, but, like the House of Commons, expressed its feelings of either approval or disapproval by making other appropriate noises. It was, I think, a good tradition and I upheld it from the chair. In more recent times this rule has been less observed.

The Sunday of Conference was a very full day. I preached at the 9.30am broadcast service in Carver Street Church. In the afternoon I went to the home of the Chairman of the Sheffield Methodist District, the Rev Sydney Booth, to talk with a group representing the Muslim and Hindu communities in the city. It was a meeting which demonstrated the quality of the interfaith dialogue which has happily grown up in the multi-faith community which is Britain today. In the evening I preached at an ecumenical service in the Cathedral attended by a huge congregation. The Bishop of Sheffield, David Lunn, and the newly-appointed Roman Catholic Bishop of Hallam, Gerald Moverley, and other church leaders were present. Bishop Lunn made a brief speech deeply regretting the failure of the Anglican/Methodist Unity Scheme.

The Conference holds a devotional session during the week and I arranged for this to be held in the Roman Catholic Cathedral. Dr Ivor Jones had prepared a most beautiful programme of music and readings.

On the Thursday afternoon of the Conference three of the Methodist schools in the District sent representatives. They sat in the gallery to see what their elders were up to. I announced a hymn so that they could hear the very fine unaccompanied singing which is a notable feature of these annual gatherings and asked members of the Conference to turn round in their seats and face the young people. In the evening of that day there was a great musical celebration in the City Hall organised by Mrs Jenny Carpenter under the title 'The Power and the Glory'. The Conference finished promptly at 12.30pm on the Friday when the traditional speech of thanks to the President was made by Ted Rogers.

The President of the Conference faces a gruelling schedule during his year of office. My detailed diary records long days of ceaseless activity; often I arrived home at midnight only to be off again by 6.30 the next morning. The day after the Conference ended I felt exhausted. A bad cold did not improve the situation so I took a day off and watched the Men's Singles from Wimbledon. Bjorn Borg beat John McEnroe after nearly four hours of play.

On the following Friday I flew with my wife to the United States for a series of engagements. I preached twice in the large auditorium at Lake Junaluska in North Carolina, in the morning to two thousand people including many bishops of the United Methodist Church, and in the evening at a service organised by the Wesley Historical Society. The temperature was in the low nineties. On the Monday I lectured to a school for preachers, did a half-hour television broadcast and then attended the South Eastern Jurisdictional Conference of the United Methodist Church. I witnessed the election of a bishop: a long drawn out procedure. Between each ballot small groups of people could be seen in earnest conclave discussing how they should vote. At the eighth ballot the Rev Paul Duffy was elected. He was carried to the platform on the shoulders of two fellow-bishops amidst thunderous applause. Then his wife was similarly escorted. Altogether a most extraordinary spectacle. The American trip concluded with a visit to Cleveland, Ohio, where I preached in the beautiful Church of the Saviour and met many old friends. Before leaving we watched on television the acceptance speech of Ronald Reagan at the Republican Congress.

The first occasion after our return was the Royal Garden Party. During my years as Secretary of the Conference I attended one of these functions every year. Those attending are permitted to take any unmarried daughters with them so we invited our younger daughter, Elizabeth, to come with us and arranged that she should meet us at the Palace gates.

96

Unfortunately she waited at the wrong gate. Supposing that she had been prevented from coming we went in with some hundreds of other guests. Elizabeth was chivvied by a policeman for 'loitering'. To make matters worse there was a heavy shower and she eventually arrived on the Palace lawns looking as if she had fallen into a bath of water. These occasions afforded an opportunity to meet some interesting people if only you could spot them amid the masses of mayors and other local dignitaries. The following year we ran into Mrs Margaret Thatcher, as she then was, and her husband. She very kindly invited us to Chequers to meet Mrs Nancy Reagan who was coming over for the wedding of Prince Charles. She said, 'I thought it would be nice for you to thank Mrs Reagan for all that the Americans have done to help us with the refurbishment of Wesley's Chapel.' The Thatchers had been married in Wesley's Chapel in the City Road, London. This Mother Church of Methodism had undergone extensive renovations after a slab of masonry had fallen from the roof following one of Dr Colin Morris' sermons, and American Methodists had contributed towards the costs, though I doubt whether Mrs Reagan would have known anything about that. In the event we could not accept Mrs Thatcher's invitation because at the time of the royal wedding I was in Honolulu presiding over the centenary gatherings of the World Methodist Conference. We did watch the wedding ceremony on American television and were much amused at the commentator's at times wildly inaccurate observations, such as, 'Here comes the Duchess of Argyle', when it was in fact the wife of a well-known politician. He also imparted spicy stories about the royal family which may or may not have been true, but certainly at that time would not have formed any part of a British television presentation.

The next set of engagements took us to Switzerland for the meetings at the Ecumenical Centre to which I referred earlier. We ran into serious trouble on the Paris motorway near Auxerre. The cable carrying the electrical wiring of the car got very hot and all the wires fused together. Clouds of blue smoke emerged from behind the dashboard and the car came to a halt. I went to the nearest roadside telephone to summon help. I had no idea whether the man at the other end of the line understood my French because I could not understand his. Moreover all sound was drowned by the thunderous roar of passing trucks. However, a breakdown van arrived and we were forced to languish in Auxerre for twenty-four hours. The man who came to fetch us from our hotel to take us to the garage to pick up our car was drunk and his driving was distinctly erratic. When I gave him a handsome tip he kissed my wife ferociously on both cheeks.

The few days in Geneva, once we arrived, were very enjoyable. Dr Philip Potter, the General Secretary of the World Council of Churches, had arranged a full programme of meetings with the various units of the Council. We had dinner at Bossey with Methodist members of staff. Philip presented me with the massive biography of John R. Mott, the Methodist layman who was one of the pioneers of the modern ecumenical movement, and a copy of the hymnbook *Cantate Domino* to which Philip's wife, Doreen, had contributed generously before her death.

Before returning we snatched a few days' holiday in Switzerland, staying in the beautiful Hotel Viktoria at Reuti-Hasliberg and going to the top of the Jungfrau Jock. As usual we received a great welcome from our children when we reached home.

The last week in August saw me *en route* for Zimbabwe where I was due to attend the Methodist Conference in Bulawayo. The day after my arrival I was received in Government House in Salisbury by the President of Zimbabwe, the Rev Canaan Banana, a Methodist minister who had become Head of State. It was interesting to see this house which had been pictured so often on British television during the troubled times leading up to independence. The well-watered lawns and flowering trees contrasted with the brown, parched world beyond the guarded gates. The President, who had been in prison until the previous November, is a small but impressive man. We had a long conversation about the need for reconciliation and reconstruction in his country. He pleaded for the exercise of greater pressure on the regime in South Africa since the peace of the whole continent depended upon the establishment of a just order there. Tea was served from a gleaming silver teapot by a black servant wearing white gloves. Driving away from this encounter I passed through several African townships and noticed a large 'segregated cemetery'. The evil of racism even accompanies people to the grave.

In Bulawayo I stayed with two missionaries from Britain, the Rev Keith Beacroft and his wife Winifred. They told me that on their arrival they had started to cultivate their garden. They were conscious that very often passersby were stopping to peer through the surrounding hedge, and after a time other gardens began to assume a new appearance of tidiness and fruitfulness: a fine case of teaching by example.

The Methodist Conference in Zimbabwe gave me a splendid opportunity to learn about the country and the work of the church. Compared with the well-ordered proceedings of the British Conference the sessions appeared rather chaotic, but there was an atmosphere of intimacy and good fellowship which made the whole experience very enjoyable. I heard much about the difficulties of finding jobs for soldiers who were no longer needed in the armed services. Trained for warfare, they were now cooped up in camps and the inevitable result was outbreaks of sporadic violence. The President of the Conference, the Rev Andrew Ndhlela, was a choice spirit. He was some time later tragically killed in a road accident. I delivered the 'Andrew Ndhlela Lecture' on 'The Part that Preaching Plays'. At the end there was a standing ovation which I found most moving.

On the Sunday morning I preached at Mpopoma, a large untidy township. A crowd of about 500 filled the church and the sermon was translated into one of the native languages, of which there are 27 in Zimbabwe. About a hundred children sat on the floor and sparrows twittered in the rafters. The women's organisation called Mananya was present in strength, all the members wearing black skirts representing sin, and red blouses signifying the cleansing blood of Jesus. Many of the women were breast-feeding their babies during the sermon. I found the strong sound of sucking rather off-putting, but at least it prevented the infants from crying.

Other engagements in Zimbabwe included an ordination service. Among the seven ordinands was the first woman to be ordained. There were visits to people in their homes and to various institutions for the care of the handicapped and the blind. I reached home on 3 September and spent the evening helping our son, John, and his fiancée paint the flat which they were to occupy. They were married on the following Saturday.

It is a tradition that the President of the Conference preaches at Wesley's Chapel in London on the first Sunday of September – the beginning of 'the Connexional Year'. I preached on the text 'Ask and you will receive' (Matthew 7:7). I never mount the steps of the pulpit in that lovely building without a great sense of the history which it represents. John Wesley's tomb is in the churchyard behind the Chapel and many of his followers are buried there. It is a place of pilgrimage for Methodists from all over the world. The little man who had no children of his own gave birth under God to a great global family now numbering some fifty million in over 100 countries.

Now began the real business of the Presidential Year: a visit to each of the 32 Districts of British Methodism. The arrangements for these visits were largely in the hands of the District Chairmen. Mary, who came with me to every District, and I were deeply grateful for the hospitality given to us by the Chairmen and their wives. The programmes arranged for us included a huge variety of events: preaching at crowded services and meetings, opening new churches, mayoral receptions, visiting homes for the elderly, speaking at schools, colleges and prisons. I presided at all the major Connexional Committees and at the Synod of my own District. I particularly welcomed the opportunities to lecture at conferences for preachers, to meet the ministers of each District and to share in 'Any Questions?' sessions. I tried to follow up the themes I had expounded in my Presidential address to the Conference. Everywhere I went I was questioned about the open letter I had published on disarmament. Gerald Priestland discussed this with me on the radio in a very sympathetic interview.

On 28 September I flew to Toronto for a meeting of the Executive Committee of the World Methodist Council. The only advantage of long 'plane journeys was that they afforded opportunities to write articles and prepare speeches. On the Sunday morning I preached to 1100 people in the Metropolitan Church in London, Ontario and in the evening at a service in Toronto attended by all the members of the Executive Committee. On returning home I went to preach in Raunds. I announced my text and then completely forgot how the sermon was supposed to begin. Since I have never used notes or manuscript in the pulpit this was a dreadful experience which I put down to fatigue. However, after what seemed like a lengthy silence, it all came flooding back and the sermon proceeded. Another unhappy moment in the pulpit occurred in Huddersfield Parish Church, when I began by saying how happy I was to be in Halifax. I wondered at the time why, looking down, I saw an agonised look pass over my wife's face.

Good health enabled me to keep all my engagements though the visit to the Cornwall District presented some difficulty. Following the great civic service in St Mary Clement Church in Truro on the Sunday morning I preached in the afternoon in the Cathedral at a service to celebrate the centenary of our Truro School. Following this I was motored to Falmouth for an evening service and a youth meeting. The following morning I was stricken with the most frantic lumbago and hobbled off for a full schedule of meetings culminating in a service in St Just where, in spite of torrential rain, a congregation of 200 had gathered. On my return to Truro late in the evening a skilled chiropractor, Mr Price, was waiting for me. An hour of his treatment brought considerable relief.

Many engagements during the year were in connection with various organisations I served. I spoke with the Archbishop of Canterbury at St Marylebone Church in London for the Churches' Council for Health and Healing. That church has special significance for Methodists because Charles Wesley is buried in the churchyard. As Vice-Chairman of the Churches' Council for Covenanting I went to High Leigh to speak at a meeting of all the Anglican bishops on the proposals for a covenant.

During my visit to the Bristol District I was able to preach at the 50th anniversary of the little church at Redcliffe Bay where my mother and younger brother were members. She, alas, was by this time too infirm to be present. I also paid a visit to Cotham Grammar School which I had attended as a boy. The headmaster looked astonishingly young! Since my time the school had become co-educational and the girls had brought a more civilised atmosphere to the place. I was welcomed at the front door, which we were never allowed to use in my day, and met a number of the senior pupils in the headmaster's study. I noticed that he called them all by their Christian names. The row of brass studs outside his door where we used to have to toe the line before being interviewed had been removed. It was an altogether enjoyable and encouraging experience to find the old school in such good hands.

In many of my meetings great concern was expressed about the high level of unemployment. I went to see Len (later Lord) Murray, the General Secretary of the Trade Union Congress. He stressed the need for the churches to think hard about the fact that increasing mechanisation and the use of computers was bound to mean fewer jobs and more leisure. I received a similar response from Sir Terrence Becket when I went to see him at the offices of the Confederation of British Industry. There was another opportunity to discuss unemployment at the annual dinner for Methodist Members of Parliament in Speaker's House.

In the Sheffield District I arrived at the country chapel in Freethorpe to find it packed with an enthusiastic congregation. The gallery had not been used for many years and was creaking under this unaccustomed load of humanity. The stewards were afraid that it might collapse, but it didn't. One of them asked if he might borrow 'John Wesley's chair'. He had been at the Sheffield Conference and when the opening session was over had stolen on to the platform to sit in the chair himself. He said that it was still warm, an intimation that caused me no surprise. In fact, of course, it never was John Wesley's chair but one donated by the Methodists of Australia, and since replaced by a rather smarter piece of furniture. I never discovered why the friends at Freethorpe wanted to borrow the chair.

The President of the Conference always pays an official visit to the Forces. For my own visit I was quartered in Drake House in Plymouth. I had not been looking forward to this. I respect the necessary work of the Chaplains but the whole of the military milieu is one in which I feel ill at ease. However, I determined to do my best and this was made easier by the courtesy of the various officers who took me in tow and the kindness of the Methodist Chaplain, the Rev Irvin Vincent. I toured HMS *Argonaut* and met some of its complement of 230 men. I learned that it cost £3,000 a day in fuel when the ship is at sea and £800 a day for electricity off the grid when the ship is berthed. The bottomless pit of military expenditure depresses me. I visited a diving centre and was given a demonstration of the workings of a decompression chamber. The bomb disposal squad fired at a parcel and blew it up. I saw the facilities of a training centre for new recruits and had coffee with twenty Methodist lads. I conducted prayers in St Andrews Church and learned that the navy had built three large chapels under the same roof: Anglican, Roman Catholic and Free Church, a ridiculous squandering of resources in these ecumenical days.

From Plymouth I went to the Naval Training College in Dartmouth. I was given a gracious welcome by Captain Julian Oswald and shown up a stately staircase to a palatial bedroom. A man servant had already unpacked my case and laid out everything with naval precision. He said, 'Sir, Prince Charles slept in this bed recently.' I replied, 'Then I shall hope to dream about Princess Diana.' Alas, in these latter days such a dream would not have the overtones of happiness that would have accompanied it then. I took the salute with the Captain at a ceremonial passing-out parade and preached in the college chapel before leaving. I came away able to believe that many of those to whom I spoke are sincere in their longing for peace and their belief that it can only be safeguarded by maintaining military strength. It is a premise that I do not share, but that is an issue which I deal with more fully in Chapter Six.

On 12 April 1981 there were devastating riots in the Brixton area of London. The next morning I toured the district with the Rev Graham Kent, our minister at the Railton Road Church. We visited people in their homes and spoke to a policeman on the beat. He agreed with the judgement expressed by many that part of the trouble was undue harassment by the local police.

The Easter weekend was spent, as tradition demands, in the Channel Islands. In Jersey we stayed with Mr Edgar Becquet, a distinguished lawyer, and his wife Monica. The Bailiff of Jersey, Sir Frank Eriant, showed us round the Parliament Building. A congregation of 700 gathered in the Wesley Grove Church for the Good Friday morning service and in the afternoon I spoke at the Odeon cinema. After the Easter morning service we went to visit Alan Whicker. He showed us pictures of his world travels and said, 'I've laid in a large bottle of apple juice, knowing that you don't drink.' He is a man every bit as charming off the screen as he is on it.

Another interesting encounter was with Mrs Madge Beuzeval who kept a confectioner's shop. She has the gift of 'Odic force' and many testified to her healing powers. She keeps a stool behind the counter on which her patients sit for treatment. She is noted for her generosity and gave us enough Mars bars to see us through the rest of the year.

We were escorted round the lovely Island by the Chairman of the Channel Islands District, the Rev Donald Lee. He was a man with great charm and flair. His car, however, was of ancient vintage and could scarcely manage the steepest hills; at one point we had to get out and push. He was President of the Conference in 1973. Once during his year of office I travelled with him on an overnight train and I was fascinated to see when he opened his case a choice array of toiletries, including bottles of aftershave and all that sort of thing. Some Presidents are more elegant than others but none more so than he.

On Easter Monday morning we went to the quayside in Guernsey to take a boat to the tiny Island of Sark. A furious gale was blowing and the boatman said that it was too dangerous to attempt the crossing. I remembered that John Wesley had stood on the beach and asked, 'Are there any souls to be saved on Sark?' I said to the boatman, 'We must go. There are sixteen Methodists on Sark and they are expecting me.' He set out reluctantly saying that he doubted whether we should be able to land. When we arrived off the Island they sent a rowing boat out to collect us we had to jump into it when it rose to the right level on the crest of a wave. We were taken by horse and trap to be received by the Seigneur and his wife, Mr and Mrs Michael Beaumont. I was in great pain, having been thrown across the deck of the boat on the journey over and injuring my thumb, which was black and swollen. The Island doctor saw me and bored a hole in the nail with a primitive instrument. This relieved the pressure and provided some relief. The Methodists had baked the biggest cake I've ever seen.

The weekend of 3 May had been kept free to enable us to catch our breath before the last lap leading up to Conference. We went down to the house at Rustington which we had bought for retirement. Our dog, Pip, a favourite with the whole family, came with us. He was very ill and, although the vet did his best, on the Sunday morning our faithful friend had to be put to sleep. This event caused an unexpectedly acute sense of loss and sadness, and our 'carefree weekend' turned out to be rather a disaster.

On Wesley Day, 24 May, I preached at Wesley's Chapel at a service attended by the Prime Minister and the Speaker of the House of Commons. Mrs Thatcher reopened Wesley's House next door following its refurbishment. I was impressed by the fact that her very appropriate speech was written in her own hand and had obviously taken some time to prepare. At 7.15pm a crowd of 2,500 gathered at the Barbican where a memorial had been erected commemorating John Wesley's heart-warming experience. I presided at the Communion service and precisely at 'a quarter before nine' George Thomas read the famous passage in which it is recorded and to which I referred in Chapter One.

At 9.50pm we set out to motor to Nottingham for engagements in the District of which my brother Brian was the Chairman. He and his wife Jill entertained us royally. On Whit Monday they took us to Cliff College for the annual event which draws thousands for services in a big marquee and in the open air. Torrential rain turned the campus into a sea of mud, but spirits were not dampened. 'It was worse when Billy Graham came', said one stalwart. I was not sure whether he was referring to the sermon or the weather. During my sermon in the marquee I happened to refer to Pope John Paul II as 'our brother in Christ'. This drew a stentorian cry of 'No Popery here' from some ultra-Protestant brother near the back of the crowded congregation.

Every year in May there is a great rally of members of the Methodist Association of Youth Clubs. The Albert Hall in London is filled several times over the weekend. There are two big displays on the Saturday and two services on the Sunday as well as other events. I attended the Saturday events and preached at both services on the Sunday. I invited all those who would like to register their allegiance to Christ, or a new decision to follow him, to stand. Several thousand rose to their feet in a quiet and impressive act of witness.

The British President presides over the Irish Methodist Conference, so at the beginning of June we went to Cork for this event. At one of the sessions there was a lively debate on 'the Irish situation'. The Methodist

Church in Ireland is one church, north and south, but the discussion became rather tense. One minister rose to say, 'Mr President, I note that the resolution we are debating says nothing about the victims of violence.' I invited him to propose an amendment to remedy this omission. This he did. Then another member with a mischievous twinkle in his eye rose to say, 'Sir, I have to point out that, alas, many of the victims of violence are dead, so our brother is inviting this Conference to pray for the dead.' The mover of the amendment turned red, leapt to his feet, and said, 'I beg leave to withdraw my amendment.' This the Conference declined to allow him to do. It was an interesting sidelight on certain strangely conservative theological concepts.

At the end of June I travelled to Norwich for the Ministerial Session of the Conference. I delivered an address on 'The Constants and Variables of Ministry'. Although the text of this address repeats several of the things I have mentioned already in this Chapter it is included as an Appendix at the end of the book because it expresses much of what I believe about the ministry, and also because it conveys something of the flavour of the Ministerial Session of the Methodist Conference. I conducted the Memorial Service for ministers who had died during the year. This is always a deeply moving hour. As the list was solemnly recited I heard the names of many whom I had known and loved.

The Norwich Conference was overshadowed for me by our having to deal with a very difficult disciplinary case involving one of our ministers. Yet humour kept breaking through, as when my old friend John Stacey, who keeps appearing in these pages, said of a previous speaker, 'Mr Brake has cut my speech by 95 per cent.' 'What a blessing,' I remarked, 'otherwise your speech would have lasted one hour and thirty-five minutes.' My colleague Frank Smith, at the end of his own arduous year as acting Secretary, said at one point, 'We are glad to see Mr Wallwork.' Knowing and loving this large and large-hearted brother so well I felt able to comment, 'Well, you couldn't very well help seeing him, could you?'

On 3 July at the opening of the Representative Session of the Conference I inducted my successor, the Rev Dr John Newton, a minister and scholar of immense distinction and one of the most gracious Christians I have ever met. I resumed the Secretary's chair. It seemed entirely right and natural to hear someone else being addressed as 'Mr President'. My year as Chief Pastor of the Methodist people was over.

Chapter Five

TRANSCRIPTS OF THE TRINITY

In 1990 I preached during the Week of Prayer for Christian Unity in Chelmsford Cathedral. Representatives from all the denominations filled the building. The service was just about to begin when a bearded man near the front rose to his feet and shouted, 'Come ye out from among them and be ye separate.' He was escorted out of the Cathedral by two vergers. But then another disturber of the peace started to shout from the back of the congregation. This went on for about ten minutes. The Provost who was leading the service said quietly, 'We will remain in prayer for our friends until the disturbance is over.' This intrusion of representatives of an extreme view which regards the ecumenical movement as evil certainly lent point and urgency to the theme of my sermon.

It is easy to grow depressed by the slowness of the progress we have made along the road to Christian unity, but as I look back I realise that in fact my lifetime has seen a revolution in the relationships between the churches. Suspicion has been replaced by trust and a competitive spirit by a desire for co-operation. At every level ecumenical councils and committees have come into being to enable the churches to work more closely together. The degree to which they actually do so varies, of course, from place to place and one encounters many distressing examples of ecclesiastical isolationism. A great deal depends on the quality of local leadership.

There has been a deepening understanding of the fact that God wills the *visible* unity of his church. Vague talk of a spiritual unity already existing is not enough: ours is an incarnational religion. Hence the long and often tiresome search for institutional forms which will reflect and express the reality of our unity in Christ. Another factor which has increasingly prompted the search for unity is the realisation that a dangerously divided world needs the ministry of a church which offers a way of reconciliation and a true path to peace. A church which is itself divided offers a poor example and lacks credibility.

In spite of the progress made there is not the slightest room for complacency. Speaking again in personal terms experience of the ecumenical movement has brought many joys but also a great deal of heartache. At the all-important local level many congregations seem scarcely aware of their fellow-Christians in other traditions. We have failed miserably in some of the national and most costly ecumenical endeavours in this country. I am also aware from my travels round the world that progress towards deeper unity is very patchy. In some places there is open antagonism between churches and even persecution of minorities by majorities. Whole areas of Christendom are scarcely influenced at all by the ecumenical spirit that has transformed life for so many of us. The great historic divisions between Catholic, Orthodox and Protestant remain, for all the world to see. Within individual denominations and indeed across the denominational spectrum theological divisions, particularly between liberals and conservatives, cause serious breaks in fellowship. Even when unions occur it is sometimes more as a result of weakness than strong conviction about the unity God wills. All in all this represents a sombre litany of failures signifying a lack of vision and at best a half-hearted response to the promptings of the Holy Spirit. The people of God are very far from becoming what Charles Wesley described in his evocative lines:

> You whom God ordained to be
> Transcripts of the Trinity.

These words depict a people who reflect both the diversity and the perfect unity of Father, Son and Holy Spirit.

In what I have written so far about my personal odyssey there have been glimpses of ecumenical encounters and endeavours. The work which the church gave me to do, however, has meant a considerable involvement in the formal structures of the ecumenical movement, and it is to some account of all this that I now turn.

Whilst the solid work for the closer unity of the churches has been done in a variety of councils and committees some of the fun has come from occasional, even chance, encounters, so a word first about some of these. There was, for example, the morning when I went up to Broadcasting House in London to be interviewed on some topical issue. As I was leaving, having said my piece, a man in a state of great agitation came rushing along the corridor saying, 'Have you heard the news? The Pope is dead.' Then, spotting my clerical collar, he said, 'Will you come into the studio and speak a word of tribute?' So I was the first British churchman publicly to express sorrow at the untimely passing of John Paul I, the 'laughing Pope' as he had been called. I expressed sympathy to the Roman Catholic Church and ventured the comment that this sudden death six weeks after his election raised vexing questions about Providence, since Cardinal Hume had returned from the conclave in Rome asserting that the new Pope was 'God's choice'. Emerging with some relief from the studio I was accosted by another man with a sheaf of papers in his hand. 'I say,' he said, 'I liked that bit about Providence. Would you come in and record something about Providence for my programme which goes out later this morning?' Thus is instant theology produced!

Another interesting encounter with the Roman Catholics occurred some years earlier when Cardinal Heenan was very ill. I received a mysterious telephone call from a layman who said, 'You and your wife will shortly receive an invitation to dine with the Apostolic Delegate.' (Archbishop Heim, the Apostolic Delegate as he was then styled, was the personal representative in this country of the Pope.) I indicated that we should be glad to accept and that we had in fact been before to his spacious residence on Wimbledon Common. The voice at the other end of the telephone then said, 'The purpose of this dinner is to gather together a group of leaders from the other churches to advise the Archbishop about which name he should submit to the Vatican as the successor to Cardinal Heenan when he dies. Some of us feel that in these ecumenical days the other churches should be consulted.' Accordingly I made a short list of my favourite Roman Catholic clerics.

The Roman Catholic hierarchy never seems to be very clear about who are the leaders of the other churches and on our arrival at the dinner party we found an odd assortment. Donald Soper greeted me with, 'Hallo, old cock, what are you doing here?' to which I replied, 'And what about you?' We had an enjoyable dinner; then, quaintly, the ladies were asked to withdraw. The Apostolic Delegate seemed ill at ease. We all talked about this and that, and Donald Soper entertained us with some of his stories. But nothing was said about what we had supposed was the reason for our being there. Eventually, about 10.00pm our host suggested that we should rejoin the ladies. As we walked along the corridor I took his arm and said, 'We are all grieved to know of Cardinal Heenan's serious condition and realise that soon you may have to advise the Holy Father about his successor. Would it be improper to mention a name?' 'I wish you would,' came the reply, so I whispered the name of my 'candidate'. I then poked Lord Soper and said, 'Your turn next.' I suspect that some of the Roman Catholic hierarchy had heard about this lay initiative and had expressed their disapproval. The man appointed was unknown to any of us. But what a wonderful choice Basil Hume turned out to be. Certainly the dinner party was an event which would have been unthinkable even twenty years earlier.

Another entertaining memory of my ecumenical adventures concerns the Conference of European Churches (CEC) of which for some years I was a member. I used to sit next to Pastor Martin Niemöller who smoked a pipe which filled the room with blue smoke. On one occasion when we were due to meet in Denmark the Secretary, Dr Glen Garfield Williams, was informed that the East German representatives would only be allowed to attend if we met in 'neutral territory'. So he hired a boat called the *Bornholme* and our meeting was held while we sailed the Baltic Sea. I shared a cabin with Dr Kenneth Slack. At dead of night a small craft approached the ship and we hauled our East German brothers on to the deck. As we rode the choppy waters the ecumenical symbol of the movement we represented became very meaningful: a little ship with a cross-shaped mast riding the turbulent waves of a restless ocean. The CEC will exercise an increasingly important role in the Europe of the future. In spite of financial problems it continues its task of bringing the continental churches into closer fellowship and co-operation. It is planning a second European Ecumenical Assembly for 1997 on the theme, 'Reconciliation as God's Gift and Source of New Life'.

As Secretary of the Methodist Conference I was privileged to address the annual assemblies of the other churches from time to time. In 1974 I went to Edinburgh to speak to the General Assembly of the Church of Scotland. At the time we were engaged in discussions of possible union between that church and the Scottish Methodist District. It came to nought for reasons which demonstrate the difficulties of uniting a comparatively large body like the Church of Scotland with over one million members and a comparatively small one with about ten thousand. The Methodists feared absorption, a fear which was not allayed by the refusal of the larger church to change its name by including the word 'united' in its title.

My reception at the Edinburgh Assembly was cordial. It is a large body of somewhat fearsome appearance. The Queen, or her representative, sits in a special seat, high and lifted up. I got off to a good start by telling them that I had recently been wandering round St Giles Cathedral. At the time there was an interregnum; they were awaiting the appointment of a new minister. I asked the verger who showed me round how they managed to fill the pulpit Sunday by Sunday during this period of waiting. He replied with a rich accent, 'We have professors from the University.' His tone of voice suggested a certain dissatisfaction with this arrangement. 'Do you ever have Professor William Barclay?' I asked, referring to that popular biblical scholar. 'Och aye,' came the reply, 'but he's no professor; you can understand every word the man says.'

My wife and I were due for lunch at the Palace of Holyrood House at 1.00pm and the Assembly did not rise until 12.55pm. We could not find a taxi to drive us down the Royal Mile so I hailed a young man driving a sports car. He rushed us to the Palace but dropped us at the wrong entrance. We found ourselves in the kitchens. However, we eventually arrived in the dining room. The whole experience left us with a vivid impression of the place held by the national church in the life of that northern part of the United Kingdom.

The Lambeth Conference of 1978, which I attended as an observer, also stands out in my memory. Encouraged by Archbishop Coggan I made a speech about the ordination of women. I shared our Methodist experience and referred to the way in which the fears of some had been put to rest by the actual experience of being ministered to by a woman.

One evening at the Lambeth Conference Alec McCowan gave his recital of St Mark's gospel and held his episcopal audience spellbound. He said that usually in the theatre there were many actors and one prompter but that now there was one actor and 500 prompters. But he needed no prompting. The only addition he made to the text was a 'plop' as the Gadarene swine plunged into the Lake. Every time I went into the hall after that I pictured the scene and heard the 'plop'.

Turning now to some of the ecumenical agencies I have served I refer first to the World Council of Churches. It came into being in 1948 as the result of the flowing together of three streams of ecumenical endeavour. The first of these was the International Missionary Council. This agency for international co-operation in mission sprang out of the Conference which was convened in Edinburgh in 1910. That event represents a watershed in modern church history. It is important not to forget that the modern ecumenical movement as we know it began with a concern for more effective mission. No-one expressed that concern more vividly than John R. Mott, a remarkable Methodist layman from America. He was described by the then President of the United States as 'the world's most useful man'. He travelled seventy times round the world. He had a gift for slogans, like 'Pray as if there is no such thing as work, and work as if there is no such thing as prayer.'

The second of the three streams was concerned with faith and order. In the years that followed 1910 there was a deepening conviction that though it was important for the churches to develop a common strategy for mission it was no less necessary for them to consider the doctrinal issues, both those on which they were agreed and those which divided them. Bishop Charles Henry Brent of America was the leader of what became known as Faith and Order. The architect of the third stream of activity known as Life and Work was Nathan Soderblom, Archbishop of Uppsala. He had a deep concern for peace and justice and sought ways of demonstrating the relevance of the gospel to a sadly divided world where so many experienced neither.

The concerns of these three movements find their place on the agendas of the WCC. Through all my years at Westminster I was in receipt of a steady stream of literature representing the work of the great international team of dedicated Christians from many traditions who have staffed the Council's Headquarters. They have been brilliantly lead by successive General Secretaries and my own life has been enriched by knowing three of them: Dr Visser't Hooft, appointed at the formation of the Council, Dr Eugene Carson Blake and Dr Philip Potter.

From the beginning the fathers of the modern ecumenical movement have sought to be what Dr Visser't Hooft called 'pan-Christians', concerned about the whole people of God, the universal dimension of the Christian faith, and the wholeness of the gospel. An inevitable difficulty is that the Movement, as represented in Geneva, has tended to move ahead of the churches. It takes years for some of the creative ideas emerging from the centre to seep down into the life of the local congregations. High-powered committees, especially when composed of people of different nationalities, tend to develop a jargon of their own and issue documents which are opaque to those who did not share in the labour of producing them.

The WCC has often been criticised for being over-politicised. In the early days of its life it was asserted that though doctrine divides, service unites. This, however, has turned out to be only partially true. The Geneva Conference on Church and Society held in 1966 was the first serious encounter between Christians from the rich North Atlantic countries and those of the poor South. It has become increasingly clear that service is not a matter of the rich distributing largesse to the poor. Christians must face the challenge of the injustice written into the systems which perpetuate and even deepen the gulf between the haves and the have-nots. There is no escape from the tension which arises from a ministry that seeks to combine reconciliation and prophetic witness about the enemies of peace and justice.

In 1971 I attended the Central Committees of the World Council of Churches in Addis Ababa, Ethiopia. During a great service in the Orthodox Cathedral I was fascinated by a gaudy stained glass window depicting an ostrich egg beneath the cross. When I enquired about its meaning I was told that the ostrich is the national bird but that the baby bird cannot escape from the hard shell without assistance. Neither can we escape from the shell of our sin without the aid of him who died on the cross to redeem us. The service was attended by the Emperor Haile Selassie. I reminded him of his sojourn in Bath during the war years when he sought refuge in Britain. Though short of stature he was an impressive figure with a quiet dignity and a majestic bearing. His days as ruler of that backward country were numbered. One member of the local church said, 'His great achievement is to pull Ethiopia out of the 13th into the 14th century.' I had long conversations with one of his daughters who said, 'We don't know what the future holds for us, but the present regime will not last much longer.' At an open-air ceremony of welcome the Emperor was seated on a golden chair while we, his guests, were on seats arranged on a huge oriental carpet. One innocent onlooker happened to step on the edge of the carpet and was viciously kicked in the stomach by a member of the armed guard: as tough a bunch of thugs as I ever saw.

A banquet was held in the Imperial Palace. A real lion sat, unchained, on the top of the palace wall. He looked too old and decrepit to be a threat to anyone. We ate off gold plates and the whole set up was medieval. I was told that the Emperor often drove in his limousine through the streets of the city throwing coins to the poor beggars whose numbers were legion.

Members of the Central Committee were able to travel a little beyond the bounds of the city and understood the difficulty of communication in a land which consists of one steep mountain range after another. I still carry in my mind a vivid image of an aged Orthodox priest standing fathoms deep in meditation outside the door of his little church in a remote village. It was difficult to relate him and his way of life to the high-powered discussions of weighty themes in the Central Committee.

In 1975 I attended the Assembly of the World Council of Churches in Nairobi. One of the speakers was the world-famous anthropologist Margaret Mead. She ascended the platform steps assisted by the long stick which she carried with her. For a moment she stood surveying the crowd in front of her: bishops in purple cassocks, Orthodox priests in flowing robes, African men in colourful costumes, Indian women in silken saris, plain Presbyterians in grey suits, and Methodists in open-neck shirts.

112

Then she uttered these memorable words: 'I reckon that this is the most unlikely conglomeration of disparate elements the world has ever seen.' There were indeed many moments when our diversity seemed more apparent than our unity. As I moved around I heard mutterings among the representatives of the Russian Orthodox Church about fellow-Christians from the USA who were 'tools of capitalism', and equally strong strictures by some Americans that the Russians were in the pockets of their communist masters. Nevertheless the churches which came together in 1948 have for the most part stayed together. Since the Second Vatican Council and its liberating influences there has been an immense growth in co-operation between the WCC and the Roman Catholic Church. At the other end of the ecclesiastical spectrum the Pentecostal Churches contribute their own lively insights to the quest for fuller understanding of the imperatives of the gospel.

Alongside the WCC there are the World Confessional bodies several of which, like the World Lutheran Federation, have their offices in the Ecumenical Centre in Geneva. The World Methodist Council (WMC) takes its place with these as an instrument for strengthening the ties between Methodist Churches in more than 100 countries and to enhance their Christian witness. It traces its beginnings to the first Ecumenical Methodist Conference held in London in 1881 attended by 400 representatives from 40 churches around the world. It now serves a Methodist constituency numbering more than 50 million. Every fifth year it meets in conjunction with a World Conference usually attended by some 3,000 people. Its various committees help the Methodists of the world to understand and share their heritage and theology, to study social and international problems and propose appropriate action, to strengthen family life, to set up bilateral conversations with other world communions, to engage in evangelism, and to think together about education, liturgy and the needs of youth. Closely associated with the Council is the World Federation of Methodist Women. There is also an exchange programme which enables ministers from one country to undertake a spell of work in another. This programme has achieved a great deal in building bridges and establishing friendships.

I have been associated with the WMC for the greater part of my ministerial life. I first addressed its five-yearly Conference in Oslo in 1961. When I came down from the platform I was met by a man with a rubicund face and a winning smile. He was a minister of the Methodist Church in the USA. His name was Howard J. Brown. He said, 'You are the man I've been looking for. I want you to fill my pulpit for a month while I'm away on holiday. You and your wife and family will live in the parsonage.' I expressed my regret that I could not accept this kind invitation since there was no possibility of our being able to afford to travel as a family. Dr Brown said, 'I shall write to you.' In due course his letter arrived. It said, 'I have mentioned to my people that a family from England is coming and that we shall want to enable them to see a bit of the country. The money has just rolled in and I now have an inexhaustible fund that will take care of all expenses.' After receiving this astonishing intimation of beneficence we decided to accept the invitation and managed to get cheap air fares across the Atlantic for £65 each. Howard Brown and his wife Helen met us in New York and for three hectic days took us all round the city and the World's Fair, ending up in Washington DC. At the foot of the steps of the Lincoln Memorial our younger daughter Elizabeth, unable to walk another yard, sat on the ground and said, 'Mummy, I think I shall die.'

Our destination was the Church of the Saviour in Cleveland, Ohio and we arrived there late in the evening. That beautiful building stood like a glorious cathedral floodlit against the night sky. The month that followed was full of excitement as we became part of the church family. I preached to a great congregation every Sunday and our 'social secretary' fed us with a daily diary of engagements which included meetings, meals in the homes of the people and visits to places like Niagara Falls. We formed friendships that have lasted down the years, strengthened by return visits. In January 1996 we went back yet again to the Church of the Saviour for the celebration of the 100th birthday of Mrs Treva Rupert, the oldest member, and still full of life and vigour.

This little interlude provides just one example of the way in which the World Methodist Council has opened doors of friendship and given an added dimension to the word 'connexion'. My own life has been enriched beyond measure by an ever-widening circle of friends, not just in America but throughout the world.

During the early years of my membership of the WMC it was often criticised as being dominated by America and Britain. Such domination was perhaps inevitable. The running of any world organisation is bound to be expensive, even when the budget is as modest as that of the WMC. The greater part of the funding has in the past come from America and Britain. Those who pay the piper often want to call the tune, even when the piper is a church council. The sometimes oppressive sense that the WMC was largely an American organisation was increased by the fact that some of the American bishops who occupied key positions were rather formidable characters. They were used to wielding considerable power in their own church and brought the same autocratic style to their work for the Council.

Over a period of time considerable changes have occurred, resulting in a more widely representative Council in which the voices of Asia and Africa are effectively heard. There are, however, very real difficulties. Procedural methods of conducting business and rules of debate vary from one culture to another. The person who presides tends to try to order the assembly by the set of rules with which he is familiar. Not all the terms he uses will be meaningful to every member, or they may carry an entirely different meaning. This is a recipe for chaos and there have been some fairly confused sessions in the Council. As in any debating chamber much depends on the quality and competence of the one occupying the chair. The Council now has a printed set of rules of procedure.

The Conferences held in conjunction with the Council every fifth year are big jamborees attended mainly by Methodists but with a sprinkling of observers from the other churches. The largest number of those attending comes from America. The Methodists are a talkative people; their favourite hymn is 'O for a thousand tongues'. Little wonder that these world gatherings leave many of those attending punch-drunk with the constant verbal battering of endless speeches. The programme is always arranged around a central theme. In 1961 in Norway it was 'New Life in the Spirit'; in 1966 in London it was 'To Know Christ and Make Him Known'; in 1971 in Denver, Colorado, it was 'Now'; in 1976 in Dublin it was 'The Day of the Lord'; in 1981 in Hawaii it was 'Gathered into One'; in 1986 in Kenya it was 'Christ Jesus: God's "Yes" for the World'; in 1991 in Singapore it was 'Jesus Christ: God's Living Word'.

The subject allocated to me for my address to the 1961 Conference in Oslo was 'The Holy Spirit and Moral Standards'. I began, 'I wish we could do something about this word "spiritual". It has, I think, been in the wrong company and acquired a stuffy smell.' I went on to criticise the 'unnatural break' so often made between the spiritual and the material and to expound the incarnational nature of the Christian religion. The spiritual man is necessarily involved in the life of the world. The address examined Christian attitudes to sex, crime and money.

At the Dublin World Methodist Conference I was elected Chairman of the Council for the following quinquennium. My closing address to that Conference was entitled 'The Day Yet to Come'. I spelt out my hopes for the future of the Council: that we should get to know each other better within the Methodist family; that we should explore the meaning of holiness; and that we should understand more fully the nature of the unity to which Christ calls us.

In 1981 in Honolulu we celebrated the centenary of the WMC. I preached at the opening service of Holy Communion from the text, 'That he might gather together in one all things in Christ' (Ephesians 1:10). I spoke about purpose, programme and promise. The welcome extended to us by the Hawaiian people was overwhelming. Before preaching I was garlanded with flowers. The service began with a procession of flags of the Methodist Churches around the world. Later the holy elements were dispensed from twenty tables placed around the perimeter of the huge auditorium. Many of the worshippers were moved to tears by the sense of belonging to this global family of Christians.

Presiding over so large and diverse an assembly presented a challenge. In the event the sessions were orderly and good-humoured. At the end I inducted as my successor Bishop William Cannon, a long-time friend and distinguished scholar who has played a significant part in the bilateral conversations between the WMC and other World Confessional Bodies.

My wife and I discovered that one could get a cheap and satisfying lunch in Woolworth's store in Honolulu. There was a notice which said that foreign visitors would receive a free parcel of goods on presentation of a passport. The next day we went to Woolworth's armed with a passport and were given an exciting-looking parcel. On our way back to the place of meeting we were stopped by a group of young people who wanted to know the significance of our Methodist badges. Thinking that here was a golden opportunity for some pavement evangelism among this group of splendid young folk I delivered a brief lecture on John Wesley. It was only when they had moved on that I realised they had filched the parcel from under my arm. I hope they enjoyed the contents.

We had arranged with a local minister in Honolulu that we should occupy his manse for a couple of weeks following the Conference while he came to England to live in ours. At the last minute the arrangement fell through because he was moved to the American mainland. However, he fixed us up at a youth camp by the sea. This turned out to be a disaster; every night about 11.00pm the place was invaded by a gang of youths who stayed till 4.00am and played loud music. After a few days we were greatly relieved to receive an invitation from a local Methodist lady. She asked if we would do her a favour. I thought she must be about to ask me to preach at her church but it was something very different. She kept an eye on a mansion owned by a wealthy business man who was absent most of the year. She had to go away for ten days and asked if we would be willing to take up residence in this palatial home. We eagerly grabbed the opportunity to escape from the youth camp and we were immediately translated to paradise. The house was on the seashore and was like one of those mansions occupied by film stars in Hollywood. There was a notice asking that the windows be cleaned every day, but this task was accomplished by pressing a button which sent a cascade of water down each of them. The bedroom was spacious and commanded a view of the deep blue ocean. The bed was large enough for six.

The Council's General Secretary for many years has been Dr Joe Hale. He and his wife Mary have, through their great capacity for friendship with people of every race, enhanced the quality of the fellowship which they serve. I have shared many adventures with Joe in different parts of the world and have never known his gentle courtesy to fail.

Some years ago the Council decided to open an office at the Ecumenical Centre in Geneva. This has provided an invaluable means of keeping in touch with the wider Ecumenical Movement. The office has been served by a number of retired Methodists, ordained and lay. The present incumbent, Mr Ralph Young, is greatly respected by the representatives of the other World Communions in Geneva and by the staff of the WCC. His quiet presence will be sorely missed when the time arrives for his retirement. I very much hope that resources will be found to continue the work of the Geneva office.

When the present Pope held a service in St Peter's Square in Rome to mark the inauguration of his ministry as the Chief Pastor of the Roman Catholic Church I went with Dr Hale and Bishop Cannon to represent the Methodists of thc world. We sat among the large gathering of dignitaries which included Princess Grace of Monaco, the King and Queen of Spain and many heads of state and leaders of churches. The square was filled with people as far as the eye could see.

At the end of the service the Pope broke away from the stately procession of Cardinals and went down to talk to a group of handicapped people who had been given seats at the front of the crowd. I had been invited, along with the leaders of other church delegations, to go into the Vatican to meet the Pope. We went first to one splendid room and then along gilded corridors to one even more splendid. We then approached the Vatican equivalent of the gates of heaven – the room where the Pope was waiting. In front of me was a small Orthodox delegation dressed in long, flowing robes. Peering through the half-open door I was dismayed to observe that their leader deposited a gift on a side table. It was a statue of the Virgin Mary. I had not come armed with a gift, no warning having been given in advance about this part of the proceedings. When I entered the chamber the Holy Father gave me a warm embrace. We had a five minute chat during which he said how much he had valued our small Methodist Church in Poland. Just as I was leaving he caught sight of the statue on the table. 'Oh,' he said, 'do please thank your Methodist people for that beautiful statue of Our Lady.' I did not feel it right for a humble Methodist to correct the Pope.

I referred earlier to the work of the WMC in promoting bilateral conversations. The earliest of these was with the Roman Catholic Church and was started in 1967. The Commission responsible for carrying forward these ongoing exchanges has published reports at five-yearly intervals. These have dealt with a wide range of subjects including mission, social questions, moral and ecclesiastical discipline, spirituality, the work of the Holy Spirit, the nature of the Church, authority, the ministry and the apostolic tradition. It is slow and painstaking work. In Britain there is a similar dialogue between Methodists and Roman Catholics. These discussions have resulted in a joyful recognition of the extent of the areas of agreement that exist and a deeper understanding of the points of disagreement. They have also meant for those involved a grateful acceptance of a rich and satisfying fellowship among themselves.

Whilst these high-level conversations may seem to be rather remote from the men and women in the pews they do, I believe, facilitate the process of growing together at the all-important local level. Roman Catholics are active members of many local councils of churches. I remember an occasion when Cardinal Heenan called together 150 Methodists and an equal number from his own communion for a day of fellowship. In my discussion group was an elderly nun. At one point she jumped to her feet, enveloped me in an ample embrace and exclaimed, 'Oh, my dear brother, I never knew before that Methodists believed in holiness!' I nearly said that John Wesley invented it! There is no doubt that in many areas Methodists enter more readily into fellowship with Roman Catholics than with Anglicans who seem so often to have around their necks the incubus of establishment status. I myself find much to admire in the openness of the Roman Catholic Church to all sorts and conditions of men and women. Class distinctions do not seem to matter as much to them as they sometimes seem to do in other parts of the church, though no doubt a few Roman Catholics experience a flush of pleasure at the movement of some well-known personages, including a Duchess, into their corner of the vineyard. I fear, however, that Cardinal Hume did the cause of unity no good when, noting the fact that some disaffected Anglican clergymen were joining his church, he described this as 'the beginning of the conversion of England'.

In addition to its dialogue with Roman Catholics the WMC is conducting conversations with the Anglicans, the Lutherans and the Orthodox. It was in connection with the last of these that I went to Russia in 1977. My wife came with me as did also Frank Northam, at that time Secretary of the Geneva Office and a world traveller with immense experience and impeccable ecumenical credentials (he had been on the staff of the World Council of Churches). Not the least of his accomplishments was his ability to consume large quantities of vodka which had seemingly little effect upon him.

It was bitterly cold as we landed on the snow-packed runway at Moscow Airport; at 5.00am the thermometer registered minus 8 degrees centigrade. We were met by Sergei, a lay member of the Russian Orthodox Church. He spoke excellent English and proved a most valuable friend, guide and adviser. We were taken to the Hotel Ukraina on the banks of the Moscow River which was frozen over. This hotel is a vast pile with 27 floors. There was a peculiar arrangement whereby access to the elevator was with the permission of a formidable looking female custodian in a white coat who occupied a seat on the landing. On arrival in our bedroom we found a welcome note and a large bottle of vodka. We explained to Sergei that we did not drink. He hid his evident astonishment under a courteous acceptance of this eccentricity, and the next day the bottle had been replaced by a huge box of chocolates. Although they were different shapes the fillings were all the same: disappointing, but a kind gesture.

On the day following our arrival we were taken through the snowy streets to the Patriarchate for a discussion with Metropolitan Juvenaly. It was an impressive occasion. We were ushered into an ante-chamber where three priests stood dressed in elaborate vestments. We were then shown into the room where the Metropolitan was waiting for us. We exchanged the usual three-fold kiss and after tea and sweetmeats had been served the conversation began. It was evident that very careful preparations had been made. There were papers containing a long list of questions about Methodist history and doctrine which I did my best to answer. At the end of the afternoon I presented our host with a specially-bound copy of the Methodist Book of Offices and he gave me a case of silver and gold drinking goblets and a lavishly illustrated book about Moscow. Mary was given a beautiful necklace and a book.

We were driven from this interesting assignment in a sleek limousine to the famous Baptist Church in the centre of Moscow. The huge building was packed with 1,500 worshippers and there were several overflows in adjoining rooms. I preached a simple sermon. We were permitted to leave before the end of the two-hour service. As we walked down the centre aisle hands were stretched out to greet us and the whole congregation sang 'God be with you till we meet again.' By the end of these varied experiences we were quite exhausted, having travelled through the previous night from meetings in Singapore and having had no sleep for 36 hours.

Our kind hosts had laid on a non-stop programme. We toured the Kremlin – the old city of Moscow – and we were impressed by the beauty of the buildings. We visited the University and also attended an unforgettable performance of *Aida*. This was given in the great hall where the Supreme Soviet held its meetings. I was told that all seats were sold weeks in advance, yet we were accommodated near the front of the audience of 6,000 people. The scenery was stunning. At the end the actress who had played the lead role stood alone on the stage silently weeping, overcome by the tumultuous applause. Another memorable part of this visit was the journey which took us out across the Steppes of Russia – endless flat plains – to the monastery at Zagorsk. Here we met some of the several hundred Orthodox priests-in-training and talked with the head of the theological seminary.

Back in Moscow we were the guests of the Patriarch in his Cathedral. I was invited to stand by the high altar and a priest who spoke some English described the unfolding liturgy in an audible whisper. When the 'royal doors' before the altar swung open I looked out over a huge congregation, all standing packed together. The Patriarch arrived late and entered on a cloud of incense. There were candles everywhere. A little old lady wearing a black shawl stood motionless before an icon picturing the Virgin Mary. A priest stood near the door with a silver phial of oil and with a small brush marked the foreheads of departing worshippers with the sign of the cross. There was glorious music from two choirs which sang antiphonally. It was a strange experience for a plain Methodist and made the average Roman Catholic service at home seem like a Quaker meeting.

*Mary and myself with Sergei Gordeev
in front of St Bazil's Cathedral in Moscow*

One of the characteristics of Orthodoxy is its tremendous attachment to tradition, and another is its sense of the reality of the eternal. Time doesn't seem to be particularly important. A thousand ages in their sight are but an evening gone. If it takes five years to set the agenda for a meeting, what does it matter? While I was in Moscow Bishop William Cannon and Dr Joe Hale were visiting the Ecumenical Patriarch in Istanbul and the result of these initial forays is that a formal dialogue has started between Methodism and Orthodoxy. As time goes by we shall learn a lot and hopefully the Methodist people will come to understand and appreciate the treasures which are to be found in the second largest of the great world Christian families. In the past the separation of east and west has been the cause of tragic mutual impoverishment; now, with the renewal of east/west relations, both the elder brother, as the Orthodox see their communion, and we, the younger brethren and sisters in the other churches, may find a new community of purpose.

I turn now to ecumenical affairs in Britain. In 1972 an event occurred which was of considerable significance for the British Churches. It was called a Church Leaders' Conference and was organised by the British Council of Churches. The venue was the Selly Oak Colleges in Birmingham, and among the 500 who attended there was a substantial number of Roman Catholics. It was this fact that gave the Conference a new dimension, and at one point a rather stormy passage. The Roman Catholics were not used to the kind of exchanges that characterised this gathering and there was fear that they might pack their bags and leave. However, this did not happen. The prepared agenda was torn up and a different one adopted with more emphasis on shared discussion and the repudiation of any attempt to pass resolutions. As we faced the dilemmas of our times and the reality of much failure there was a good deal of plain speaking. I remember clearly the moment when Cardinal Heenan was being pressed about how long it would be before non-Catholics would be able to receive Holy Communion in his church. He replied that he could only conceive of this in exceptional circumstances such as a concentration camp. This drew from Canon Bernard Pawley, that master of dry wit, the response, 'It seems, then, that we must pray for the multiplication of concentration camps.'

Archbishop Michael Ramsey had to go off to attend the funeral of his predecessor, Lord Fisher, so I was asked to make the closing speech. I felt bound to criticise the failure of the churches to send more women. I said, 'We must, I think, take seriously the unrepresentative nature of this gathering. Male dominance is one of the most pervasive and disastrous defects in the whole Christian tradition. The equal partnership of men and women is plainly the mark of that true humanity which is God's design and purpose. The practical denial of it has resulted in all manner of error and dire impoverishment.' I thanked two men who had made outstanding speeches, Bishop Ian Ramsey of Durham and Professor T. F. Torrance of the Church of Scotland, describing them as 'the Tigris and Euphrates of the Conference'. Bishop Ramsey, I said, had taken us to the heights and 'was last seen with his back towards us, making steadily in the direction of God'. They were prophetic words; a few days later he died.

Few, I think, would have disagreed with my summing up: 'Most will surely recognise the will of God in a new pattern of leadership – a leadership which listens. As the word "collegiality" edges its way into our vocabulary, the hand on the helm will be steadier, and maybe the conditions for a new Pentecost will be created. I came here believing church union to be right; I go away believing it to be inevitable. I believe God has revealed to us more clearly our resources in faith. The reward of accepting the disciplines of ecumenical encounter is a richer understanding. My judgement is that God will send no one away empty from this Conference.'

During my Westminster years the main instrument of inter-church co-operation in the United Kingdom was the British Council of Churches. It was served by a succession of extremely able General Secretaries: David Say (who became Bishop of Rochester), Kenneth Slack (who became Director of Christian Aid), Bishop Kenneth Sansbury, Harry Morton, and Philip Morgan. I have vivid memories of them all. Kenneth Slack was a commanding figure, a fine preacher and broadcaster who was very skilful with his pen. His time at Christian Aid was overshadowed by a miserable legal dispute with a clever but rather opinionated layman called David Smithers. Dr Slack had criticised Mr Smithers in connection with his relief work in Africa. A completely unnecessary dispute went on interminably wasting time, money and a great deal of nervous energy. I tried to persuade Mr Smithers not to continue with his attacks on the integrity of his critic, but without success. It is a good job that all those public figures who are inevitably subject to criticism don't feel it incumbent upon themselves to pursue their critics with threats of litigation. Towards the end of his life Kenneth Slack was stricken with a wasting disease which robbed him of his powers, and when he died we lost a gifted friend and leader.

Harry Morton was another man of outstanding gifts. His lucidity of thought and ability to present a penetrating analysis of a situation were wedded to a truly prophetic sense of mission. But the ministry he exercised exacted a heavy price. He suffered from spells of deep depression, what he called his 'black dog', and his colleagues, who supported him with deep loyalty, sometimes found him testy and uncertain. He was felled by a debilitating stroke. Just as Millicent Slack had nursed her husband with great devotion, so Pat Morton cared for Harry with unfailing tenderness. When the British Council of Churches celebrated its 40th anniversary in St Paul's Cathedral Harry was pushed down the aisle in a wheelchair by Kenneth Slack, so soon himself to be a victim of illness.

No-one who was present at the thanksgiving services for these two men will ever forget them. Kenneth was remembered in Westminster Abbey and Harry in Wesley's Chapel. Colin Morris' tribute to his friend Harry Morton was the most brilliant and evocative I have ever heard. He recalled his first meeting with this remarkable man, when they were both candidates for the ministry. Harry was standing under the statue of John Wesley in Richmond College where they were both being interviewed. Of the two of them, Colin asserted, Wesley looked the more nervous. He went on: 'When I professed my utter unpreparedness for the coming ordeal he gave me an impromptu tutorial which in five minutes ranged from a masterly survey of the state of New Testament scholarship to the Methodist doctrine of ordination. And it was redeemed from any trace of pretentiousness by his final sentence – "If all else fails," he concluded sarcastically in a broad Yorkshire accent, "thee can always limp. They can't resist a war hero!"' (Colin had just completed his war service.) The address ended with these words: 'All in all, a God-obsessed man. He walked with God; he loved God's world; he cherished God's children; he stood for God's truth; he served God's church; he led God's people; he followed God's Son; he prayed for God's Kingdom; he proclaimed God's victory. He dwells with God.'

The Presidency of the British Council of Churches was held by the Archbishops of Canterbury; Geoffrey Fisher, Michael Ramsey, Donald Coggan and Robert Runcie. It was always made clear that there was no constitutional reason why the incumbent of the See of Canterbury should automatically assume the leadership role and on occasion the matter was discussed. There was, however, never any likelihood of some other arrangement being accepted. The association of the Archbishop with the Presidency gave the Council a certain standing.

I served for a time as Chairman of the Executive Committee of the BCC and on various other Committees and Working Parties. The Council achieved some success in enabling the member churches to think, speak and act together and it certainly provided a forum in which the church leaders could get to know one another well. It could not, of course, legislate for the member bodies, but its pronouncements on some of the great issues of the day represented a general Christian consensus. Some of its detailed work, particularly on international relations, was extremely competent and well-informed. Whilst it kept a sympathetic watch on the attempts of member churches to bring about organic union the Council did not itself feel it right to be directly involved in any such negotiations. I felt that it was often overcautious in this matter. The BCC has now been replaced by the Council of Churches for Britain and Ireland and by separate ecumenical instruments for the four parts of the United Kingdom.

The BCC was involved in the historic visit of the Pope to Britain in May 1982. There had been doubt almost to the last minute whether he would come. Britain was at war with Argentina over the Malvinas (the Falkland Islands). Most British people hadn't the remotest idea where they were until they appeared in the headlines. The Pope did not wish to appear to be taking sides in a conflict that sadly divided the two nations and in which members of his church were killing each other. He summoned leaders of his communion in the two countries to meet him in Rome. They talked together and celebrated mass in a spirit of penitence and reconciliation. Then the Pope decided that he must visit both countries and preach the gospel of peace to both sides.

There was a great service in Canterbury Cathedral. Those of us who were taking part gathered in the crypt to robe; I recall chatting with Dr Billy Graham as we waited for our instructions. There was some difficulty in finding the right person to carry a candle. A prominent Baptist was asked if he would do it. He turned pale and said, 'I dare not, with all those television cameras watching.' I stepped into this amusing dilemma and suggested that Dr Philip Morgan would make an admirable candle-bearer. So the General Secretary of the BCC stepped into the breach. I represented the Free Churches as Moderator of the Free Church Federal Council and stood before the high altar with the Pope and Dr Runcie and led that part of the service where we recited our baptismal vows together.

When the service was over a group of us repaired to the Deanery for lunch. To our disappointment Dr Runcie announced that the Pope would take his meal alone in a separate room. Then the door opened and the Holy Father came in saying, 'I do not wish to be alone.' Dr Runcie invited him to sit next to me which afforded a wonderful opportunity for an hour-long conversation. We talked about the war and his forthcoming visit to Argentina. I gave him £3,000, a Methodist gift across the battle-lines for the relief of poverty in that country. He used it to help a struggling village community there.

Before leaving, the Pope invited the BCC to send a delegation to Rome in company with representatives of the Roman Catholic Bishops' Conferences of England and Wales, and of Scotland. This invitation was gladly accepted and in April 1983 I went to Rome together with Mr Martin Conway, the Rev Martin Cressey, the Rt Rev John Habgood, the Most Rev Alastair Haggart, Dr Philip Morgan and Mrs Elizabeth

Templeton. The Roman Catholic companions were Bishops Alan Clark, Cormac Murphy-O'Connor and Francis Thomson, together with the Revs Michael Richards and James Quinn. We were given a wonderful welcome in the Vatican. Over five memorable days we sat in on meetings of the various 'Congregations' or Departments, each headed by a Cardinal and dealing with a wide range of subjects such as unity, justice and peace, relationships with other faiths, and so on. It was very interesting to note that some of the Departments were quite liberal in their outlook and others more conservative, depending, perhaps, on the views of the presiding Cardinal.

One day we moved from the Sacred Congregation for the Doctrine of the Faith to the Secretariat for non-Christians. The first encounter took place beneath a massive crucifix hung on red damask. To reach the second we walked along a corridor full of symbols of the great religions of the world. I was fascinated by a diminutive Japanese priest who told us that he had been converted to Christianity from Buddhism. 'But,' he said, 'much of what I learned as a Buddhist was true and I have carried that truth into my Christianity.' It was a powerful witness, pointing us in the right direction in our search for right relations with people of other faiths.

A gift from the Pope at the Vatican, 1983

At the end of our discussions we were received by the Pope. With a mischievous twinkle in his eye he said, 'And what do you think of my Curia?' There was a long silence so I said, 'I imagine, Your Holiness, that this is a rhetorical question?' at which he laughed. On that day, as on so many others, the Pope was receiving distinguished visitors from all over the world. It seemed to me that the Vicar of Christ is expected to carry an impossible burden of a kind that no man should be asked to carry. Alastair Haggart said to me, 'Has the poor man no place where he can just let his hair down and be an ordinary chap?'

I was left in no doubt that the Pope exercises very considerable influence. I talked to one of his speech-writers who told me that often drafts are sent back full of corrections and sometimes with requests to start all over again. I heard complaints that this much-travelled occupant of the throne of St Peter is away from Rome too much. He is a charismatic figure and, I suppose, the biggest crowd-puller in the world. His conservatism has, however, been a brake on progress in some of those areas where many had hoped for advance: for example, the ordination of women and the matter of birth control. For all that, the entry of the Roman Catholic Church into the Ecumenical Movement has brought a sea-change in relationships and prospects for closer unity. It was Alastair Haggart who summed up our hope by quoting from Christopher Fry's 'A Sleep of Prisoners':

> The frozen misery
> Of centuries, breaks, cracks, begins to move;
> The thunder is the thunder of the floes,
> The thaw, the flood, the upstart Spring.

This visit to Rome was made even more enjoyable by the fact that my wife and younger daughter Elizabeth came with me. While I was busy in the Vatican they stayed in a delightful Anglican convent, a haven of peace in a rather rough part of the city. One day they received an invitation to join our group to see the Sistine Chapel. I left them careful instructions to meet me under a certain arch where a Vatican car would be waiting. Rome is full of arches and they waited under the wrong one. As a result they had to make their way to the Vatican on foot. It was a very hot day and in the middle of our inspection of the Sistine Chapel a door burst open and they entered looking distinctly overheated. John Habgood looked down from his Olympian height and said, 'Is this your wife?' I confessed that it was. I don't think that she remembers her visit to the famous Chapel with unalloyed rapture, and, truth to tell, neither do I. I thought that it was very dark, even dingy. It has since been cleaned.

The hardest part of my ecumenical commitment has been the task of seeking with others to move things forward in Britain. I have already referred to the work of the BCC. I was also closely associated with the Free Church Federal Council (FCFC). Its roots go back into the Victorian age when Nonconformity was seeking to establish its full and rightful place in the life of the nation, often against the spirited opposition of the established church which felt threatened by the success and growth of the Free Churches. Various attempts were made to bring these churches into closer association. The FCFC was a union in 1940 of the two major organs of Free Church unity: the Free Church Council and the Federal Council.

Whereas in the earlier days Methodist leaders like Dr Scott Lidgett and Dr J. E. Rattenbury had played leading parts in the movement for Free Church unity, during my time that enthusiasm had waned. The largest Free Churches – Methodist, Baptist and United Reformed – were fully involved in the life of the BCC and it seemed to many of us that our main energies should be given to developing the work and influence of this more widely representative body. The need to fight our Free Church corner over against the Established Church did not seem any longer necessary in an age of greatly improved relationships between all the churches. The Baptist Church representatives found themselves more at ease in the FCFC than their Methodist and United Reformed colleagues and provided during my time three admirable General Secretaries: the Revs George Mann, Richard Hamper and David Staple. The smaller Free Churches also valued their chance to be represented on a Council where they seemed to have more influence than they did on the BCC.

The situation has been improved by establishing a much closer working relationship with the BCC and in more recent times with its successor bodies. The FCFC has been able to undertake pieces of work on behalf of the BCC and has made funds available for various ecumenical projects. (It has benefited from the generosity of that great Baptist Churchman, the late Sir Cyril Black and his father before him.) The FCFC has done much good work in the educational field and particularly in the oversight of Free Church hospital chaplains.

In 1981 I became Moderator of the FCFC. This post is significant in that often on national matters of concern it is possible for the Moderator to issue joint statements with the Archbishops of Canterbury and Westminster, thus representing the three major strands of British

Churchmanship. In my Moderatorial address to the Council in Newcastle I spoke about 'The Changeless as the Instrument of Change'. Often at meetings of the FCFC some of the members of a rather aged assembly would talk about the need to maintain 'the Free Church emphases'. When I inquired what these were there was never any very clear answer, which is not surprising since most of the emphases that matter are now shared right across the ecumenical spectrum.

In spite of the progress made in bringing the British churches nearer together there has only been one actual organic union of separated denominations and that was between English Presbyterians and Congregationalists which produced the United Reformed Church (URC). This new church came into being in 1972. The gathering to consummate the Union was held in the Methodist Central Hall at Westminster and was addressed by the Archbishop of Canterbury, Dr Michael Ramsey. The Presbyterians and Congregationalists came out of the Hall clothed in their new identity and crossed the road for a great service in Westminster Abbey where the leaders of the other churches pledged themselves to the search for fuller unity. In his sermon the newly-elected Moderator of the new church, Dr John Huxtable, pleaded with others to join them in a more united fellowship. I wrote in my diary, 'Here is a brave new church which is writing its death warrant into its birth certificate.' Alas, there has been no rapid response to Dr Huxtable's invitation.

Up and down the country local URC and Methodist Churches have united. But although a national union of the two churches has been discussed there has been no great enthusiasm for this on either side. I think that this is partly due to the fact that local unions have not always been trouble-free. The bringing together of different traditions and constitutions is never easy. I think also that there has been a deep sense of reluctance to be exposed to the danger of failure of the kind experienced by Anglicans and Methodists when their Scheme for organic union finally collapsed.

Conversations between the Church of England and the Methodist Church had begun in 1955. An 'Interim Report' was published in 1958 which recommended that the goal should not be inter-communion but organic union. The definitive Report was published in 1963. The signatories declared their conviction that in spite of different emphases there was enough agreement on doctrine to make organic union possible. The Report suggested a procedure whereby this could happen in two stages. In the first stage ministers and members would be 'reconciled' and the two churches would enter into full communion with each other. From the beginning of Stage 1 all new ministers would be ordained by an Anglican bishop in the historic episcopate and certain Methodist ministers would be consecrated as bishops. Stage 2 would be the joining together of the two churches in a 'Service of Reconciliation': the members and ministers of the two churches would accept each other, the ministers, including the Anglican bishops, by the laying on of hands. There followed a period of lively debate in both churches. Along with many others I addressed crowded meetings and commended the Scheme. In 1965 both churches declared that the Report had indicated the right way forward and appointed a further team to produce a fully-articulated Scheme including an Ordinal. Some of those in my own church opposed to the Scheme had formed an organisation which they rather presumptuously called 'The Voice of Methodism' (VMA). They mounted a concerted attack, asserting that the very heart of Methodism was endangered. Votes were taken at Parish and Diocesan levels by the Church of England, and at Circuit and District levels in the Methodist Church. Some objected to the ambiguity in the Service of Reconciliation which allowed it to be interpreted as in fact a service of ordination, or not, according to the attitude of the person making the judgement.

The decisive vote took place simultaneously in the assemblies of the two churches in July 1969. It had been decided that a vote of at least 75 per cent was needed for approval. I remember the dramatic moment in the Methodist Conference when the President, the Rev Brian O'Gorman and the Secretary, Dr Eric Baker, left the platform to telephone the Archbishop of Canterbury in London. The voting in the Methodist Conference had been over 78 per cent. They came back to tell us that the Anglican vote was just under 70 per cent. The Anglo-Catholics and the Evangelicals had united to vote against the Scheme for quite opposite reasons: the former because the Service of Reconciliation was not an ordination; the latter because they thought that it was and believed that Methodist ministers were properly ordained already.

The supporters of the Scheme made one more attempt three years later. I sat in Church House, Westminster with Dr Baker and heard Michael Ramsey make what was probably the finest speech of his life. 'I pray,' he cried, 'that the answer will be "yes".' But, as before, the Anglican answer was 'No', or, at least an insufficient 'Yes'. I walked across Parliament Square with Dr Baker to a press conference. He suddenly looked ten years older.

What was now to be done? None of us who were committed to the Ecumenical Movement could accept that the failure of the Scheme after so many years of toil was the end of the road. It was a great opportunity lost: a judgement which, so far as I am concerned, the years since have confirmed. There was a great sense of disappointment among the Methodists. There were similar feelings in the Church of England, mingled in some hearts with a sense of shame. Nevertheless it was not all loss. A majority in both churches had desired union. During the protracted discussions much had been learned, and fellowship had been deepened.

A new initiative came from the 1973 General Assembly of the newly-formed United Reformed Church. An invitation was sent to all the churches in England to engage in 'talks about talks'. Those who attended these talks came from a very wide spectrum and they approached their task with varying degrees both of enthusiasm and misgiving. However, the decision was made to set up a body called the Churches' Unity Commission' (CUC). It consisted of representatives from the Baptists, Churches of Christ, Church of England, Congregational Federation, Methodists, Moravians, Roman Catholics and United Reformed Church. These participants agreed together to fund the work of the Commission for three years, eventually extended to four. Dr John Huxtable was appointed the Executive Officer.

The CUC was asked to examine Local Ecumenical Projects, to try to stimulate ecumenical activity in areas where little co-operation was evident, and to discover whether there was any way by which the national churches could move closer together. The result of much labour was the publication in 1976 of the Ten Propositions. Part of the drafting was done in my Westminster office. They read as follows:

1. We reaffirm our belief that the visible unity in life and mission of all Christ's people is the will of God.
2. We therefore declare our willingness to join in a Covenant actively to seek that visible unity.
3. We believe that this search requires action both locally and nationally.
4. We agree to recognise, as from an accepted date, the communicant members in good standing of the other Covenanting churches as true members of the Body of Christ and welcome them to Holy Communion without condition.
5. We agree that, as from an accepted date initiation in the Covenanting churches shall be by mutually acceptable rites.

6. We agree to recognise, as from an accepted date, the ordained ministries of the other Covenanting churches as true ministries of word and sacraments in the Holy Catholic Church, and we agree that all subsequent ordinations to the ministries of the Covenanting churches shall be according to a Common Ordinal which will properly incorporate the episcopal, presbyteral and lay roles in ordination.
7. We agree within the fellowship of the Covenanting churches to respect the rights of conscience, and to continue to accord to all our members, such freedom of thought and action as is consistent with the visible unity of the church.
8. We agree to give every possible encouragement to local ecumenical projects and to develop methods of decision-making in common.
9. We agree to explore such further steps as will be necessary to make more clearly visible the unity of Christ's people.
10. We agree to remain in close fellowship and consultation with all the churches represented on the Churches' Unity Commission.

Five of the churches which had laboured in the CUC agreed to go forward to the implementation of these Ten Propositions. They were: the Church of England, the Methodist Church, the Moravian Church, the Churches of Christ and the United Reformed Church. The Methodist Conferences voted overwhelmingly in favour; the Anglicans less enthusiastically. A Churches Council for Covenanting (CCC) was formed with Bishop Kenneth Woollcombe as Chairman, Mr Philip Capper as Secretary and Mr Arthur Chapman as Treasurer. The first meeting was held on 24 November 1978. Consultant observers were appointed by the Baptists, Roman Catholics, Lutherans and a number of church agencies. The Rev John Coventry of the Roman Catholic Church proved to be a particularly valuable adviser.

In 1980 the CCC published its Report under the title: 'Towards Visible Unity: Proposals for a Covenant'. It contained the text of a proposed Order of Service for the Making of the Covenant at national level and for regional and local responses to the Covenant. There were suggestions for joint services for Confirmation and Reception of Members, and a Common Ordinal. There was also a Memorandum of Dissent signed by three of the Anglican members: the Bishop of Truro (the Rt Rev Graham Leonard), the Rev Peter Boulton and Mr O. W.

H. Clark. This was tabled just before the Report was due to go to the printer.

This Report with its Proposals was submitted to the five churches. The responses of the Moravian and United Reformed Churches was positive. So also was that of the Methodist Church. Every attempt was made by the Methodist Conference to ensure that the whole church was consulted and the Proposals were, in fact, widely studied at every level. The voting in Conference was 497 for with five against and five neutral: an overwhelming endorsement. But once again the vote in the Synod of the Church of England, while registering a majority in favour, failed to reach the reduced level of 66 and two-thirds per cent which had been agreed.

The final meeting of the CCC in Church House, Westminster, was a sad occasion. We met to acknowledge our failure. Some of the Anglicans wanted us to have one more try. As the leader of the Methodist team I felt compelled to say to them, 'You have asked us to march our Methodist people to the top of the hill and down again once. By the grace of God we have done it a second time. But do not ask us to do it a third time, for they will not follow.' I think that was right. Our people had most loyally supported us in pressing ahead with the Covenanting Proposals though I was aware that many entertained doubts about the ability of the Anglicans to deliver. The sense of disillusionment was now widespread.

The meeting was informed that David Brown, the Bishop of Guildford, who had led the Anglican team, had arrived feeling unwell. Before the end of the meeting Bishop Woollcombe told us that David had died. It is the only time in my life that I have seen a room full of church leaders many of whom were weeping. We had little doubt that he had died of a broken heart. His death demonstrated that a heavy price can be paid for full commitment to the Ecumenical Movement. I had known him as a boy in Bristol. I walked from the meeting with a leaden heart.

Some time after this Cardinal Hume telephoned me and said, 'The Covenant has failed; we must do something.' He invited me to join him for lunch together with Robert Runcie and the other Free Church Secretaries. It was, I thought, significant that the initiative for some fresh move came from the leader of the Roman Catholics in England and Wales. The lunchtime meeting was an occasion for frank speaking. I said that in personal terms neither of the Archbishops had helped the Covenant Proposals to succeed. Basil Hume had come at my invitation to Newcastle to address the Free Church Federal Council Annual Congress.

He had said in effect, 'A Covenant, yes; but not this Covenant.' In the Anglican Synod Robert Runcie had been lukewarm in his commendation. Cardinal Hume now suggested that we should have a weekend when all the church leaders should come together to pray, an idea that was later carried into effect. We agreed, however, that more than that was needed. Dr Runcie asked Cardinal Hume if a group of us from the British Council of Churches could be invited to the Roman Catholic Bishops' Conference to try to move them nearer to acceptance of the idea that their church should become a full member of that Council. The Cardinal replied that he could not immediately issue such an invitation. It appeared that the Bishops' Conference was very much a closed shop. However, not long afterwards such an invitation was sent and a splendid meeting was convened in a Convent. The Bishops welcomed those of us who attended from the BCC with great warmth and cordiality. It's the only time I've ever been conducted to my sleeping chamber by a bishop! Our discussions were frank, and at times moving. Archbishop Derek Warlock made this confession: 'We believe that all the essentials of the Christian Church are found in the Roman Catholic Church, but we acknowledge that some of those essentials are found even more fully expressed in other Churches than in our own.' I record these words from memory and may not have recalled them with complete accuracy, but the sense of them is as I have indicated.

The Roman Catholics had long hesitated about taking up full membership in the BCC although they had contributed richly to working parties and as observers at the Council's meetings. They had doubts about the Council's stance on some social issues. Moreover the BCC was not a Council as they understood the term, that is, a body empowered to make decisions. Our meeting with the Bishops helped to promote deeper understanding and trust and the end result was the creation of the successor bodies to the BCC in which the Roman Catholics now play a full part.

It is not easy to see where the Ecumenical Movement will take the British churches in the years ahead. The entry into that Movement of the Roman Catholics has in one way been a great encouragement and enrichment. On the other hand it has faced us with a much more complex scenario. There is no doubt in my own mind that the search for full communion must bring us in the end to a full sharing of ministry, mission and sacramental life with the Roman Catholic Church. In correspondence with Cardinal Hume some years ago he referred to 'the real but imperfect communion we already have with each other' – meaning, of course, our two churches. Well, all our Christian fellowship is imperfect and always must be. At the personal level I have grown increasingly restive at the slow progress towards that point where Roman Catholics can come together to the table of the Lord, free of all restraints. I know all the arguments. I am aware that the Roman Catholic Church sees the Holy Communion as evidence of a unity already achieved and not as a means towards achieving that unity. But our bilateral discussions as well as our everyday experience at the local level demonstrate how much we have in common both in terms of basic doctrine and love of our Lord. If we wait for complete doctrinal agreement we will wait for ever. Not only that, but some differences on important issues run right across all the denominational boundaries. I have respected the rules of the Roman Catholic Church but every time I attend a mass, joining wholeheartedly in most of the hymns and prayers, I am conscious of the pain of being separated from the rest of the congregation at the very point where we should be rejoicing in our oneness in Christ. I feel that I am conniving at a form of spiritual apartheid which is no longer tolerable.

I am not worried, as some are, by the thought of accepting the primacy of the Pope. Someone has to take the lead in any organisation. It is a sign of hope that in my lifetime the Church of Rome has changed more rapidly than any other. Perhaps not under this Pope, but maybe under the next, the Roman Catholic Church will feel able to follow the logic of its commitment to ecumenism and remove some of the barriers to fuller fellowship which cause so much heartache to so many.

So far as the more immediate future is concerned it is being claimed that the prospects for reviving the proposal for organic union between Anglicans and Methodists are improving. It is suggested that the departure of some Anglo-Catholics to Rome will have removed some of the stumbling blocks on which previous proposals came to grief. It is to be hoped that those who are entering into a new round of talks will test the ground thoroughly before inviting the two churches to embark once again on a concrete shceme. Anglicans lost the initiative through the failures recorded earlier in this Chapter, and Methodists, understandably, lost interest in formal schemes of union. It will be important to ask if there is any new approach which could produce more positive results. It must not be forgotten, too, that the Covenant Proposals went further than the earlier Anglican/Methodist Unity Scheme and involved three other churches. They must be involved in any new advance. The need for advance can scarcely be exaggerated. There is the constant danger of a purely parochial view of the church. Locally the degree of inter-church co-operation varies enormously. The local, national and global aspects of the search for unity cannot be separated. If the all-important area of witness is the locality, as I believe, then progress at this level is bound to be inhibited by weak leadership at the top. There is great need for a new multilateral move at the level of national leadership.

A report entitled 'Commitment to Mission and Unity' published in 1996 is the work of an Anglican/Methodist group set up on the initiative of the Methodist Church. It reaffirms the goal of visible unity and details the familiar issues to be resolved. This report is to be studied by both churches and other churches are invited to comment. Following this it is hoped that a decision will be made to begin formal conversations in 1998 aiming at a Declaration of mutual recognition and solemn committment. Ecumenical observers, as in earlier conversation, will be asked to contribute.

There is no reason at all why Christians should fear the imposition of uniformity. It is odd that this fear is often most fervently expressed by people who accept a fairly dull uniformity of practice within their own denomination Sunday by Sunday and week by week. Closer relations with the other churches can only result in a richer and more diverse experience.

The hope for the future lies in the fostering of a deep dissatisfaction with things as they are, springing from the conviction that the Holy Spirit will not allow us to stay the way we are. The goal is a visibly united church which begins to look more like a transcript of the Trinity, a perfect unity in a creative diversity.

Chapter Six

STILL A VISION

The decision made in 1939 to register as a conscientious objector was not arrived at without much travail of heart and mind. It is never altogether easy to stand with the minority though, in fact, it is an inescapable condition of Christian discipleship that we should be willing to do so. The church itself, though millions strong, nevertheless represents a minority of the world's population. It is incontestable that many of the great ideas which have moulded the life of nations and changed the course of history have been the possession of minorities. The abolition of slavery, the battle for the female franchise and numerous other significant advances have been pioneered by small but convinced minorities. Our Lord himself referred to his small band of followers as the leaven in the lump. Again and again history has demonstrated that majorities can be wrong and minorities can be right.

Throughout my life I have felt compelled to take the minority position on a whole range of issues. When I have found myself siding with the majority I have championed the right of the minority to express their views. I think that is consistent with democracy.

Nevertheless, while what I have just written was clear to me in 1939, I did not find it easy to stand with the minority who rejected military service. The pressure to conform was immense. The constant outpouring of jingoistic propaganda, the drive for recruitment to the armed forces, the harnessing of the endeavours of the whole nation in support of the war effort, all had a most powerful effect. In all kinds of ways the suggestion was conveyed that to refuse to fight was a cowardly and unpatriotic thing to do.

Within the church at both local and national levels, though the right to conscientious objection was upheld, there was little sympathy for the pacifist view. The notion that Britain was engaged in a just war and that fighting it was a Christian duty was little questioned. Within the family circle I received much support even from some who could not share my position. At work any opposition was couched in language which showed a degree of respect for a stand that was generally regarded as odd and unrealistic. As colleagues went off to the war I was left to shoulder some of their responsibilities.

As the war advanced towards its dreadful climax, and as the stories of German and Japanese atrocities multiplied, the voices of opposition were drowned in the din of conflict. I attended a large meeting in the centre of Bristol addressed by Mr Ernest Bevin. He said, 'For every bomb the Germans drop on us we'll drop two on them.' The whole audience rose to its feet in a frenzy of cheering and clapping. I was the only one to remain seated, horrified by this eruption of hysteria.

To stand against so strong a tide of patriotic fervour was not easy, but there were other reasons why I found it hard to do so. I was aware that in Nazism we were facing a monstrous evil. I recognised the sincerity of many of my fellow-Christians who went off to fight and supported the war in other ways. Many young men, of course, enlisted in the armed forces unthinkingly and without questioning the non-stop national propaganda in support of the war; some thought of the whole thing as a great and welcome adventure. But there were those who became part of the war machine with deep reluctance but believing that evil must be resisted and that this could only be done effectively by resort to arms. They were sustained by a long tradition of Christian participation in warfare.

In these days when there is no conscription and the prospect of Britain being involved in a major war seems remote it is difficult to engage the minds of young people on the issues which those of my generation had to confront with sharp urgency in the 1930s under the looming shadow of approaching conflict. I am sometimes invited to lecture on pacifism in public schools and other such places, but the whole approach of those who invite me seems to be that of academic interest. But in those earlier days the issue was one requiring decision.

Looking back I ask myself what it was that led me to the position which I adopted and to which, with deepening conviction, I have adhered ever since. There was, of course, the influence of home, to which I have already referred. I do not remember that I had much intellectual conversation with my parents on the question of war, but I had their quiet example and unfailing encouragement. I was fortunate in my friends; John Stacey and George Lockett, who eventually went with me into the ministry, were both pacifists. We were able to argue together and the mutual support we derived from this was of inestimable value. We often shared night duty as firewatchers at the Bristol Homeopathic Hospital. We were not remote spectators of the war. We watched Bristol burn. Arriving home at 6.00am one day after a night at the hospital I saw from afar a huge heap of rubble outside our home. My heart stopped beating.

On closer approach I saw that it was the house of our neighbour opposite that had been bombed. He was lying dead in the ruins.

My thinking in the 1930s had been influenced by a number of men and women whose opposition to war was eloquently expressed in speech and writing. Eric Loveday, who later became Vicar of St Martin-in-the-Fields in London, was the Rector of the downtown church of St Peter in Bristol. Every Thursday he held a lunchtime service for city workers. It was always packed until, alas, it was destroyed by bombing. It was here that I first heard Donald Soper speak. Arriving just before the service began, I was shown up to the front pew. During the opening hymn I heard an extraordinarily powerful sound which seemed to make the woodwork vibrate. It was Donald Soper, singing! All down the years that rich voice has challenged Christians to think and act. My debt to him is beyond calculation. To have enjoyed his friendship and to have shared with him the work for peace has been one of life's great privileges.

Lord Soper has used the Upper House of Parliament as a platform for an informed and Christian witness on many of the great issues of the day. Like John Wesley, who lived through storms of opposition, was often violently attacked in the open air, and who in old age became a venerated national institution, so Donald Soper, the great controversialist, has become a figure almost universally respected and admired, and indeed loved by many.

There were other speakers and writers who challenged me to define my own position. Canon Charles Raven, with his superb intellect, presented the case for pacifism with impressive cogency, as did John Middleton Murray. Dick Sheppard, one-time Dean of Canterbury, toured the country as the founder of the Peace Pledge Union, which I joined. He was supported by Canon Stuart Morris, an eloquent apologist, and by Vera Brittain, one of the finest women orators of the century. In my own local church I derived inspiration from a small group of like-minded people headed by a layman, Leslie O. Brown, who reminded me of the Apostle Peter. He had a quick temper but was able to use his fiery energy in the cause of peace.

Surrounded, then, and upheld by this small cloud of witnesses I prepared my submission for the tribunal before which I had to appear. It was presided over by a tough character called Judge Wethered. The tribunal had not long been in existence and he listened to my presentation with considerable attention. (He became less sympathetic as the months went by.) I was asked a number of questions designed to test my sincerity, and then granted unconditional exemption from military service.

Later on my brother Brian appeared before the same judge. He was granted exemption on condition that he worked on the land. So with David Stacey, John's brother, he ploughed the field and learned to master a huge and temperamental cart-horse – splendid preparation for two men who were to become, respectively, a District Chairman in the Methodist Church and a College Principal.

During the years since the Second World War I have never ceased to think about the issues relating to peace and war. They are central to my ministry and inseparable from my understanding of the meaning and the demands of the gospel. It was the prophet Habakkuk who said, 'There is still a vision for the appointed time' (Habakkuk 2:3). It is the vision of a world freed from the scourge of war that has sustained my involvement in the work of a number of peace agencies and the writing and speaking on this theme which I have undertaken. I turn now to some account of these activities, which reflect not only developments in my own thinking but those within the church and society generally.

I believe that the life and teaching of Jesus Christ reveal a non-violent God and that the power of non-violent resistance to evil is the outstandingly radical element in the gospel. In the early days of the Christian church this seemed to be recognised and I am convinced that the recovery of that insight is an urgent necessity if the church is to make an effective contribution to the overcoming of violence. Few will doubt the need to attempt to do so; many believe that the very survival of humanity depends upon it. The World Council of Churches has shown prophetic wisdom in setting up its 'Programme to Overcome Violence'. This is the crucial issue for the churches and indeed for the whole world as we approach the beginning of the 21st century. The 1996 Methodist Conference commended to the churches the study of and active participation in the Programme to Overcome Violence. It referred to the Methodist Council for consideration and reported the judgement of the WCC's Central Committee that 'this may be a time when the churches together should face the challenge to give up any theological or other justification of the use of military power'.

Until at least the first quarter of the second century the church, in conformity with its understanding of the gospel, taught that the way of obedience rendered participation in warfare inadmissible. Justyn Martyr (c150AD) wrote, 'While Christians will gladly die for Christ we refrain from making war on enemies.' That attitude mirrored the teaching of Jesus which requires Christians to love their enemies (Matthew 5:44) and his example in going to the cross rather than heading a military revolt.

140

Although there have always been Christians who have remained faithful to the original repudiation of violence by the early church the official position shared by the great majority of Christians changed after the conversion of the Emperor Constantine in 312AD. Christianity became a state religion, accepted patronage from the Emperor, and in return was reconciled to Caesar's claims. The change is reflected in the words of Athanasius, 'the Father of Orthodoxy': 'Murder is not permitted, but to kill one's adversary in war is both lawful and praiseworthy.'

In spite of valiant attempts by all sorts of people to stimulate reasonable discussion about peace and war, two things have become inescapably clear. One is that misuse of the Bible is endemic among us. The following are typical of the comments one hears: 'The Bible speaks of "wars and rumours of wars", so there will always be war to the end of time. There is nothing we can do about it.' 'There are plenty of examples of holy wars in the Old Testament in which God supported the chosen people against the enemy (for example, 1 Samuel 15:2-3). So Christians are fully justified in taking up arms in defence of a good cause.' 'Jesus told his disciples, "[Whoever] has no sword, let him sell his cloak to buy one" (Luke 22:36), so obviously Jesus was in favour of fighting.' 'The bible is not concerned with political and social matters; it is all about the relationship between the individual and God. So it's no good looking to the holy scriptures for guidance on modern issues like nuclear war.'

The indiscriminate flinging about of biblical texts is the enemy of sound thinking as is also the strange idea that all parts of the Bible are of equal value. But even among those who approach the Bible with knowledge and serious intention there is often a wide diversity of judgement. The question, therefore, of how the Bible is to be used in seeking to arrive at clear judgements on important issues is of immense importance: a point already made (p.47) in reference to the debate on homosexuality. Unless there is a right understanding of the nature of biblical authority its use as a book of moral guidance is seriously impaired. Any such understanding must begin with an examination of what the Bible is, of the diversity of writings it contains, and of the way in which those writings reflect a progressive comprehension of the divine mind and purpose, culminating in the revelation brought by Jesus Christ.

The other fact that has been demonstrated repeatedly is the reluctance among Christians to face up to complex and controversial issues. As I said in Chapter Three, the ability and willingness of Christians to debate difficult questions within the bonds of unbroken friendship is one of the tests of the reality of Christian fellowship. Many

Methodist Churches have in recent times introduced a peace candle which stands on the Lord's table and is lit before the service begins. It is usually a very small candle lest any ultra-Protestant member of the flock should think that we are moving towards Rome! In spite of this symbolic witness to peace, however, the silence of the pulpit on the matter of the legitimacy or otherwise of destructive weaponry is for the most part almost deafening.

A rather more significant symbolic gesture has been the establishment by the World Methodist Council of an annual peace award. When the Council and its accompanying Conference met in Dublin in 1976 the 'peace women' of Ireland, as they were called, staged a march through the streets. Almost all the Methodists attending the Conference, nearly three thousand in all, joined the marchers. Out of this came the proposal to make an award each year to someone who had made a notable contribution to the cause of peace. The award consisted of a modest cheque for $1,000 and a medallion. The first award was made to Sadie Patterson, a Belfast Methodist who devoted her life to the work of reconciliation in Ireland, often exposing herself to danger. I went to Belfast with Dr Joe Hale to make the award.

I also went on a similar errand to Cairo in 1978 to make the award to President Anwar Sadat who had just made his courageous journey to Jerusalem to address the Israeli Parliament. I was astonished on arrival at the airport to find an official car and an armed guard waiting for me on the tarmac. I was whisked off to an expensive hotel on the banks of the Nile and the armed guards remained on duty outside my suite of rooms day and night. When I went out I was handed over to a police escort who dashed me round the city with sirens screaming. This excessive security made me feel distinctly insecure.

The day of the presentation came and I was transported to the Abdin Palace. Seated on gold chairs were the members of the Egyptian cabinet and the leaders of all the main religious bodies in the city. The President arrived by helicopter and after I had made my speech he responded. He said he was deeply moved by the fact that a Christian organisation was making this presentation to a Muslim. He shared his dream of a great peace accord to be signed on Mount Sinai and said that he would invite me to be present. Of course, President Sadat's peacemaking efforts were deeply unpopular with some and I was saddened when not long afterwards he was assassinated. His dream was never realised but it may be that his efforts played some part in moving the Middle East a little nearer to the peace that has for so long eluded it.

142

Presenting the Methodist Peace Award to President Anwar Sadat, Cairo 1978

The WMC continues to make this annual award but the choice of recipients has not always been easy. The officers who are responsible for deciding have not always agreed on their approach. Some have argued that the purpose of the award is best served by choosing some distinguished and well-known figure; there is then a good chance of media attention. The presentation to President Sadat, for example, was the first item on all the Egyptian television news bulletins. Others have taken the view that the award should be made purely on the quality of the individual's contribution to peacemaking. The choice of President Jimmy Carter as a recipient highlighted the compromises that have to be made. Mr Carter is a man of integrity, and, especially since his retirement from office, he has been used as a troubleshooter in several very difficult situations such as the one in Haiti. But, as American President, he was commander-in-chief of the most powerful military force in the world. The proposal to make the award to Gordon Wilson, the brave man who lost his daughter in the Enniskillen bombing, was a much easier one for the officers to make. The choice of Lord Soper on another occasion gave me great pleasure.

The symbolic gestures which I have been describing are not to be despised, but they fall short of the radical reassessment of the church's theology and teaching about peace which I am anxious to promote. As I mentioned earlier, for some years I have been Chairman of the Methodist Peace Fellowship (MPF). This is an organisation of pacifists within the Methodist Church and an integral part of the ecumenical body, the Fellowship of Reconciliation. It produces literature and holds occasional conferences. It organises a public meeting at the time of the annual Methodist Conference – usually a very lively and well-attended occasion. There has been a lengthy discussion about whether the MPF should open its membership to non-pacifists who are interested in practical peacemaking. I am myself keen on maximum co-operation of individuals and organisations in the search for peace, recognising that there are differences of approach and judgement. But I believe that the MPF is right to maintain its position as a focus of pacifist witness within the church.

One of the functions of the pacifist minority is to persevere in trying to keep the issues of peace and war alive in the churches, and to argue the case for a reassessment of traditional teaching. I do not accept the distinction which Dr David Edwards makes between pacifists and 'realists'. He is glad that 'many Christians have a simpler faith' (pacifism) but in this very complex world the rest must perforce be 'realists'. (*The Futures of Christianity,* Hodder 1986, p.370). The so-called realism to which Dr Edwards refers involves the acceptance of military options in defence of peace and justice. But it is precisely that thesis which I want to challenge both on the grounds of its theological assumptions and its practical effectiveness. As this violent century draws to its close it is difficult to escape the view that trust in the military option has proved singularly ineffective in safeguarding peace. Even more important is the question whether war fought with modern weapons can be justified at the bar of either Christian theological assessment or moral judgement.

I refer to war 'as fought with modern weapons' because, although I believe that violence in all its forms is wrong, I think that, for those Christians who accept the just war theory, there are new issues to be faced. They arise because modern warfare cannot be fought within the restrictions of the just war doctrine. Quantitative advances have raised qualitative considerations.

The criteria which define just war have been refined and developed over the years. They are:

144

1. Last resort. The use of arms can only be justified if all other just means of settling the dispute have been tried.
2. Just cause. The goals which the war seeks to achieve must be just.
3. Right attitudes. There must be no desire for revenge but only for the restoration of peace with justice.
4. Prior declaration. There must be a formal declaration of war by legitimate authority.
5. Reasonable hope of success. There must be a reasonable probability that all the things for which one is fighting will not be destroyed in the process.
6. Civilian population. No military action may be aimed directly at non-combatants.
7. Proportionality. There must be a reasonable expectation that the good achieved will exceed the inevitable harm done by the resort to arms.

Ever since the Christian church first felt constrained to sanction the use of armed force it has sought to place limitations on the conduct of warfare. The doctrine of just war represents the attempt to define the situations in which military action may be legitimate. In practice, of course, the rules of warfare have been breached repeatedly, not least by nations claiming to be Christian. During the Second World War there was a steady escalation in the scale of destruction and in the end the saturation bombing of both German and British cities meant that there was no longer any pretence of aiming at military targets only. Some sixty thousand people perished in the city of Dresden as a result of this largely indiscriminate form of attack.

The process of escalation reached its grotesque climax in the destruction of the Japanese cities of Hiroshima and Nagasaki. Whole populations of men, women and children were wiped out as if a giant blowtorch were being applied to an ant's nest. It was a long time before the world was allowed to know the full details of what had happened. What emerged was a picture of destruction on a scale never before realised, and a volume of human suffering made worse by the long-term effects of atomic radiation which still continue. The case in favour of dropping the bombs on Japan has been made often enough. It is claimed that the 'courageous' action of President Truman brought the war to an end and that had it continued huge numbers of people on both sides would have been slaughtered. This reading of history has been questioned by a number of writers who claim that Japan was about to sue for peace anyhow and that from a military point of view the dropping of the bombs was unnecessary.

Whatever the truth may be about Japan's intentions it is surely clear that the resort to nuclear weapons finds no endorsement in the Christian doctrine of the just war. That is the judgement repeated in many official statements by churches of every denomination. As long ago as 1957 the British Methodist Conference stated: 'The dreadful devastation caused by such weapons and the consequent and persistent effects of radioactive contamination make it extremely doubtful if a war so waged could achieve a good outweighing the evil it would involve.'

Many Christians who condemn the use of nuclear weapons as immoral nevertheless believe that their possession acts as a uniquely effective deterrent which has in fact 'kept the peace in Europe for over fifty years'. From the standpoint of Christian ethics it is very doubtful whether, if it is wrong to use a weapon, it can ever be right to threaten its use. If there is no intention to use, then deterrence is based on a huge bluff. When as President of the Methodist Conference I visited the Dartmouth Naval College I was asked by the commanding officer to speak to some of his men who actually handle nuclear weapons. They assured me that their sole purpose was to deter. One of them said, 'We have a slogan – if we fire, we've lost.' I was not impressed.

Much of the discussion of nuclear weapons as deterrents overlooks the fact that the dropping of the two bombs in 1945 initiated the nuclear arms race – one of the most appalling and senseless episodes in human history. The superpowers wasted huge resources in building up arsenals far beyond the requirements of any theory of deterrence; indeed to the point where the whole planet could be destroyed many times over. Other nations began to seek the means of possessing these uniquely effective deterrents. Now we are forced to recognise the deadly danger of nuclear proliferation. Urgent attempts are being made to introduce a Comprehensive Test Ban Treaty and there were widespread protests recently when France to conducted a series of nuclear tests in the Pacific.

The World Court Project is an attempt, supported by many of the peace organisations, to get the use of nuclear weapons declared contrary to international law. A group of concerned people succeeded in obtaining from the International Court of Justice at the Hague a judgement that the use or threatened use of nuclear weapons is 'generally contrary to international law'. The only possible exception would be the extreme circumstance of self-defence in which the very survival of a state would

146

be at stake. This perhaps represents a modest step towards a world freed from the horrors of nuclear war.

One of the results of my constant immersion in discussion and debate of all these issues over the years has been an increasing awareness of the evil influence of the international arms trade, described by Cardinal Hume as 'The Death Trade'. Sir David Steel is on record as saying, 'There is something appallingly hypocritical in the sight of developed nations pouring arms into the Middle East . . . and then collectively wringing our hands the moment they are used.' (*The Arms Bazaar in the Nineties*, Anthony Sampson, Hodder 1991, pp381-2).

In an attempt to deepen public awareness of this evil trade I wrote, as President of the Methodist Conference, an open letter to the Methodist people. This was published in the *Methodist Recorder* and the Editor, Mr Michael Taylor, gave me tremendous support and encouragement by printing a large volume of comment and correspondence on the matters I raised. I pleaded with Christians of every shade of opinion to make common cause. The letter began: 'Let me state with the utmost clarity what this letter is NOT. It is not a plea for pacifism. Some Methodists are pacifists, some are not, and the Methodist Church recognises both positions. But that is not what this letter is about.

'It is not a public airing of purely private views. The President of the Conference has a responsibility to try on occasions to speak representatively. I have pondered long, consulted widely, noted what the Synods have said, and believe that there is now a growing consensus in favour of what this letter proposes.'

I then set out a series of established facts. I pointed out that many poor countries were spending five times as much on arms as on agricultural machinery; that the cost of one jet fighter could build 40,000 village pharmacies; that 12 million children die every year before their fifth birthday. I then commented on the disastrous build-up of nuclear and other weapons. I concluded by appealing for support for the World Disarmament Campaign (WDC) and said, 'Not to be involved in the discussion of disarmament is surely to fail the Lord who commissioned us to be makers of peace. No Christian anywhere is exempt from the implications of that dominical command.'

The response to this appeal was encouraging. Only one of the many who wrote letters to the *Methodist Recorder* sounded a sour note. He scolded me for flinging 'an atomic war scare into the midst of the Methodist people', and went on to lay the blame for our parlous situation on the churches for failing to preach the infallibility of the Bible. He assured us that all would be well because the Lord would return and subject everything to his righteous rule. This letter exemplified the kind of escapist religion which accords not at all with the teaching of the Methodist Church. Many Methodists joined the World Disarmament Campaign and some much-needed financial support was obtained for this young organisation.

In November 1980 I addressed the British Council of Churches on the matter of disarmament and moved a resolution calling for support of the World Disarmament Campaign. Archbishop Robert Runcie spoke in support. He said, 'It may be possible to have a just war, but there can be no such thing as a just mutual obliteration.' He deplored the fact that developed nations were spending some of their best brains and a large proportion of their budgets on planning the 'lunatic unthinkable'.

My own connection with the WDC began in 1980. One day Lord Brockway (Fenner Brockway) came to see me in my Westminster office. With that other octogenarian peer, Philip Noel Baker, he had launched a campaign based on a petition addressed to all governments and to the United Nations Organisation. It read:

We, the Peoples of the World, demand:

1. The abolition of nuclear weapons and all weapons of mass destruction.
2. The abolition, by agreed stages, of conventional arms, leading to
3. General and complete disarmament.
4. Transference of military expenditure to end world poverty.

Fenner Brockway was a remarkable man. All his life he had campaigned in support of the underprivileged of the world. In Africa he was almost worshipped by many of the people whom he had helped. He had two great qualities. One was that he would never take 'No' for an answer. When he said, 'Kenneth, my friend Philip Noel Baker has died, I am lonely, and I want you to become co-Chairman with me of the WDC', I could not refuse. His other quality was an indomitable spirit which refused to acknowledge the possibility of defeat. He travelled the world with the Peace Action Programme which he devised. When he was well into his nineties I received an enthusiastic postcard from him posted in Japan. It read, 'Just addressed 1,000 peace activists in Hiroshima; off to India tomorrow to talk with Indira Gandhi.' He had a great gift for inspiring the friendship and loyalty of others. I have known him rise to his feet at the end of a rather dull meeting and in a brief speech rouse everyone to enthusiastic applause.

Inevitably, as the years took their toll, Lord Brockway became more infirm. His hearing failed almost completely. He would arrive at meetings with a contraption like a small meat-safe attached by wires to both ears. I had to assume increasing responsibility for the oversight of the Campaign. We began preparing a large celebration for Fenner's 100th birthday, and a statue was erected in Red Lion Square. He attended the unveiling and spoke from his wheelchair. Several tramps on a nearby seat mingled with the crowd who had been invited to a reception in an adjacent hall. I have never seen alcoholic refreshment disappear as quickly as it did down the throats of those uninvited guests. But Fenner would not have minded even had he noticed.

Lord Brockway died just before reaching his centenary and I became President of the WDC. It has continued its work though constantly hampered by lack of finance. It would have ceased operations altogether but for the small band of loyal and hardworking men and women who form its Executive Committee. There is no doubt that the work of the various peace agencies suffers because, like the Churches, they remain separated. Attempts at closer co-ordination of effort have been only partially successful. Each claims to have its own specific agenda and its own particular constituency. In 1994 I felt compelled to relinquish the Presidency because of pressures on my time and was grateful to Lord Archer of Sandwell for his willingness to take over. A multiplicity of other commitments had prevented my being able to give adequate time to the Campaign and I accepted the honorary position of a Vice-President.

The WDC launched an annual weekend of services and vigils for peace now observed by many churches and cathedrals throughout the land. Another notable achievement was the holding in 1990 of a National Convention on Human Survival to celebrate the Campaign's tenth anniversary. We gathered together a panel of distinguished speakers which included the Bishop of St Andrews, the President of the Methodist Conference, the Moderator of the Free Church Federal Council, Bruce Kent, Ken Livingstone, Simon Hughes, Judith Hart, Sir Richard Body, Dr Frank Barnaby and Professor Ken Coates. The speakers at this Convention covered a large number of interrelated issues and during the day seminars were held under the titles: Towards Sustainable Development, Environmental Security, New Political Dimensions of the

Arms Race, and The Future of the United Nations. We certainly demonstrated that the search for peace cannot be undertaken in isolation from all the factors upon which security and stability depend.

In 1982 I wrote a book entitled *The Big Sin: Christianity and the Arms Race* (Marshalls), a fairly comprehensive review of the facts concerning the advances in military technology and the ramifications of the international arms trade. The more I examined the facts the more convinced I became that the trade in arms is one of the most sinister and unprincipled that the world has ever known. Some of the details of its operations are regularly catalogued by the Campaign Against the Arms Trade which does a valuable work in alerting the public to what is going on. The book also gathers together a number of church statements indicating a steady movement of thought and increasing uneasiness about British defence policy. On 24 November 1980 the Assembly of the British Council of Churches had stated: 'The doctrine of deterrence based upon the prospect of mutually assured destruction is increasingly offensive to the Christian conscience.' In a subsequent series of resolutions the Assembly has at various times made concrete proposals about the control and reduction of weapons.

In a letter to the *Times* dated 21 October 1981 I made a point which I believe to be important. It read:

> The tendency to don labels and to make black and white distinctions between what are seen to be opposing policies can sometimes obscure an important truth. The present polarisation between those who espouse the cause of multilateral disarmament and those who plead for unilateral disarmament is a case in point . . .
>
> There is little likelihood of progress on the multilateral front without some willingness to undertake unilateral initiatives. The test of real statesmanship today is the readiness to contrive and then to take the unilateral steps that will deliver us from the political impotence that allows the monstrous and idiotic arms race to escalate.

In the middle part of the letter I referred to President Sadat's unilateral action. In the years since there have been a number of such initiatives that have helped to reduce tension and the risks to humanity caused by the piling up of destructive weapons.

A war situation on which I made public comment was the conflict with Argentina over their invasion of the Falkland Islands. There was diplomatic incompetence on both sides. The question of the sovereignty of those far-away Islands should have been settled before it became a matter of military action. At the end of the conflict there was a service in St Paul's Cathedral, and Cardinal Hume telephoned me to say that he and I (as Moderator of the Free Church Federal Council) were being asked to participate along with the Archbishop of Canterbury who would be preaching the sermon. He was troubled by the fact that Mrs Thatcher was to read the lesson and feared that this would give a political slant to the service. He asked me to convey these anxieties (which I shared) to Dr Runcie. I did so and the invitation to Mrs Thatcher was withdrawn. Cardinal Hume and I were responsible for the prayers and we included petitions for those who had lost their sons in the war – both British and Argentinean parents. A number of Tory members of Parliament criticised us for this. However, I had moved among the congregation at the end of the service and was touched by the fact that a number of parents who had suffered bereavement came to thank me for remembering those in Argentina who were suffering in the same way. I shared this fact with the representatives of the press. The critical noises from the members of Parliament suddenly ceased.

I have from time to time been able to use the monthly column that I have been privileged to write for the *Methodist Recorder* to highlight aspects of the debate about war and peace. In December 1990 I presented a Christian critique of British policy following the invasion of Kuwait by Iraq. It concluded:

> The whole effort of the international community must be geared to the finding of a rational and peaceful way of resolving the dispute. The invasion of Kuwait was an evil act and must be redressed. But Iraqi allegations relating to boundaries and oil rights need to be impartially examined. The importance of the role of the United Nations cannot be overstressed. If compromise is involved, so be it. The whole of international and national politics involves compromise. That is the nature of the game.
> The crowning irony of the present situation is that Iraq is armed to the teeth with weapons supplied by Russia, France and other Western nations. It will be no comfort to weeping British mothers and fathers if our lads are killed by weapons bearing a British or Western trademark.

After war with Iraq had started I wrote:

We are now being subjected to the saturation bombing of the mind by war news and propaganda. All of us who have lived through earlier wars know that lies, half-truths and selective reporting on both sides are an inevitable concomitant of armed conflict. So also is the horribly euphemistic language which produces such phrases as 'surgical strikes', thus prostituting a word normally associated with one of the most honourable professions in the world.

In another article I raised the question why war is very largely a male activity:

War and religion have always been mixed up together. The children of Israel went to war with the name of God upon their lips, for was he not the Lord mighty in battle? Have you ever tried to count how many times the word 'battle' occurs in the Old Testament? It is a bloodstained book, and it is almost exclusively the men who spill the blood.

Is not one reason for this that we have thought of God as masculine and we have thought of masculinity in terms of battle bravery?

Religion, sex and war: these three have always been inextricably intertwined. Now, as never before, the male leadership of the churches has been questioning whether war can ever be just. The most outspoken judgement has come from the Pope – head of the most male-dominated of all the major churches, yet saved from the worst consequences of that imbalance by devotion to Mary the mother of Jesus. The Bishop of Rome stands in judgement over the Pentagon spokesman who after several hundred civilians were burnt alive in the shelter in Baghdad said that he was 'quite comfortable with the decision to bomb that bunker'.

Women, oh women, who have borne so much of the world's pain, rise up and shatter that comfort. Make us uncomfortable, for only so can we hope to hear the comfortable words of our Saviour Christ: 'Peace I leave with you, my peace I give unto you.'

In recent years, as I have pondered the state of the world and the threats to humanity's future posed by the addiction to militarism as a means of security I have come to see that what is needed is nothing less than radical conversion. For some Christians the word seems to stand for a personal experience of God's grace which apparently overlooks John Wesley's assertion that 'there is no holiness but social holiness'. Unless Christian conversion means a change of mind which challenges the popular concept of security and sees a better way, it is difficult to see that it has much to contribute to the construction of any new world order.

The word 'conversion' is increasingly used in connection with the effort to convert defence industries to other functions. A number of studies indicate how this might be done and give examples of successful diversification already achieved. With the ending of the Cold War and the disappearance of many jobs in the defence field practical schemes for redeployment are an urgent necessity. But my major point is that nothing less than deep conversion to a new way of living and looking at life will suffice. Since the churches are by their own profession in the business of conversion they must take this challenge seriously. The need to do so is all the more urgent because of the dawning realisation that in our search for military security we are helping to destroy the environmental security on which our survival depends.

I call up another memory from the Lambeth Conference which I attended as an observer. The address delivered by the late Barbara Ward was unforgettable. The substance of her message is contained in the last two paragraphs of her splendid book *The Home of Man* (Penguin 1976):

> If man has learned to be loyal to his nation as well as to his family and his town, do we have to argue that no further extension of loyalty is possible – to the planet itself which carries our earthly life and all the means of sustaining it?

> This is perhaps the ultimate implication of the underlying unity of scientific law first discerned by the Greeks, of the underlying law of moral brotherhood and obligation most passionately proclaimed by the Hebrew prophets. Today they come together in a new fusion of vision and energy to remind us of our inescapable unity even as we stand on the very verge of potential annihilation. The scientist and the sage, the man of learning and the poet,

the mathematician and the saint repeat to the human city
the same plea and the same warning: 'We must love each
other or we must die.'

'There is still a vision for the appointed time'. For this appointed
time the vision I cherish is of a world set free from the scourge of war and
a church leading the world towards that emancipation.

Chapter Seven

A MARKED MAN

Ralph Waldo Emerson said, 'No man is the whole of himself; his friends are the rest of him.' Certainly no man can sit down to write the story of his life without becoming aware of his debt to innumerable men and women who have left their mark upon him. I once talked with Kenneth Griffiths, the actor. He told me that he had been back to the chapel in Wales which he attended as a boy, and as he knelt in the familiar pew he discovered his initials scratched into the woodwork with a penknife – no doubt when he was bored by the sermon. 'I left my mark on the church,' he said. 'I think, too, that the church left its mark on you,' I responded.

I never mount the pulpit steps without pondering the fact that one mind can influence another. My sermon has not been cribbed from any volume published to assist busy preachers who haven't time to prepare their own, yet I am aware that I have borrowed consciously or unconsciously from the thoughts and words of others. And then, as I preach, the thoughts that I have been given are mysteriously transferred to those who, hopefully, are awake to what I am saying.

Throughout the preceding chapters I have written much about people and places. Even so I am left with a huge jostle of memories concerning both. This chapter, therefore, contains an account of a few of the many encounters that have given me pleasure and profit, and occasionally irritation. Some of those mentioned are folk to whom passing reference has been made on earlier pages, but I want to say a little more about them. Many of those whom I remember with affection and gratitude were or are people little known outside their own immediate circle, but the sort of folk who enrich the lives of all who know them. I give two examples.

Herbert Jones was the Warden of Eastwood Grange, a conference centre in Derbyshire run by the Midland Temperance League. He was a man of gentle spirit with a slow winsome smile and eyes that glowed with the light of an inner integrity. I used to go every year to Eastwood Grange to help run a Christian Leadership Course. My colleagues were the Secretaries of several of Methodism's Headquarters' departments. There was Allen Birtwhistle of the Mission House, an artist with pen and brush who long ago designed the 'Drinka Pinta Milka Day' advertisement. Len

Barnett was at that time the dynamic leader of the Methodist Association of Youth Clubs. Philip Potter, who later became General Secretary of the World Council of Churches, added weight to our team. Many of the young people who attended these annual gatherings went on to occupy positions of leadership in church and society. Ivor Jones, for example, attended a number of courses. He became one of Methodism's scholars, is Principal of Wesley House, Cambridge and, as mentioned earlier, was one of the architects of the 1983 *Hymns & Psalms.*

Our week's course always ended with a camp fire under the stars. The simple service held in the open air was always moving. One year as we assembled Herbert Jones came to welcome us and he carried a brown paper parcel. Slowly unwrapping this he produced a charred ember. 'Last year,' he said, 'when you had all gone I rescued this from the embers of the camp fire. I present it to you with the prayer that the Holy Spirit will this year kindle again a sacred flame on the mean altar of your hearts.' It is impossible to remember Herbert Jones without a thrill of pleasure.

A very different character, though equally memorable, was Mr Horace Duke, known to some as 'Lord Lancing'. He used to stand on street corners in Worthing immaculately dressed in striped blazer, white flannels, natty bow tie, monocle and straw boater. With his white-gloved hands he would direct the traffic. Sometimes he would be wearing earphones and conducting the London Symphony Orchestra with tremendous panache. If you waved to him he would give a courtly bow which would have put the head waiter of the Strand Palace Hotel in the shade. One very cold day I stopped for a word with this eccentric character. 'Take care,' I said, 'I don't want you to catch a chill.' 'Quite right,' he replied, politely removing the red nose he was wearing that day, 'there aren't many of us left, you know.'

I wish that I had got to know Mr Duke better. By all accounts he was a lonely soul. I learned that he died of cancer in a hospice; if I had known I would have gone to hold his hand. He added to the sum of human laughter. Maybe he cherished dreams of greatness. There must surely be a place in heaven for a clown like him.

I have worked with many of the church leaders of the past forty years. Earlier references will have revealed my deep regard and affection for Lord Soper. The way in which he has maintained his open-air work and so many other aspects of his continuing ministry even though his mobility is seriously impaired has only added to the lustre of a life of brilliant Christian advocacy. On his ninetieth birthday, a Sunday, Michael Foot and I paid tribute to him at a service in Hinde Street Methodist

Church in London, now the headquarters of the West London Mission. In the afternoon a great crowd of us went to support him in Hyde Park. During the usual cut and thrust of argument a rather vicious heckler shouted contemptuously, 'So you're ninety; what do you think your main achievement has been?' 'Putting up with people like you,' came the instant response, accompanied by a broad grin. It reminded me of the only occasion when I stood in for Donald Soper at Speaker's Corner. Our elder daughter, Susan, was with me. I, too, was fiercely heckled and she had to be restrained from attacking my assailant with her umbrella. She has always been a loyal supporter of mine!

Leslie Weatherhead, like Donald Soper, was widely known, not just in this country but across the world. I cherish a recording I have of extracts from sermons preached by Sangster, Soper and Weatherhead, that great triumvirate of Methodist preachers who drew large congregations to their London churches. Each of them had the gift of compelling speech but their styles were very different. I went often to hear Weatherhead at the City Temple. The hour of worship was always meticulously planned, and the glorious music provided by the organist Dr Thiman and the choir, together with the moving prayers, brought the congregation in a spirit of expectancy to the sermon. Weatherhead was an impressive figure in the pulpit and his voice had a haunting quality which compelled attention. His writings have helped many. Alas, sometimes lesser preachers have tried to copy some of his sermons. There was an embarrassing occasion in Croydon where Weatherhead preached a sermon which had been published in one of his books, and the following Sunday a lay preacher reproduced it word-for-word in the same church. But it was rather like playing Handel's *Messiah* on a tin whistle.

It was in the field of healing and the linking of religion and psychology that Leslie Weatherhead made a significant contribution to the thinking of the church. He also wrote bravely about sex before the avalanche of contemporary comment, good and bad, descended upon us. I valued his encouragement, often conveyed in little notes written in green ink. He wrote a Foreword to one of my books. When Leslie's wife died he was devastated. Mary and I called to see him shortly before his own death. He had suffered much pain and wanted only to be released into that heaven about which he had often written. He wept as we prayed together. I remembered the huge crowds that had hung on his words and told him of the blessing he had brought to so many. As we left his face was shining.

One great preacher whom I never met but who nevertheless greatly influenced me was Dr Harry Emerson Fosdick. For many years he was the senior minister at the Riverside Church in New York. I devoured his volumes of sermons with titles like *Adventurous Religion*, his book on the Holy Land and many of his other writings. His thinking and approach and the way in which he made the ancient text of the Bible meaningful for the contemporary world appealed to me enormously. He sustained a weekly radio ministry over many years in the USA which established him as that country's outstanding preacher. On my first visit to America as a young man I went to the famous Riverside Church. I arrived as dusk was falling and as I reached the door the janitor was locking up for the night. 'Sorry sir, the church is closed,' he said. I told him that I had an ambition to stand in Dr Fosdick's pulpit. His heart softened and he led me up the long aisle of the darkened church. I stood for a few moments in the pulpit from which such a torrent of inspired oratory had poured. It was a moment to cherish.

During my Westminster years I came to know and work with successive Archbishops of Canterbury. I did not know Geoffrey Fisher well. He never lost the manner and appearance of a headmaster. During the period when Anglicans and Methodists were talking together about organic union I used to receive periodic letters from him telling me how mistaken we were and explaining that in his famous 1946 Cambridge sermon he had talked not of union but of growing together into full communion between still separated churches.

It was Dr Fisher's successor, Michael Ramsey, who made the greatest impression on me. He, too, was often in receipt of critical letters from his predecessor. The story goes that on emerging from Madame Tussaud's, having had his image cast in wax, he met a newspaper reporter who said, 'How did it go, Your Grace?' 'Famously, famously,' replied Ramsey, 'they'd run short of wax, so they had to melt down Geoffrey Fisher to do me.'

At the time of Michael Ramsey's death in 1988 I paid tribute to him in the *Methodist Recorder*:

> I have known many wonderfully good men and women and a few who were both good and great. Michael Ramsey was one of the latter.
>
> A short time before he resigned the See of Canterbury he wrote me a letter in his own spidery hand. It read, 'I shall soon be retiring; my brain has grown tired. I wanted you to know before the public announcement is made.'

There followed various farewell dinners. I recall an earlier dinner given by the then Prime Minister, Mr Harold Wilson. My wife and I were invited. Michael made a delightful speech. 'When I was here before,' he said 'there was another Harold in residence. The difference between Prime Ministers and Archbishops is that the former come and go, and the latter go on for ever – or what seems like for ever.' He said how glad he was that his two sisters had been invited. 'It has,' he said 'been a source of unending surprise to them that their brother became Archbishop of Canterbury.'

At the farewell dinner in his honour which I arranged he spoke of the unpredictability of life, saying that his own ministry had turned out to be very different from anything he had expected. He talked of his teaching ministry. 'People say that I speak very simply,' he said. 'Well, I need to speak so that I can understand what I am saying because if I can't understand it I reckon no-one else will either.'

Michael Ramsey was a cartoonist's dream. There was no need for them to caricature him. With his great domed head and beetling eyebrows he looked exactly as archbishops are supposed to look. He had a mischievous sense of humour and seemed to delight in poking fun at the more pompous aspects of Anglicanism. On one occasion at Lambeth Palace an expansive American lady looked out of the window and, spotting a flowering tree, asked me the name of it. I confessed my ignorance and suggested that she should ask Dr Ramsey. Later in the evening I enquired how she had got on. 'Oh,' she exclaimed, 'that dear man hadn't even noticed it was there. That's what comes of having your mind on higher things.'

Dr Ramsey came at my invitation to address the Ministerial Session of the Methodist Conference in Norwich in 1981. He arrived the night before and we had a long conversation which began with the enquiry, 'Now tell me, how is Runcie doing?' I asked him what he intended to talk about the following day. 'The minister's prayer,' he said. He developed that theme and held five hundred ministers in the hollow of his hand. In his address he revealed the secret of his greatness: he walked closely with God.

We entertained Michael and his wife Joan to lunch at a carvery in the city. The waiter asked the Archbishop whether he would like his beef well done or a little bit red. Michael seemed to like the phrase 'a little bit red' and kept repeating it to himself throughout the meal; a quite extraordinary phenomenon but entirely characteristic.

When I was about to retire from the Secretaryship of the Conference I received a letter from this truly great man. He wrote: 'You may feel some regrets as you move away from the centre of things, but I know that, like me, you will now in a strange way come closer to the centre of things.' For him the centre of all things was God.

Donald Coggan succeeded Michael Ramsey after more than thirteen years as Archbishop of York. He is a man whose goodness and integrity shine from his face. He lacks the eccentricities which made his predecessor a cartoonist's delight and sometimes caused his friends to despair. No-one would ever describe Donald Coggan as bringing in his guest's morning tea 'looking like an untidy haystack'. He is a man of humble spirit. I treasure memories of a walk through the snow in Edinburgh when he insisted on carrying my case, and of an evening he and his wife Jean spent in our home. I motored them back to Lambeth Palace where we had to knock three times on the great wooden door – 'one for Father, one for Son and one for Holy Ghost'.

Coggan's gifts as a biblical scholar were well used by the Bible Societies and he was Chairman of the Joint Committee which produced the New English Bible. The titles of many of his sermons and addresses reflect his evangelical convictions. The word 'Convictions' characteristically is on the title page of a collection of these published in 1975. His 'Call to the Nation' did not evoke a very great response, and the 'Nationwide Initiative in Evangelism' with which he was prominently associated did not fulfil the hopes that many held for it.

Robert Runcie, Donald Coggan's successor, is a very human person with a wonderful warmth and a gift of self-deprecation. At a conference at the Hayes Conference Centre in Swanwick he told us that he had wandered into the kitchen to thank the staff there. A little Yorkshire lady who was washing up said, 'Ah, tha's taller than tha' looks on the telly.' 'Oh,' said the Archbishop, 'is that so?' 'Yes,' she replied, 'I allus thought tha' were a little shrimp of a chap.'

Like any leader who lives in the public eye Runcie had his critics. He seemed at times to lack decisiveness. Margaret Duggan comments perceptively in her book *Runcie: the Making of an Archbishop* (Hodder 1983, p.228): 'He does not have the single-mindedness of the great campaigner, for he has never lost his compulsion to listen to all arguments and to acknowledge that the other side (unless it is an obvious evil) might also have a case.' During his years at Lambeth he often had a very bad press. The attack on him in the Preface to Crockford's *Clerical Directory* published on 3 December 1987 provided sensational headlines in the popular press. Phrases like 'the Archbishop is usually to be found nailing his colours to the fence' were bound to be hurtful. Although by tradition the author of the Preface remains anonymous it soon leaked out that this sour and unworthy contribution had been written by Dr Gareth Bennett. His subsequent suicide only served to underline the tragic aspects of the affair. In my view the whole idea of an anonymous Preface is half-baked. The *Daily Mail* printed a banner headline, 'For God's sake, go.' Robert Runcie preserved a remarkable serenity during these turbulent periods and appeared, at least outwardly, to be indifferent to the malicious claptrap churned out by journalists who often seemed to have no real understanding of the issues on which they pontificated.

Robert Runcie made a fine master of assemblies and was deeply appreciated by the members of the British Council of Churches during his Presidency. He took his ecumenical responsibilities very seriously though, as I say elsewhere, a more resolute line on the proposals for a covenant of unity might just have tipped the scales in the General Synod of the Church of England. His Chairmanship of the Lambeth Conference was said to have been outstanding.

Robert Runcie led a small BCC delegation to China and on arrival there he was stricken with lumbago. The story goes that his companions told him that the Chinese had a sure cure – acupuncture – and that they would be sending a practitioner round in the morning. 'They do it through the eyeballs,' his informant added. The Archbishop hobbled off to bed but came down the next morning completely recovered!

Many of us were profoundly grateful for the sermon which Robert Runcie preached in St Paul's Cathedral following the war with Argentina to which I referred in the previous chapter. It did nothing to improve his relationship with the Prime Minister. He said:

> War, demonstrably irrational and intolerable, has left a terrible mark on this century, it has claimed tens of millions of victims and even now occupies some of the best talents and resources of the nations. The great nations continue to channel their energies into perfecting weapons of destruction, and very little is done to halt the international trade in arms which contributes so much to the insecurity of the world . . .

People are mourning on both sides of the conflict. In our prayers we shall quite rightly remember those who are bereaved in our own country, and the relations of the young Argentineans who were killed. Common sorrow could do something to reunite those who were engaged in this struggle. A shared anguish can be a bridge of reconciliation. Our neighbours are indeed like us.

One of the haunting anxieties that burdened Robert Runcie was the taking hostage of Terry Waite who had gone on an ill-advised errand to gain the release of hostages in Beirut. During the long weary months of waiting Robert Runcie never deviated from his belief that Terry was alive and would return.

When I retired Robert Runcie gave a dinner for my wife and me in Lambeth Palace. He began his speech, 'We are meeting in the Guard Room: that will not be entirely to your liking, I am sure.' On arrival at the Palace a man in a frock coat said, 'Mrs Runcie is giving a recital tonight.' (She is an accomplished pianist.) 'Oh, how nice,' I replied, 'is it to be in the music room?' 'Ah no,' he said, 'she is giving it in Folkestone.'

When Robert Runcie himself retired in 1991 the Free Church Federal Council gave a dinner to which he and his wife Lindy came. Free Church people held him in high regard. I was grateful to be asked to make the speech thanking them both for their friendship and leadership. Referring to the tensions caused by diversity I said, 'You have had to keep disparate elements together.' I mentioned in particular the issue of the ordination of women and said, 'This has rumbled on during your Chairmanship of the Synod like a thunderstorm that will not go away. The rest of us watch with sympathy tinged with impatience.' The storm eventually broke, of course, during the archiepiscopate of his successor, Dr George Carey.

Cardinal Basil Hume is another leader who has friends in all the churches. He personifies all that is best in the Roman Catholic Church of today. In him the phrase 'the Roman obedience' comes alive. One gets the strong impression that he would have liked to escape the demands of the leadership of the Roman Catholics in England and Wales. No-one can doubt that he is a holy man. When, as Free Church Advisers to Thames Television, we were discussing a series on 'Saints' one of my colleagues said, 'Why don't we ask Basil Hume to come on the box? There's something about sanctity that lights up the screen.' He has no oratorical gifts but his manner of speech conveys a deep sincerity of conviction and purpose. He once came to dinner in our home and I asked him to pray at the end of the evening. When he did so it was a benediction.

I have met many fine Christian leaders in different parts of the world. Bishop K. H. Ting is the President of the China Christian Council. When the British Council of Churches celebrated its 40th anniversary with a service in St Paul's Cathedral he led a small delegation of Chinese Christians. There was great disappointment when it was announced that their arrival had been delayed. Then part way through the service they appeared. It was a dramatic moment when this small group of diminutive figures walked down the length of the nave to be embraced by Archbishop Runcie. Bishop Ting turned and addressed the great congregation in his fluent English. This visit marked the beginning of the resumption of relationships between the Chinese Church and the rest of the world after the long years of silence.

During our visit to China to which I refer later in this chapter I spent a good deal of time with Bishop Ting. I was impressed by the respect paid to him by members of the Chinese Government. He explained some of the difficulties which the church had suffered during years of persecution under the communists. Now there was a degree of freedom not known for many years. The church had adopted the Three-Self Movement: self-propagation, self-government and self-support. I asked about tales I had heard of American evangelists smuggling Bibles into China and he replied that any such operation was unnecessary since the Chinese Church was publishing large quantities of Bibles every year. Outside interference, he said, was not welcome and was regarded with distaste and suspicion by the Government. 'The time has come,' he asserted, 'for the Chinese Church to be itself.' I visited the Bishop in the theological College in Nanjing where he was the Principal.   In the entrance hall was a large picture of the dove of peace. I was invited to inspect some of the art work done by the students and noted that Jesus had a Chinese face.

One of the outstanding Christian leaders of our time is Archbishop Desmond Tutu. During our visit to South Africa my wife and I spent an hour with him in his study. He came out in his shirt sleeves to welcome us as if we were the only people in the world. He was frantically busy but acted as if he had all day to give to us. He invited us to kneel for prayer and then opened his heart concerning the future of his country. Apartheid still held South Africa in its miserable embrace, Nelson Mandela was still in prison, but we knew that we were talking to a man who was certain that right would triumph. The evil of the system he was fighting was evident in the way it divided people at every level. I had heard Tutu described as 'a liar and an impostor' by white people who were not fit to tie his shoelaces. We came away from this conversation feeling that we had been taken by him into the presence of God.

Some time later I shared a platform with Desmond Tutu at a meeting in Nairobi. Now we saw the great orator in action. His theme was justice. The media folk were there in force waiting for the latest political pronouncement from this turbulent priest but he took us through the Bible, illustrating how God is always on the side of justice. It was a *tour de force*. At one point he told us, with many a characteristically dry chuckle and with the slight stutter that develops when he is excited, how the white man came to Africa. 'The white man had the Bible and the black man had the land. The white man said, "Let us pray." And lo, when they opened their eyes, why, the black man had the Bible and the white man had the land.' Then, holding his own big Bible aloft he said, 'Is anyone going to tell me that was a bad bargain? Why, you gave us the most subversive thing in the world. And now the white man wants it back. Too late, too late!'

I was for many years a member of the All Souls Club founded by Nathaniel Micklem. This was a little group of fifteen men occupying various positions of leadership in the churches. We met three times a year. At each meeting one of us would act as host, provide the dinner and read a paper. So I had regular contact with men like Sir Godfray LeQuesne, Paul Rowntree Clifford, Sir Robert Birley and Gonville ffrench Beytagh. The last of these, who had achieved some fame as the former Dean of Johannesburg, addressed us on the subject of church buildings. He deplored modern concrete monstrosities full of harsh white light. 'Where,' he growled, 'are the dark corners where a man can weep?' Michael Ramsey, crouched in a corner, announced his subject as 'Christianity without history. Question mark.' He began, 'I shall set up a number of skittles and then I shall proceed to knock them down one by one.' This he did with consummate skill and evident relish.

Another rich experience of fellowship, this time within my own denomination, was provided by the meetings of the St Ermines Club. This was founded by Dr Leslie Davison and funded, I believe, by Lord Rank. We met every few weeks for dinner in the St Ermines Hotel in Westminster. Leslie Davison was a creative thinker. His wife died of cancer during his year as President of the Methodist Conference and he succumbed to the same disease soon after his year was over. He showed tremendous courage through these afflictions. The other members of this small group were Dr Eric Baker, Dr Harold Roberts and the Rev W. Walker Lee. These were all men at the heart of the life of Methodism and each in turn had been President of the Conference. We would discuss the problems and opportunities facing the church. In the years leading up to my own accession to the Secretaryship of the Conference this provided me with a most valuable training; it was also extremely enjoyable.

From time to time I found myself on the other side of the door of Number 10 Downing Street during the premierships of Harold Wilson, Edward Heath and Margaret Thatcher. I recall a dinner hosted by Mr Heath when he had invited a group of cathedral choristers to sing between courses. After the meal he showed us his yachting trophies. I have always liked Edward Heath and in written exchanges found him the soul of courtesy.

When Mrs Thatcher became Prime Minister it was arranged that a small group of us representing the British Council of Churches should go to see her to establish contact and explain the work of the Council. We were warmly received. After I had outlined the way the Council worked I called on several of my companions to speak about particular aspects of the work that we thought would be of interest to the Prime Minister. The first speaker was Derek Pattinson, the Secretary General of the Anglican Synod. He had only uttered two sentences when Mrs Thatcher interrupted him to put him right. This was the experience of all who spoke. One could not but be impressed by the Prime Minister's ability to talk at length about everything. At the end of the conversation, which overran the allotted time and brought a secretary tapping at the door, I asked Harry Morton, the General Secretary of the BCC, to close in prayer. He assumed his most thunderous frown and began, 'God bless Britain.' On one occasion, following dinner at Number 10 Mrs Thatcher announced that she would be leaving at 10 o'clock for another engagement. As we took our leave my wife said to her, 'You must be tired.' The astonishing reply was, 'I never get tired.'

There is no doubting Margaret Thatcher's enormous ability, but I used to get a bit tired of Americans saying to me in the porch of their churches after I had preached, 'We do love your Iron Lady', indicating a complete lack of any informed Christian critique of her policies. The restiveness of many church leaders at some of the trends and policies of the Thatcher Government was entirely understandable. When she suggested that there was no such thing as society that epitomised an emphasis on individualism and a stress on personal success that can overlook the needs of the disadvantaged and those who lose out through no fault of their own, and the responsibility of the rest of us towards them. The apparently uncritical acceptance of the rightness of the decision to use force at the time of the Falklands crisis and the way in which this episode seemed to restore her political fortunes left many of us feeling very unhappy.

There is about some politicians an arrogance of power. No party should ever assume that it rules by divine right; in a democracy its rights and obligations spring from the will of the people. I have an unpleasant memory of an occasion when I went with two other churchmen to see Lord Hailsham. Our purpose was to state the case for raising the level of aid for overseas development. His Lordship said, 'Now, look here, you men, I get rather tired of people coming here asking for money: it's the nurses one week and the dustmen the next, and now you.' I felt constrained to say that the Government had no money save what the people gave it and that anyhow we were not asking for anything for ourselves but merely exercising our democratic right to suggest how the cake should be sliced. He then said, 'But why don't you ministers stick to your last and preach the gospel and leave politics to us?' It seemed to me to be a strange dichotomy coming from so intelligent a Christian, and quite unacceptable as a definition of the proper responsibility of a Christian minister.

When Wesley's Chapel was reopened after extensive renovations the service was attended by the Queen and the Duke of Edinburgh. Since the Chapel would be full to overflowing the minister, Dr Ronald Gibbins, arranged for troops from the nearby barracks to tramp through the gallery to test its structural soundness. It passed the test. I was conducting the service and during the first hymn noticed that there was no Bible on the lectern. The Queen had asked that her husband should read the lesson. I felt highly embarrassed but need not have worried. I discovered later that the Duke had indicated that he would be bringing his own Bible.

When the service was over a number of us went across to the military establishment on the other side of the City Road to take tea with the Queen. It had been arranged that I should present about twenty selected Methodists to Her Majesty and the rest of the crowd of about two hundred – mainly Americans – were restrained behind a scarlet rope. All went well at first but then, impatient of British protocol, some of the Americans behind the rope started reaching forward. 'Shake yer hand, Mam. Elmer T. Boltinghorse, Junior, from Texas' was a typical greeting. We eventually emerged from the ordeal and I said, 'I fear, Your Majesty, that was a bit of a scrum.' She smiled and professed to have enjoyed it all, adding with a twinkle in her eye, 'I noticed that your Methodist people sing with a strong American accent.'

There was an occasion when my wife inadvertently stood in for the Queen – for a fleeting and embarrassing moment. It was at a service in the Dutch Church in London. The event coincided with a rail strike and the city was choked with traffic. I had to leave Mary stuck in the car on London Bridge where nothing was moving, and race to the church on foot. I met the other clergy in the vestry. Dr Runcie came panting in just after me. We robed and processed into the sanctuary. It was then announced that the car carrying the Queen and the Duke with their guests, the Queen of the Netherlands and her husband, was also stuck in a traffic jam. After about twenty minutes there was a stir at the back of the church and we stood. The door opened and in came my wife, having miraculously found a parking space. She would, I am sure, have been glad if the aisle had opened up and swallowed her. The Queen arrived five minutes later.

From time to time the Duke of Edinburgh invites a group of men from various walks of life to dine with him at Buckingham Palace and engage in discussion. When I attended one of these pleasant occasions the discussion was at first rather slow; then he felt that it was obviously time to be provocative. I had said something about the great work of relief and development being done by the churches through Christian Aid. 'Well,' he responded, 'I think we did very much better when we had an Empire.' After that the conversation became extremely lively!

Among those present on that occasion was Robin Woods, a most colourful character and a friend of the royal family. He came into my office one day and to the astonishment of my secretary said, 'Get me Prince Charles on the telephone, will you?' His booming conversation with the Prince could be heard all along the corridor. Robin Woods did fine work as Dean of Windsor in creating a Conference Centre in St George's House. When I attended a course there I was not certain whether all the members of the Windsor establishment were entirely happy about the invasion of their pitch by an assortment of earnest Christians from the outside world.

As I have compared our British system of government with others around the world I have concluded that the monarchy, with all its flaws, is worth keeping. Its standing in the public eye has depended in the past on the maintenance of a certain distance between the royals and the rest. Now that the younger members seem unable to resist using the television studio as a confessional one wonders if it can survive unscathed. In the end it can only function effectively if it has a degree of public regard and support.

The only American President I ever met was Dwight Eisenhower. A group of Methodists was invited to visit him in the rose garden at the White House. 'What do you want me to talk about?' he asked. I think the reply was, 'Anything you like, Mr President.' This seemed to leave him stumped, but it was a pleasant occasion and I came away with the impression that if one got close to him one would discover a very amiable character.

Turning now to the subject of travel I recall again John Wesley's saying, 'I look upon the world as my parish.' His own journeys were, of course, mainly within Great Britain and on the back of a horse. His one visit to America with his brother Charles was a disaster. The voyage, taking many weeks, was uncomfortable because of fierce storms and uncongenial fellow-passengers. His evangelistic efforts among the American Indians were a failure and he experienced a disappointing love affair.

I contrast that with my own experiences of travel to various parts of Wesley's world parish. What took him weeks can now be accomplished by aeroplane in a few effortless hours. In 1956 I crossed the Atlantic by ship in company with Ted Rogers. We sailed from Liverpool in a magnificent liner called the *Empress of Scotland*. I remember a number of interesting features of the journey. There was the map which indicated how far the ship had progressed each day. There was the fact that halfway across the Atlantic the daily prayers ceased referring to the Queen and substituted the name of the President of the United States. There was a free concert given by Liberace, the flamboyant entertainer. I stood in a long queue but first-class passengers were given priority. By the time I reached the door of the concert hall every seat was taken and I was turned away. I quickly recovered from this rejection.

The food on the ship was more luxurious than anything I have experienced elsewhere. Alas, in mid-Atlantic we ran into a terrible storm. The numbers in the dining room dwindled to about six, one of them being Ted who continued to eat his way through the menu. I lay in my bunk not caring whether I lived or died. The storm subsided and when we woke in the morning the ship was as steady as a rock. I called out to my travel companion in the lower bunk, 'Seems the storm is over, Ted.' 'Either that or we're on the bottom,' came the lugubrious reply from one who was always able to see both sides of an argument.

During the years when I worked in the Department of Christian Citizenship my travels took me to many countries including Norway, Sweden, Denmark, Finland, Belgium, Germany, Switzerland, Italy, America, Canada, Jamaica, Nigeria and Ethiopia. In nearly all these places I met the leaders of the Methodist churches. Many of them were remarkable people, like Bishop Ferdinand Sigg who presided over the Central European Methodist Conference and travelled ceaselessly from one country to another. He was a brilliant linguist who could move effortlessly from one language to another. At the end of one tiring day he started translating English into English! Nearly all these leaders were men, and even now there are far too few women in the national leadership posts in the churches.

During my term as Secretary of the Conference my travel schedule grew heavier. As I mentioned in Chapter Four I continued to visit churches all over the United Kingdom for weekend and midweek preaching and speaking engagements but also undertook three or four overseas visits most years. This pattern has continued on into retirement years. Some of the visits to other countries have been referred to at earlier points in my narrative but others which have been of special interest and significance merit a rather more detailed account.

My second visit to Nigeria took place in 1975 and almost started disastrously. When I arrived at Gatwick the man who took my ticket asked to see my visa. For some unaccountable reason I had forgotten to apply for this essential document. He intimated that I would not be allowed to board the aircraft. I told him that I had a most important engagement in Lagos the following day. 'Well,' he said, 'they are very strict there and if I let you travel they will only put you on the next plane back to London.' After further argument the official said, 'Do you know anyone of importance in Nigeria?' I replied that I knew the Lord Chief Justice. I had met him briefly on my previous visit. 'In that case I'll let you go, but you must mention your friend as soon as you arrive,' came the response. I did not know that the gentleman concerned was at that very moment in a London hospital having his leg amputated. I sat up all night in the plane composing speeches to get me through the formalities at Lagos Airport. In the event all went smoothly. I was met by a man who said, 'I've been sent by the Patriarch. Please follow me; we don't go through customs or any of that.'

The discerning reader may ask how I came to be the guest of a Patriarch. The answer is that I was going to participate in and preach at the ceremony inaugurating a new-style Methodism. The revised constitution was the brainchild of Professor Bolaji Idowu, a Methodist minister who had been trained in England. The reasons for change were spelt out in a series of broadcast talks which he gave and in a small book entitled *Towards an Indigenous Church*. How to rid Nigerian Christianity and Methodism in particular of its Western cultural trappings was the issue which he sought to tackle. What emerged was an elaborate and highly colourful set of proposals. Dr Idowu himself became the first Patriarch with the title 'His Pre-eminence'.

The inaugural ceremonies extended over two sweltering days. More than three thousand people crowded into the Tinubu Square Church for the induction of the Patriarch, the Archbishops and Bishops of the new church. I preached on the humility of a Christian bishop. I had to put the mitres on the newly-created episcopal leaders. The Patriarch himself was vested in the most glorious apparel and carried in his hands the 'keys of the Kingdom'. The string of wooden beads which I had to put around his neck broke and as they scattered around the area in front of the Lord's table constituted a considerable hazard for the officiating clergy.

I came away from this unusual experience with very real misgivings about the direction that Nigerian Methodism was taking. My fears were later confirmed when the Methodists of the Eastern Region broke away to form a separate church which would 'remain loyal to John Wesley'. As Chairman of the World Methodist Council I arranged for a three-man peace delegation to visit both sides to try to effect a reconciliation. They were not immediately successful. Happily, under the direction of Dr Idowu's successor, the Rev Sunday Mbang, the two parts of the church have been reunited. Nigeria has suffered much from harsh military rule and the corruption encouraged by tin-pot dictators and it certainly needs the witness of a strong united church.

In 1975 I paid my second visit to Australia, this time to deliver the Cato Lecture. This lectureship was endowed by Fred J. Cato who was born in a miner's tent but became a person of wealth and influence. It provided for the lecturer and his wife to travel across Australia and on into New Zealand. We landed at Perth where we had arranged to meet Mary's cousin and her husband. It was an interesting experience to meet our relatives. Up till then we had only received an occasional letter which was usually full of information about sheep and the various problems of the farm. We also had a picture of a little lady in a faded sun-hat. Now the pictures that we had formed in our minds came alive though we were not entirely prepared for the vast distances and the remoteness of the farmhouse in which they entertained us; their nearest neighbour was twenty-five miles away. While travelling we were nearly killed by an enormous grain lorry which came hurtling round a bend on a lonely road. Other adventures included a meeting with a kangaroo in a public toilet and an encounter with a plague of mice. There were literally millions of these little creatures; they covered the road like a moving carpet and, of course, brought great worry to the farmers whose grain crops were being eaten.

With His Pre-eminence Bolaji Idowu, following his consecration, Logos, Nigeria in 1975

After preaching in Perth we set out on the long and exacting journey across the country, preaching and speaking in every major city and meeting crowds of enthusiastic Methodists. We visited the North and South Islands of New Zealand and were entranced by the beauty of that strangely English country. One of the pleasant aspects of those weeks of travel was that many of the people with whom we stayed were members of the General Conference of the Methodist Church of Australia and so we caught up with them again at the Conference which was held in Sydney. It was an historic Conference – the last in the history of Australian Methodism. The Methodists were entering into union with the Presbyterians and the Congregationalists to form a new church. Excitingly, it was called 'The Uniting Church', indicating the hope of further movement towards wider unity in the future. The opening session of the Conference was held in the Sydney Opera House and there was a great sense of anticipation as the members addressed the theme 'Moving With Tomorrow'.

The venue for the Cato Lecture was a large modern hall known as the Willoughby Civic Centre. On arrival I was astonished to find a long queue of people waiting to get in. The Lecture was timed to last ninety minutes with a short break in the middle. It was entitled *When the Spirit Moves* and was a study of the work of the Holy Spirit in the past and in some of the movements in the modern world. It was later published by the Epworth Press in Britain. I have rarely addressed an audience that responded so magnificently. The following day we had to say farewell to the Conference. In thanking our hosts for overwhelming kindness I said, jokingly, 'You have given us everything but a didgeridoo.' Half-an-hour later a member appeared on the platform with one of these strange instruments. It was hand-painted and had been hurriedly purchased from a nearby emporium. An Aboriginal minister came forward and produced an impressive sound by blowing down the length of the tube. It made a magnificent send-off.

In the spring of 1976 my wife and I went on a tour of Caribbean Methodism, beginning in the little island of Antigua. It was from this place that Nathaniel Gilbert sailed for England in 1760. He was a distinguished lawyer and the purpose of his journey was to hear John Wesley preach. On his return he called his slaves together and, instead of addressing them from his balcony, he entertained them in his living room. He told them about the message of the Wesleys and they were converted. From Antigua Methodism spread across the Caribbean. We stayed with the President of the Conference, whose home on the top of the highest hill commanded a view of almost the whole of this beautiful island. I had one misfortune during our stay: I was riding what I thought was a friendly donkey when it suddenly threw me over its head. The main casualty was my spectacles case which was smashed.

The short hops in a small plane from one island to the next gave us wonderful views of the seabed. In Kingston, Jamaica, I preached on Easter Day in the Coke Memorial Church. It seats 2,000 and was packed, with many worshippers standing round the open windows unable to get in. The Governor General, the Most Honourable Florizel Glasspole and his wife were present and later entertained us in their home. In Nassau we stayed with Lady Freda Roberts, the widow of Sir George who had been the Speaker of the Parliament. Her palatial home overlooked the turquoise sea. My engagements included services and meetings with civic leaders. I addressed 1,700 students from a balcony at Queen's College and felt rather like the Pope giving his blessing, 'Urbi et Orbi'!

But the most enduring memories are of the days spent in Haiti. There we journeyed over rough, boulder-strewn tracks. At one point we saw a little shack half-buried under a huge rock that had crashed on to it; a family was still living in the other half. Everywhere we encountered desperate poverty. I spoke at open-air meetings at which donkeys, pigs, goats and chickens joined the congregation. Later we visited La Saline, an appalling slum built on a bog. The people lived in tiny hovels with no adequate sanitation and the stench was abominable. We were conducted around this squalid settlement by a courageous Methodist deaconess called Sister Paulette. She took us to see the medical centre built with money from the British Methodist Relief Fund. It was run by a little lady dressed all in white. They called her 'the angel of La Saline'. A small boy with bright eyes came up to us and asked if we would take him to England 'so that I can learn'. If only we could have responded with more than a smile.

Our most demanding assignment was a visit to an island called La Gonave. We left at 5.00 am in a small motor boat because the tides later in the day made the 3½ hour crossing dangerous. When we arrived off the island a man wearing a loincloth came out to meet us in a craft made from a hollowed-out tree trunk, and took us ashore one at a time. The people lived in small shacks built mainly on the beach. We spent the night in a concrete shed on a rough wire mattress. There was no glass in the windows and we were eaten alive by mosquitoes. The island is very arid and the water to make coffee was scooped from a muddy hole in the ground. The toilet was another hole in the ground. A relief agency had built a desalinisation plant to condense sea water for drinking, but I noticed that many of the glass panels were shattered and there was no-one to replace them. The Methodist minister from the mainland had built a stone water tank with his own hands; it had a padlock on the tap. I preached on Maundy Thursday in a little tin chapel. When we left at 4.30am on Good Friday dawn was breaking and the strains of 'There is a green hill far away' were drifting across the water from the congregation that had already gathered.

Back in Haiti we heard horrendous tales of the cruelty of the military regime. We passed the white palace, home of the infamous Papa Doc Duvalier, and later of his son. We stayed in a Methodist manse where the minister took us out into the hills to talk about some of the atrocities he had witnessed because he could not trust his servants not to betray him to the secret police. We have watched more recent developments in that unhappy island and hope that they presage a better future for a long-suffering people.

In 1978 I went to Argentina and Peru. I spent some days in the theological seminary in Buenos Aires where eight different denominations train men and women for the ministry. I learned a great deal about the problems of ordinary people living under another harsh military regime. Many people told me of loved ones who had 'disappeared' after they had publicly criticised the Government. Bishop Pagura, our local Methodist leader, took me to the large Methodist church in the centre of the city. This rambling building housed a counselling centre for drug addicts and alcoholics, a club for the lonely, a theatre group and other facilities: a fine demonstration of practical Christianity. Half the population of Argentina are crammed into that city and all the miseries of humankind abound there. The streets were filthy and full of potholes. I came across many lamas and was told that they are carriers of syphilis. Some young men have contracted the disease through sexual contact with them.

Boco, the Italian quarter of the city near the docks, was fascinating. Passing through a gate in a grim facade I was astonished to find myself in a quiet courtyard owned by the Methodist Church. Two elderly ladies welcomed me to their modest apartment. Their walls were covered with exquisite oil paintings each illuminated by an electric light. One of them showed me a treasured letter from her husband written shortly before he died and while she was away. It read, 'Come quickly for the sun does not shine when you are away.' They served me with lemonade and were vastly amused when, unable to speak their language, I thanked them in English, French and German.

The city cemetery filled me with dismay and disbelief. There the rich were buried in elaborate tombs arranged in streets. This city of the dead was in stark contrast to the squalid dwellings of the living poor.

Everywhere I preached the welcome was overwhelming and I got used to being kissed on the cheek – the customary salutation. After one of the services a group of refugees from Chile were waiting to see me. They were on hunger strike to draw attention to their plight. They had fled their own country because, as socialists, they were in danger from the harsh conservative regime there. I felt very sorry for these men with pale, tense faces. I accepted the document they handed to me and conveyed it to the Court of Human Rights in Geneva.

An interview had been arranged for me with the Minister of a newly-formed Government department on family life. On arrival at the entrance of the public building in which he worked I was asked for my passport. I had left it behind so I was immediately placed under armed guard. After an uncomfortable wait of twenty minutes I was taken through a series of locked doors and eventually into the Minister's office. He turned out to be a very friendly fellow and we talked at length about family planning and other matters. On leaving his office I had to ask a young man at the bus stop which bus I should catch. He insisted on going with me and paying my fare.

Every now and then as I travelled in Argentina someone would mention a group of offshore islands called the Malvinas. They all seemed to think that they belonged to them and looked upon Britain as an occupying power with no right to be there. I had not the slightest inkling that before long our two countries would be at war over the sovereignty of those isolated islands.

From Argentina I flew to Peru to share in a conference on evangelism in Lima, another great sprawling, shabby city where everything seemed to be falling down. I went straight to a modest hotel. Five minutes after arriving I received a telephone call directing me to take a taxi to the First Methodist Church. My caller said it would cost 70 soles. The hotel receptionist said it would cost 150; the taxi man charged 200. The church provided lunch and supper each day for the participants in the conference. The staple diet was rice with a little goat meat, washed down with Coca Cola, the water being unfit to drink. The toilet at the church was labelled 'Prohibe Piso' so I wondered what it was there for. When I returned to my hotel I discovered the world's most uncomfortable bed, and pillows that appeared to be stuffed with powdered concrete. I felt some sympathy for Jacob and understood why, with his head on a stone, he dreamed of a ladder stretching up to heaven. In spite of all these little inconveniences it was a privilege to meet many wonderful Methodists doing such marvellous work for God and the people on very slender resources.

In 1982 I spent two weeks in the Holy Land. Each evening my party of pilgrims met together to talk about all that we had seen and experienced during the day and to set it within its biblical context. I urged my companions not to be put off by the multiplicity of churches and mosques built over the sacred sites but to see them as evidence of age-long devotion. Neither should they be too concerned about precise locations but bear in mind the maxim: 'Here, or hereabouts, it happened.'

Every day was memorable but some aspects of our pilgrimage were outstandingly so. I preached to a very large congregation in the Garden Tomb. The song of the birds in the trees added to the joyous sound of human voices. On the Mount of Transfiguration we seemed in a strange way to be very near to heaven. We looked down upon the great stretching plain so long the strategic route between Egypt and Mesopotamia, Africa and Asia. It is called Armageddon, the place where, according to devout fancy, the last battle between good and evil will be fought. But that battle is being fought all the time in the hearts of men and women. As dusk fell a stork flapped its way lazily across the sky. 'Carrying a baby to Bethlehem,' ventured one of our number. Hour by hour the story of the life of Jesus became more meaningful as we nailed the articles of our creed to the floorboards of history.

In the spring of 1985 I was in America for a variety of engagements which included lectures to five hundred preachers. I took the opportunity to attend a service conducted by a negro preacher from the deep South. 'Let the people say Amen,' he boomed as he entered the pulpit, and from the large congregation there welled the sound of a grand 'Amen'. In his dramatic sermon he spoke of the danger of riches. His diamond ring flashed in the light as he drove home the point! He told us of a rich woman, the pile of whose carpet was two feet deep, and at this point he seized the pulpit microphone and proceeded to wade through the opulent pile of this imaginary carpet. He spoke movingly of how as a little boy he longed to be white, for was not the black sheep the bad sheep, and a black mark a bad mark, and to be blackballed to be cast out? As he moved to the climax of the sermon there was much audience participation. 'Yes, Sir, tell the story!' the congregation shouted. I wondered what the reaction would be back home if I tried the same method in Stoke Poges or some other quiet English town.

During a half-hour radio interview I was asked about the salaries of Methodist ministers in Britain (we call them stipends). It is a subject that always seems to fascinate the Americans. When I tell them that all our ministers are paid roughly the same they seem unable to believe it. 'Where is the incentive to move up?' they ask. They seem to believe that no minister would want to move from one job to another unless it meant an increase in salary. Big churches pay big money. I am grateful that in British Methodism it is not so. Parity of stipends removes some of the danger of false ambition and contributes to the sense of ministerial fellowship.

For some years the British Methodist Conference and the General Conference of the United Methodist Church in the USA have had a reciprocal arrangement whereby four American representatives sit in our Conference and we send four to theirs which meets every fourth year. I attended the Conference in Baltimore as one of the British representatives. The sessions were held in the vast auditorium of the Baltimore Civic Centre. I was not impressed by the way in which the business was conducted. An immense amount of time was spent on procedural wrangling and a process known as 'perfecting' resolutions. The Conference timetable ran seriously behind schedule and sittings continued till very late at night. Towards the end important issues were rushed through with scarcely any time for debate. Individual members of the church as well as church bodies can petition Conference. There were no less than 30,500 petitions which had to be screened by committees and then reported to the full assembly. It seemed to me like democracy run mad.

On an earlier occasion I had addressed the General Conference on the subject of homosexuality. I said that I thought they were in danger of instigating a witch-hunt among the clergy. On many subsequent visits to America I have met people who remembered this speech and quoted it with approval. Now in Baltimore there was renewed discussion focused on the question of whether the Conference should allow the admission of avowed practising homosexuals to the ordained ministry. In the end the Conference adopted by 525 votes to 442 a statement which included the words, 'Since the practice of homosexuality is incompatible with Christian teaching, self-avowed practising homosexuals are not to be accepted as candidates, ordained as ministers or appointed to serve in the United Methodist Church.' Following this vote chains of gay and lesbian supporters lined the galleries, unfurled a huge banner and sang quietly, 'We shall overcome . . . one day.' The issues that were debated will not go away.

A major engagement during this visit was the service at the Lovely Lane Church in Baltimore to celebrate 200 years of Methodism in the United States. The church was the setting for the famous Christmas Conference of 1784 when two of John Wesley's preachers, Francis Asbury and Thomas Coke, were consecrated bishops. This marked the

177

real beginning of American Methodism as an organised church. It has, of course, unlike the Mother Church in Britain, been episcopal ever since. When I arrived at 9.00am for the 9.30am service I discovered to my astonishment that all the approach roads were jammed with people and that the large building was already filled to suffocation. After the service we welcomed several outriders who had travelled on horseback along the routes taken by the early pioneers of Methodism in their country.

When I visited Germany I recorded in my diary the unpleasant experience of visiting the sites of two of the infamous concentration camps. In 1984 I went to Buchenwald (beech wood). It is as grey as hell. I went to lay a wreath in the cell once occupied by Pastor Paul Schneider who preached to his fellow-prisoners before he was murdered there along with several hundred thousands of others. I was accompanied by fifty youth leaders from all over Europe and there in the Valley of the Shadow of Death we dedicated ourselves anew to the tasks of peace. As we entered the gate through which so many passed never to return we all fell silent and a darkness descended on our souls. How could this foul brutality ever have been perpetrated? But then, one asks, who are those today who create the bloody obscenities of video nasties; and are those who take pleasure in watching them concentration camp commanders in embryo?

Two years later I had a similar experience when visiting the Mauthausen concentration camp. There is a huge quarry there in the area where prisoners were forced to work till they dropped with exhaustion. They were often shot by their cruel overseers. Reporting on this visit in the *Methodist Recorder* I wrote:

> The young man who showed us round the cells, the gas chambers and the furnaces spends his life telling the same terrible tale again and again. He does not seem to have gone mad – yet. Why do they spend money to preserve the evidence of the foulest crimes committed by large numbers of their fellow-countrymen during that shameful era when a nation was seduced by evil men whose light was darkness and whose weapon was torture? Is it a protracted attempt to purge a guilt that time cannot remove? Or is it that all who walk, stony-faced as we did, though these halls of death, may learn a lesson? And what lesson are we to learn?

Our silence was broken by a young German lad. He sounded shaken and ashamed. He said, 'You were right to make war on us, weren't you? We were evil. The American soldiers in their tanks who liberated the camp were our saviours.'

But this is what I was thinking: Thank God for every act of courage whether in war or peace. But the spirit of violence is a corrupting force of frightening potential. It can destroy reason. It can turn human beings into monsters.

I reflected that the liberation of the camp was not the last thing the Americans did. After they had dropped the bombs on Japan thousands died lingering deaths, a torture as bad as anything that happened up there on the hill called Mauthausen.

I concluded that violence, once unleashed, cannot be controlled or contained. I asked whether God has any way of stopping it except by persuading millions of his followers that they must renounce it altogether, as Jesus did.

I was thinking this as well: Jesus said, 'A city that is set on a hill cannot be hid.' But in truth it can be very effectively hidden (as Mauthausen up there on the hill was hidden), if enough Christians look the other way. Our journey to that place had taken us through glorious country and little villages with charming churches nestling beneath majestic mountains. No doubt while the devil's work was being done at the top of the hill the godly villagers were reading their Bibles, and saying their prayers, and making sure they kept politics out of the pulpit.

1985 was a particularly heavy year so far as overseas travel was concerned and included visits to Denmark and to Greece where I led a pilgrimage 'In the Steps of St Paul'. There were also two journeys of major importance. The first of these was to the Ivory Coast where I represented the British Methodist Conference at the ceremonies granting full autonomy to the Methodist Church in that country. I had to make a speech in French. The British Ambassador said that he could understand it!

The story of Methodism in the Ivory Coast is remarkable. About the turn of the century an evangelist from Liberia called the Prophet

Harris came to preach to the Ivorian people. Many were converted but the Government of the country, thinking that he was stirring up trouble, sent him packing. As he left he said, 'Wait for the man with the book.' William Platt, a British Methodist minister, heard about this and asked the Methodist Missionary Society to send him out. He arrived – 'the man with the book' – and did a great work in establishing the church in that corner of Africa. Now a community of 100,000, the Methodist Church of the Ivory Coast was being given its independence. There was a great rally in the football stadium in Ibadan. Miles of 'freedom cloth' had been printed and all the Methodists were colourfully arrayed in costumes made of this cloth. Dr Platt, who had served the United Bible Societies with great distinction, was there as a guest of honour. The President of the country, M. Hophouet-Boigny, was present on the platform and later summoned Dr Platt to his residence to invest him as a Commander of the National Order of the Ivory Coast.

The meals during the Conference were served under a large thatched canopy. I was relieved to see that all the water was served from blue bottles – until I saw a small black boy replenishing the water in the bottles from a bathful of brown liquid.

The greatest test of endurance was the ordination service. There were four ordinands and each gave a twenty minute testimony in French. The perspiration dripped from my face in a steady stream. A young missionary from England made the interesting comment that preaching was easier there than at home since everyone believed in God in some fashion. 'The problem here,' he said, 'is not faith but discipleship.'

My visit to China was different from all my other journeys in that I did not go on strictly church business. I received an invitation as President of the World Disarmament Campaign to attend a forum on 'Preserving World Peace' organised by the Chinese Association for International Understanding. My wife was invited to accompany me, and we went with several other WDC colleagues. The forum was held in Beijing and was attended by about 40 peace activists from all over the world. We learned a great deal from each other but at first our Chinese hosts were reluctant to speak. When, however, they brought in one of their leading economists to talk to us it was a different matter. He told us how the Russian pattern of communism had been adapted and declared that the imposition of a central agricultural policy made no sense in a country as huge and diverse as China.

On the first Saturday evening I told our hosts that I would like to attend a church service the following morning. In all seriousness they enquired, 'Do you want Christian or Catholic Church?' They intended no discourtesy but seemed to think that these were two different religions. We were motored to a large church that had been Methodist but was now non-denominational. The church was full and I spoke through an interpreter.

Mary and I went shopping in the crowded centre of Beijing. We felt entirely safe and experienced the greatest courtesy in all the shops. We visited the Great Wall and spent a day at a 'Children's Palace'. These establishments are educational centres to which young people go for a day of special activities. Each of us attending was allocated a child to escort us round. All the children were beautifully dressed and some of them presented a first-class theatre show. The young magician aged nine who produced bowls of goldfish from nowhere at all was a great hit. The children were taking part in a painting competition on the theme of peace. On our departure we tried to thank our little guides, and to our astonishment one of them said, 'Not at all!'

We stood for a long time in Tiananmen Square pondering the history and significance of this great country which is home to more than a quarter of the world's population. On one side of the Square is the Great Hall of the People where we were entertained to a banquet by the Vice-Premier of China. Over to our left was the tomb of Mao Tse-Tung with a queue of people waiting to gain entry to view his body. At the far end of this enormous area was the Gate of Heavenly Peace with its massive picture of Chairman Mao over the spot where he stood in 1949 before a million people to declare the foundation of the People's Republic of China. Behind us was the Chinese Museum. We toured this very large and quite admirable depository of Chinese history and tradition, tracing the rise and fall of the various dynasties. I realised that China has never known anything remotely approaching what we call democracy. We visited Beijing University and talked with some of the students there in a room near the library where Mao served as librarian for a time. We wondered how much longer they would put up with the rigidities and limitations on freedom imposed by the old regime and its elderly leaders. Not long afterwards, of course, there was the terrible massacre in the very Square where we had stood. It will be a long time yet before China develops a way of life consistent with the ideals of freedom which we hold dear. In the meantime there will continue to be abuses of human rights. The attitude of the world community of nations towards China will be very important for the future and everything should be done to keep open the channels of diplomatic and other relationships.

181

Mary and I meet the Vice-President of China, Bejing 1978

Every day of our visit was packed with interest and activity. We were driven round Beijing in a little bus, and at every crossroads the police gave us priority. Sometimes several hundred cyclists were held up to allow us to speed on our way. We were taken for a trip up the Yangtze River in Mao's own boat and saw the spot where he swam the two miles from one bank to the other to prove his virility. We climbed the steps to see the impressive memorial to Sun Yat Sen, the man who established the first Republic. He overthrew the Imperial House but failed to subdue the war lords. We visited a number of Buddhist temples; most of the monks looked very poor. I referred earlier to Bishop Ting. What a task confronts him and his fellow-Christians! We were told that the Christian community numbers about six million, though estimates vary enormously. Over against this one has to set the fact that there are perhaps twelve million Muslims and one hundred million Buddhists. For the rest the vast population of China has no religion involving the worship of God as we understand that term. There are, of course, quite strict ethical standards derived from the teaching of Confucius. The Christian Church is growing and I feel a deep admiration for those who carry the message of the gospel on their lips and in their lives.

For our longer journeys in China we travelled by train and plane. We visited Xian and viewed the astonishing terracotta warriors, some of them still being excavated. The poor Emperor Chin must have felt very insecure even in death to have so many dummy soldiers guarding his tomb. We went to the great commercial city of Shanghai and remembered Uncle Hugh, my mother's brother, who, as I recorded earlier, worked there for many years.

When I went to China I had one very human mission to execute. A friend of ours in the peace movement told me that years ago she had fallen in love with a Chinese student who was studying in London. They were intending to marry but he had returned home to fight in the war against Japan and they had lost touch. He was now living in Beijing and she had a telephone number. She asked if I would convey her greetings to him. It seemed a tall order in a city of 10 million people. I picked up an ancient telephone in the hotel where we were staying and dialled the number. A voice at the other end spoke in Chinese. I spoke in English – slowly and loudly as we tend to do when abroad. The voice at the other end said, 'I will come round.' Within half-an-hour a sleek, chauffeur-driven limousine drew up and out stepped a high-ranking government official. It was the wrong man. I was profuse in my apologies, but he responded most affably, saying that it was an honour to meet us and so on. He also said he would help to track down the man we wanted. By some magic he was able to do so and the real man came to see us. He had only recently married and showed us pictures of his little child. He still entertained a deep affection for our friend back in England and entrusted to us a lovely letter to her which we duly delivered.

The only part of our Chinese experience which was less than enjoyable was the food. Most of the time we could not identify the items on the plate and our stomachs rebelled against the strange invasions to which they were subject. But for the rest, there are abiding memories of so many things and so much kindness: images of a peaceful walk through an agricultural commune, an elderly sage with straw hat and wispy beard – a corner of a willow-pattern plate come to life – and, best of all, the smiling faces of thousands of children whose parents long for them a future of peace, a longing so intense that perhaps the God they do not know will accept it as a prayer.

On our journey home we stayed for several days in Hong Kong, visiting the Methodist community there. The whole place hums with ceaseless activity and is vibrant with life. We discussed the understandable fears of those who wait, some rather nervously, for the takeover of the reins of government by China.

Early in 1986 we went for a visit lasting several weeks to South Africa. It was one of the most searing experiences of our lives. The ostensible purpose of the visit was to celebrate the thirtieth anniversary of the founding of the Methodist Department of Christian Citizenship in that land. Actually that Department had arranged for us to visit every part of the Republic and for me to speak in support of those who were fighting apartheid.

My first appointment was in Soweto, he largest of the black townships. The Rev Austen Massey, the courageous leader of the Christian Citizenship Department, told us *en route* that there might only be a handful at our meeting because the police often broke up public assemblies. On arrival we found a hall packed with 450 mainly young people. They told me much about police harassment. One said, 'Minister, what do you think of our schools boycott?' They had been absenting themselves from school as a protest against the inferior standards of education offered to blacks as compared with those available to whites. I told them that I sympathised with them but I added, 'If you want to rule your own country in the future, it is important to remember that knowledge is power and, therefore, to stay away from school is to forfeit the chance you have, poor as that may be, to gain knowledge.' I was relieved to know that the boycott ended soon afterwards.

In the valuable briefing given to me by the Methodist Church Overseas Division I had been warned that, if I preached the gospel faithfully, I would meet opposition wherever I went. It proved to be true. I realised that apartheid was an evil concept that created division of every sort. We stayed in luxurious white homes in some of which we encountered the most vitriolic racial prejudice. We visited the slums of Crossroads and other places which made us weep. At Onfervacht, a large resettlement area, we were taken by the local Methodist minister to see the children's cemetery, a huge area on a barren hillside. Some of the headstones consisted of bits of old street signs. On one the arrow pointed to heaven. Each tiny grave had a bottle on it, symbolising the tears of the parents. We were seeing the unacceptable face of an intolerable system. I preached in affluent white churches where the minister would say, 'I wouldn't dare say what you have said, for if I did so, half my people would leave and take their money with them.' The opponents of sanctions applying their own sanctions to the church! I spoke in impressive white educational establishments and to the Divinity Faculty in Capetown

University. I preached in black churches all over the land and spoke at gatherings of ministers. The whole experience left us drained, but it was a tremendous encouragement to meet so many Christians, black and white, who were working for reconciliation and the introduction of democracy.

We met many of our fine Methodist Church leaders, like Stanley Mogoba, now the President of the Conference, and Bishop Peter Storey. The latter was at the time the minister of the Johannesburg Central Hall. I preached for him at a wonderful service attended by hundreds of people both black and white. I still recall the singing of the choir of a hundred voices and the peace candle, surrounded by barbed wire, that burned symbolically on the Lord's table.

We had a brief respite part way through our tour and spent several days in the Kruger National Park. In this area, which is the size of Wales, we saw every kind of wild animal. We nearly came to grief when an angry elephant charged towards our car. Our driver had had difficulty with the reverse gear, but happily on this occasion it worked!

Our journeys took us to the north of Namibia and its border with Angola. The sound of gunfire reached us from a mile or two away. It was there that we came upon a small Methodist chapel built of sticks and mud. There were no pews and the pulpit was made of bits of an old bedstead tied together with rope. We were told that when it rains the chapel collapses and has to be rebuilt. There had been no significant rainfall for seven years but on our 600-mile journey back to Wyndhoek, the capital, a tremendous thunderstorm broke. In no time the dry sandy river beds were rushing torrents and we had to make a diversion to avoid the floods. The local people seemed to think that we were rain gods.

On the evening of our last day in South Africa a press conference was arranged. A surprising number of representatives from press, radio and television were present. I was asked my views about sanctions and other controversial issues. One journalist asked if I would be reporting back to Mrs Thatcher. I did write to her on my return and she arranged a helpful interview with the man in the Foreign Office with responsibility for British policy towards South Africa.

The result of widespread reporting of this press conference was personally unhappy. The kind white folk who had allowed us to use their home as our headquarters – it was a palatial residence – took me to task. We had thought it courteous not to discuss politics with them while enjoying their hospitality. The conversation at the breakfast table before we left was quiet and polite, but they were obviously pained by what I had said publicly about their Government's apartheid policy. It was yet more evidence of the corrosive and divisive effect of that policy.

The Sunday after my return I preached in the Chapel of Eton College. Crossroads seemed a long way away.

In 1990 we had the unusual opportunity of spending two weeks in Oberammergau. I served as Free Church chaplain at the Ecumenical Centre in that lovely village while the famous Passion Play was being performed. My Anglican and Roman Catholic colleagues and I had to meet the coaches that came pouring in each afternoon bearing pilgrims from near and far, and invite them to a service of preparation before the play, followed by coffee. My wife washed up thousands of cups. Every other coach seemed to have half-a-dozen Methodists on board. Seeing a vaguely familiar face they would lean out and shout their greetings. No-one ever greeted my two friends. In the end they said, 'Do you know everyone in the world?' 'No,' I replied modestly, 'It's just that you are seeing the Methodist Connexion at work.'

In the same year we went to the Kennedy Space Centre in Florida and witnessed the launching of a space craft. The earth trembled as this mighty machine lifted off and we were thrilled as it presently became just a dot in the sky, racing off to climes unknown. While we were there we saw the magnificent film called *The Dream is Alive*. How easy it seems to be now to soar into the skies and admire the beauties of mother earth from a distance. How difficult to solve the problems that threaten that beauty and even the very existence of this beloved planet.

In Bulgaria in 1992 I witnessed something of the struggle of our small Methodist community in that country which has known much repression. I was present for the award of the Methodist Peace Prize to Pastor Beslov, the Methodist leader imprisoned over many years for his faith. He looked very frail and died not long afterwards. We later spent a whole day riding the tram round the rather shabby streets of Sofia. A ticket costs only about five pence. We attended a service in the Orthodox Cathedral, where I was told that many, even of the faithful, do not really understand the complex liturgy. A group of younger Orthodox clergy were in open rebellion against the conservative and reactionary leadership of their church. Outside the Cathedral a little man with a fiddle, which he scraped untunefully, led a poor brown bear muzzled and on a rope: a most unhappy spectacle. It is not easy to be a member of a small minority church in a land dominated by a national church which scarcely seems to notice the existence of other Christian communities.

In October 1994 the officers of the World Methodist Council met in Tallin, Estonia. On the first night of our stay we admired from our window a beautiful ship called the *Estonia* which was at anchor in the docks. Next morning the berth was empty and we heard the shocking news that the ship had gone down in the Baltic with the loss of over 900 lives. This terrible tragedy cast a pall of sadness over the nation and over our meetings. On the Sunday I had to preach to a congregation bowed down with grief.

The people of Estonia are no strangers to suffering. Years of Soviet domination have left their dismal marks even on the fabric of the city: decaying buildings and down-pipes that have rusted away. But our Methodist people are full of courage. We saw two wonderful new building projects which will not only be centres for worship but also of services of various kinds to the community. These modern Methodists stand squarely in the Wesley tradition.

As I have recalled all these people and places, and so many more which are excluded for want of space, I realise that I am indeed 'a marked man'. In all kinds of ways, recognised and unrecognised, I have been influenced: in the way I think and feel, in the manner of my response to different situations, in my ability to understand others, and in the convictions that have guided me.

Much of this varied experience has been the result of my being immersed in Methodism and Wesley's World Parish. I am, however, grateful that one can only be a true Methodist by being an ecumenist, and one open also to that secular ecumenism which is the world community of nations with its stresses and achievements, its politics and strivings after peace and justice. Thus I acknowledge an unpayable debt to Christians in traditions other than my own, and to the secular world which offers so much to educate the mind and challenge the human spirit.

Chapter Eight

WITHOUT PORTFOLIO

On 29 June 1984 I presented my last report to the Methodist Conference meeting in Wolverhampton – that of the Law and Polity Committee. It involved the moving of an innocuous resolution directing members to wear labels bearing their names. The decision to issue this direction had been made by the Conference of the year before and I had been instructed to prepare a simple Standing Order giving effect to it. To my astonishment Dr Peter Stephens came striding to the tribune to make a speech opposing this 'childish device'. He made the whole issue sound as important as a proposal to abolish the Lord's Prayer. In reply I said that it would surely make the Conference look a little foolish if it countermanded what had been decided the year before. For my part, of course, I didn't care a button what was decided. Dr Stephens' objection was upheld by a small majority.

The next morning I made my farewell speech to the Conference. Our dear children had risen very early and travelled to Wolverhampton to be present. I told them that I wished that they had arrived the night before in time to witness my near victory in the great name-tag debate! I could have wished to be defeated in a greater cause.

I inducted the Rev Brian Beck as my successor. He is a scholar of distinction and has brought great gifts to the leadership of the church both as Secretary and during his Presidential year (1993-4). There were presentations, gales of laughter and, against all the rules, much clapping and a standing ovation. I found it all very moving, but what delighted me most was that Mary was called to the platform, in recognition of our partnership in ministry to the church that we love. So, in a moment of time I, who had been a member of every one of the Connexional committees of the Methodist Church, ceased to be a member of practically all of them. I was also no longer a member of the Conference itself, a body that I had sought to serve in various capacities for nearly forty years. I was a 'minister without portfolio'.

This sudden release from official duties has not meant any lack of employment. Some of the journeys and engagements described in the previous chapter were already planned when I retired. Unlike some ministers I did not find that retirement left me with a sense of lostness; there was still so much to do. I think, though, that I would have been wise to take a complete break. This I failed to do and when I left the Westminster scene my diary was already fairly full for a further two years. The church has continued to make large demands of me and I have not been good at saying 'no'. Because I was for thirty years 'a Connexional man' my post-retirement ministry has been largely shaped by the invitations from near and far. I have been heard to remark that retirement is a job for a younger man!

Our grandchildren: Sophie, Kirsty and Chloe

I have often been asked the question, 'When are you going to retire?' I have never known quite how to reply. The questioner usually seems to imply that retirement means ceasing all work but there does not seem to be much point in living unless you can be useful. There have, of course, been some enhanced opportunities for leisure, though I do not think that I have exploited these as well as I might have done. I have enjoyed doing DIY jobs about the house and have also done a little work with stained glass. There is a list of hobbies that I would like to explore,

189

if ever there were time. Mary and I have been deeply grateful for more time together; because my work meant so much separation we resolved that in retirement we would travel together whenever that was possible, and this we have done. We have also enjoyed family holidays. Our three little granddaughters, born to Elizabeth, our younger daughter and her husband Alan, have brought great joy to the whole family. And anxiety, too. When Kirsty, the eldest of the grandchildren, was about nine months old she was stricken with meningitis. Her parents kept vigil by her bedside night and day. There came the day when we saw her smile again, and she made a wonderful recovery.

On leaving Croydon where we had lived for thirty years we moved to the seaside village of Rustington in West Sussex. We already knew the locality because friends of ours had allowed us to use their flat in the village from time to time. Urged on by them, we bought a small flat near theirs. Later we sold this and bought the house which we called 'Redcroft' after our first married home in Tonypandy. It was a splendid choice. Mary has always loved the sea and wanted to be within sight of it when we retired. My study looks out over the English Channel. The church, library and shops are conveniently near and the train takes us to London in an hour-and-a-half. Gatwick is only an hour away. In the next road stands the distinguished house where lived Sir Hubert Parry, the composer of the tune 'Jerusalem'. Felpham, where lived William Blake, is a few miles along the coast. He wrote those stirring words, 'And did those feet in ancient time?'

Certain fixed notions have guided me in retirement. One is that one should never get under the feet of one's successor. I take a poor view of ministers who interfere with those who follow them. Equally we have made it clear that when we attend the local church in Rustingdon our place is near the back of the congregation. Inevitably over the years we have come to know and love a great many local people and we have been glad to share in the pastoral work of the church, but it has always been with the knowledge and blessing of the minister and as a supplement to his work as the chief pastor of the flock.

I have greatly appreciated the privilege of preaching or presiding at one of the ordination services each year and have travelled to the Conference city for this purpose. I also continue to speak at the Methodist Peace Fellowship Conference meeting.

When I became a 'minister without portfolio' the Editor of the *Methodist Recorder*, Mr Michael Taylor, invited me to begin a series of monthly articles in that paper. I suggested as a title, 'Without Portfolio'. I did not imagine then that after twelve years it would still be going strong. After ten years the original title was dropped, having served its purpose. My only instruction was to 'write for the family reader'. I have valued this opportunity to write about a variety of issues and to share some of the adventures of a very full decade. Letters from readers continue to come in from every part of the UK, most of them full of warmth, with just occasionally a spirited objection to something I have written.

Looking back over these years of writing a monthly column I am intrigued to notice the kaleidoscopic variety of subjects on which I have sought to entertain and sometimes to challenge my readers. I have dealt with serious issues like the Irish situation, but since these are expertly dealt with in the paper's leading articles I have only handled them when I had a particular personal view to express.

In April 1995 I wrote about boxing:

> What is the matter with those people who are prepared to go in their thousands to witness spectacles that are more offensive than those of the Spanish bullring (where the human casualties, at least, are rare)?
>
> We are told that people get injured in other sports. Of course they do. They also get injured cooking chips at home. But those injuries are the result of regrettable accidents. In boxing, however, contestants are bound to injure each other because injury is of the essence of the game.
>
> And it is the brain that often suffers most, that marvellous and exquisite instrument with its unbelievably sensitive mechanism and creative capacity.
>
> Let's be clear, then. We are not talking about sport, we are talking about savagery. Moreover we are describing a rotten trade that prospers because it makes huge sums of money – blood money.

Some of my contributions have been in lighter vein. In April 1987 I wrote from hospital:

> With me falling asleep is a slow, gentle process, rather like taking the luggage lift from the fourth floor of the Westminster Central Hall down to the basement.
>
> But recently I went to sleep with a speed like that of the lift in the Empire State Building; a needle in the hand and a

191

plunge into darkness and total oblivion. My signature on a piece of paper had granted temporary lease of my body to a gifted surgeon. My stay in hospital was necessitated by a little local difficulty and I have made a good recovery. Having only missed one preaching appointment in over thirty years I have cause only for gratitude.

Meals, for those able to get as far, were served in the day room. By great good fortune I sat next to a delightful man who entertained the quaint notion that butter is not good for one. He regularly passed his small pats over to me, providing a much-needed supplement to the modest NHS menu.

The blood lady with her trolley full of test tubes was a bundle of bustling efficiency. I can't claim that my blood is of the same group as that of 'the precious lifeblood of the master spirits', but it's precious to me. So, when she had gone at me for the umpteenth time I said, 'I shall charge you for the next one.' Oddly enough, she never came again.

There were some choice spirits among my fellow-patients, many of them suffering with quiet, brave endurance, wired up to all the strange apparatus of modern medicine. One walked around with a drip-feed at the top of a long pole, a bit like Cleopatra. Another carried a little box with a flashing light similar to those which aeroplanes have on their wings: a cheerful chap sending out messages of hope.

Then there was the dear old man of 83, tall and dignified, though stripped of all the outward trappings of dignity. His wife came to see him, went home, took out her knitting, and died. He handed me a slip of paper on which he had written this simple shattering intimation, for he could not bring himself to speak. I put my arm around him and could not restrain my tears – I who looked so eagerly for the visits of my own wife who came with unfailing regularity.

This light-hearted description of a short sojourn in hospital does not convey the whole story. I had gone in for the very common prostate surgery. Subsequent analysis revealed that some of the cells removed were cancerous and I had to undergo daily radiotherapy for nearly seven weeks. At first I seemed to be doing well but then I began to feel ill. I did not miss any of my engagements but had almost to crawl to some of them. Even so, there were the humorous moments. One of the nurses who administered the daily treatment was a Methodist, and the week after I completed the course I was due to preach at the church she attended. I said, 'Next Sunday you will see me with my trousers on for a change.' The treatment was continued for several days too long and damaged the bowel, which has caused periodic difficulty since. I had to have a further small operation. However, the cancer was cured and for that I am very grateful. It was an experience that made me very aware of our mortality and the need to value each day as a gift from God.

It is strange that some of the more unusual themes on which I have written have provoked a most lively and interesting response. For example, I did a piece on Wesley's horse which produced quite a spate of correspondence. After all, I don't see why all the credit, humanly speaking, for the Methodist revival should go to John Wesley. Surely his long-suffering horse deserves a look-in? After a visit to France where we visited an oyster farm I described all that we saw. I was amazed to discover how many Methodists were interested in oysters!

It is said that some people are born with a silver spoon in their mouths. I must have been born with a pen in my hand. During the past eleven years I have continued to write articles for journals of one kind and another as well as sermon scripts by the score. I wrote a short life of Jabez Bunting, that intriguing character to whom I referred in Chapter Four. I also wrote a book called *What shall I cry?* – a look at some of the crucial social and moral issues of the day.

While I held representative office in the church I felt inhibited from joining a political party, though not from voicing my judgements on political issues. When I retired I felt free to join the Labour Party. I do not subscribe to all the positions taken by the Party nor do I believe that there are political solutions to every problem. I do hold, however, that socialist principles accord most nearly with the social inferences of the message and mission of Jesus Christ.

I have undertaken several new responsibilities in fields where I have not had much previous experience. I was astonished at my time of life to be invited to become the Chairman of the European Methodist Youth Council. This body calls together the full-time youth leaders of the Methodist Churches in Europe to discuss, and where possible co-ordinate, their work. Mary and I have travelled to many European cities and have come to know some of the very fine leaders of Methodist youth work on the Continent. They were very patient with my lack of knowledge of their languages. If I had my time over again I would try to gain proficiency in several European languages. It is only in French that I have any real grasp of the structure and pronunciation of the language.

On one occasion we travelled to East Germany for meetings, in the days before the demolition of the Berlin Wall, and the crossing of the border was made very unpleasant by the inquisition to which we were subjected. The return journey was hair-raising because one of our number was smuggling out papers relating to a young man who was seeking to escape to the West. Discovery could have meant imprisonment for our friend.

The largest new commitment which I have undertaken has been the Chairmanship of the Governors of Southlands College in Wimbledon. The College was established in 1872 and was set up to cater for Methodist women students; it began to admit men in 1965. It stands full square in the tradition of the Methodists who from the days of John Wesley have been involved in education. It has maintained consistently high standards both academically and in terms of its community life, and has sent many well-equipped people into the teaching profession.

When I was invited to take up this voluntary work in 1986 I thought that it would be a challenge and an opportunity to operate in a field in which up till then I had had little experience. I did not realise how absorbing the task would become. It was pleasant to renew my contact with a place I had known since the days when I used to lecture to the students on sex, marriage and the family. Then it was an exclusively female establishment with a fairly cosy Methodist atmosphere. Our elder daughter Susan received her training as a teacher there.

Recent years have seen great changes in the educational field and often bewildering switches in Government policy. The pace of change has accelerated during my period as Chairman of Governors. In 1975 when many colleges were either closing or merging with other establishments Southlands became one of the four partners in the Roehampton Institute of Higher Education (RIHE). The other three members of the Institute are Digby Stuart (Roman Catholic), Whitelands (Anglican) and Froebel Institute Colleges.

Our entry into this Federation was forced upon us by Government policy which was to combine smaller free-standing colleges in larger units. There are obvious advantages in this: shared resources and more comprehensive and diversified curriculum being the most immediately apparent. But there are also the negative aspects of federation; bigness is

194

not always a virtue, and the preservation of individual collegiate identity is not easy. Valuable traditions may be lost.

At first I was often puzzled by references to the Institute on the one hand and the Colleges on the other, and would point out that the former had no existence apart from the latter. Clearly there are difficulties in establishing the right relationships between the central government of a large institution and its constituent parts. It requires a great deal of patience and understanding, and the temperaments of the holders of the main offices of the organisation can make a substantial difference to the success or otherwise of the attempt to create a unity of fellowship and purpose. I believe that during my time there has been a steady growth of trust and co-operation. Many people have played their part in this and, in spite of cuts in Government funding and other frustrations, the future of the Institute is full of promise. The RIHE has been well served by its Rectors, first Dr Kevin Keohane and then by the present incumbent, Dr Stephen Holt, both brilliant men. The latter introduced a system whereby the Principals of the four Colleges became Pro-Rectors of the Institute, helping to ensure the full participation of the constituent parts in the central government of the whole.

The Institute has established a close relationship with Surrey University while at the same time striving towards university status for itself. There have been grave disappointments. A rash of new universities was created by elevating the status of polytechnics. Then, fearful of lowering the standards of university education – a fear fully justified – the Government imposed more stringent criteria on those applying to become universities. These new criteria included an increase in the number of completed PhDs required and the imposition of a three-year probationary period once the approved standard has been reached. It has been frustrating to be denied university status when it is widely recognised that the academic standards of the Institute are superior to those of some of the new universities. I have often wondered whether university status any longer represents a prize worth winning.

Soon after I became Chairman the point was reached when real questions were being asked about whether the Methodist Church should continue to sustain the work of the College. There were those who thought that the resources tied up in Wimbledon could be better deployed in educational work elsewhere in the Connexion. The difficulties of maintaining a Christian ethos within the College led some to feel that we might just as well leave it to the secular authorities.

Along with others I felt very strongly that it would be wrong to yield to pressure to abandon ship. We should be breaking faith both with the past and the future. My colleague, the Rev Christopher Hughes Smith, felt very keenly the responsibilities he carried as General Secretary of the Division of Education and Youth and the chief representative of the Trustees on the Southlands governing body. Discussions about the future of the College have been made more difficult and complex than they need have been by reason of a dual system of control. As mentioned earlier, we got rid of this in respect of local churches when the Methodist Church Bill was enacted. The College, however, has had to be responsible to two bodies: the Governors and the Trustees. The trusteeship of the College properties has been vested in the General Committee of the Division of Education and Youth. They have exercised their responsibilities with courage and wisdom, but it has not always been easy for Governors and Trustees to keep in step. There is the additional fact that the College is also responsible to the Roehampton Council, the governing body of the whole Institute.

In 1989 discussions had begun concerning the possibility of moving the Whitelands and Southlands Colleges on to the sites occupied by the Froebel and Digby Stuart Colleges which are next door to each other on Roehampton Lane. In many ways this proposal made sense. Our existing buildings were beginning to decay and there were no adequate financial resources available to refurbish them. The cost of bussing students round such a scattered campus was considerable in terms both of money and time. There were obvious potential advantages for the four parts of the Institute in being closer together.

In 1990 the firm of Vigers carried out a detailed feasibility study on the proposal to move Whitelands and Southlands to the Roehampton location. Estimates were provided of the value of the properties and detailed comments about every aspect of what would be involved in adopting a plan to sell up and rebuild. On 21 February 1991 the Southlands Governors registered the judgement that this was the right course to take.

The Methodist Conference of 1991 was apprised of the situation and passed the following resolution:

> The Conference welcomes the action of the President's
> Council in authorising the formation of an advisory group
> to consider the policy of Methodism concerning the future

of Southlands College and its relationship with the Roehampton Institute.

Having regard to the place of the College within the life of the church and its importance as a Methodist resource, Conference directs the General Secretary of the Division of Education and Youth upon appropriate consultation, to satisfy himself, before proceeding with any new arrangements, that any undertakings entered into on behalf of the church relating to the College and the Institute ensure that the Christian purposes of the foundation are fully secured, and in the event that this is not possible, to report to the Conference of 1992.

The Rev Chris Hughes Smith acted with great wisdom in setting up a small group under the leadership of Mr John Fox, formerly Chief Education Officer in Nottinghamshire, to provide us with an independent judgement. To my personal delight it supported the view taken by the Governors. It said:

The closure of Southlands College in the mid 70s would have been a cause of regret but it would have come as no surprise as so many Colleges of Education, both county and voluntary, were being closed at that time. But the closure of a college at this time of expansion in all aspects of higher education, including the training of teachers, would cause many questions to be asked about the church's commitment to higher education, and its true motives for withdrawing its assets. It is often said that we live in an age when the price of everything is known but not its value: the accusation could be levelled at the Methodist Church that its prime reason for closing Southlands was to gain control of the financial proceeds.

The Fox Report then went on to examine various options and concluded that the course already approved by the Governors was the right one to take.

From this point on we were plunged into a tremendously demanding programme of complex committee work presided over first by Bill Hart and then by his successor, Mr Mike Leigh. It has been a rewarding experience to work with these two Principals and with Janet

197

Dyson, the Deputy Principal. Their deep Christian faith and commitment to all that is finest in education has been an inspiration to us all. Their work has been enhanced by the support of a loyal staff. I have been particularly grateful to Jackie Macquisten, the Principal's secretary, whose imperturbable presence is a great comfort when we feel that we are about to drown in a sea of paper. The constant help and support of the Southlands trustees, led by Mr Roger Smith, has been beyond praise. One of them, Mr Barrie Hookins, who is also a Governor of the College, has given hours and days of his time making his professional skills freely available to us.

It has fallen to Mr Leigh to steer us through the complexities of planning the actual shape of the new College. Hour after hour we sat with architects and quantity surveyors; then the day came when we were able to see the scale model of the new building. There have been disappointing delays, the most serious of which was the failure of Laings, the purchasers of our site, to obtain planning permission from the Wandsworth Council to demolish the main Chapman building. I led a well-briefed delegation to plead for a reversal of this decision, and we were successful. Without that planning consent we could not have realised the full commercial value of the site. I laid the foundation stone of the new Southlands on 13 June 1996 – a gloriously sunny day. Our firm hope is to open the new College in September 1997.

Laying the foundation stone of the new Southlands College, 1996

198

One very happy feature of all this work has been the wonderful co-operation of our Roman Catholic friends at Digby Stuart College from whom we have purchased the land on which our new building will stand. Sister Bernadette Porter, the Principal of Digby Stuart and her colleague Sister Velda Lee have been helpful and encouraging in every possible way. We actually held a short service of dedication of the new site conducted by the President of the Methodist Conference, the Rev Brian Hoare, a few days before contracts had been exchanged! A less happy fact is that because so many of the Whitelands buildings are listed their selling price would not provide a sufficient sum to enable them to move. They, will, therefore, remain on their present site, geographically removed from the main centre of operations.

An important contribution to the life of the Institute is made by the three chaplains. The move to the Roehampton campus will facilitate an even closer relationship between them. It has been exciting to be involved in the planning of the chapel for the new College. The stained glass windows have been designed and executed by the Art Department of the Institute.

On one occasion when I was asked to address the religious group which meets regularly at Southlands I took note of the fact that the greater part of the time was taken up with the singing of choruses. When all three chaplains attended the Council I asked whether the general approach of students with a commitment to Christianity was of this rather circumscribed kind. The answer was 'Yes.' Our Methodist chaplain, the Rev Philip Richter, made the very helpful comment: 'We begin with them where they are and seek to lead them on to broader and deeper understandings of the faith?' Mr Richter's successor, the Rev Robert Jones, has entered the life of the College at a particularly exciting and demanding time. He will share our concern that the big move will not seriously disrupt the community life of the students.

The work of a college chaplain is no sinecure. He has no settled congregation. He ministers to a community that consists mainly of students with no commitment to the church. All the secular challenges faced by the established churches present themselves even more sharply in the world of higher education. But this very fact means that there are opportunities for adventurous and explorative ministry of the highest value.

I have enjoyed my close association with Southlands College and the Governors – a fine and supportive body of men and women. I have learned a great deal and been particularly grateful to some of the students who have served on the Board. There have been some lively debates in our meetings. Two issues which highlight the problems of serving a student community in the name of Methodism may be mentioned. Strong representations were made to the Governors to permit the installation of contraceptive slot machines on the campus. The student representatives argued that this would merely be in line with Government policy and an insurance against AIDS. I argued that if we granted permission this would send out the wrong signals. Some might feel that we were encouraging promiscuity. Anyhow, I suggested, contraceptives were available in chemists' shops. At first the Governors declined to grant the permission sought, but later, by a majority vote, reversed that decision. My subsequent enquiries revealed that the machines are little used.

The other issue was that of establishing a licensed bar, a facility already available in the other Colleges. As a total abstainer, I would prefer that people did not drink, but, of course, most students do, and some of our students were going out to public houses, not all of which were very desirable meeting places. Moreover, Wimbledon Common is not altogether safe after dark. A bar was set up under careful supervision. It is an attractive rendezvous and has not presented us with any problems.

One incidental bonus that has attached to my work at Southlands is that I have often travelled up to meetings with Sir Robert Boyd, a near neighbour. He is one of the world's leading space scientists and a man of humble Christian faith: a splendid combination. As he has talked to me about the marvels of the universe and tried in basic English to explain such simple matters as Einstein's theory of relativity, the car has seemed to expand and my mind has soared to worlds unknown.

These mind-bending conversations, and indeed the whole of the Southlands experience, have still further enriched for me the significance of the word 'connection'. To gain glimpses into the interconnectedness of the various subjects taught in the Institute has been an exciting experience. I have tried repeatedly to stress the connection between education and a Christian view of life and its purposes. At the stonelaying ceremony I said, 'I believe that academic excellence is very important and I rejoice in the attainments of the College and the Institute in this regard. But I do not attach any great value to that alone. I want to see us sending out into the community a constant stream of gifted, well-equipped men and women who know what they were educated for – to serve their fellows.' If that indeed is the result of all our labours and rich hopes, then Methodism will have been fully justified in ensuring the continuance of Southlands College.

EPILOGUE

For several years past I have carried two small stones in my cassock pocket. I often finger them as I stand in the pulpit before beginning to preach. One of these stones is from Michigan in the United States of America. It was given to me by a Methodist archaeologist following a service in the church which he attends. 'Put this in your pocket,' he said, 'it is four million years old and so it will remind you every Sunday that you are preaching to the infant church.'

As I have worked at this brief account of a busy lifetime as a Christian minister my small brown Michigan stone has given me a sense of perspective. The followers of Jesus may sometimes wish that they had been in at the beginning, sharing with the early apostles the risks and exhilaration of the opening years of the church's history. But what is a mere two thousand years compared with the vast stretches of time that lie behind us? We are still in the early stages of the Christian enterprise. And if the past be that long, what of the future? May we not look forward to what Michael Ramsey in a sublime phrase called 'the great Christian centuries to come'?

Some Christians may react impatiently to that assumption. They predict the imminent return of the Lord and the winding up of history, some going so far as to name the actual date – in view of the past history of millennial forecasts, surely a most foolhardy thing to do. Since all of those who have predicted our Lord's early return, including the first disciples, have been proved wrong, it seems not unreasonable to assume that God is in no hurry to bring the human story to an end and may intend history to run for some time yet, maybe for millions of years. In that case the church is still very much at the beginning of its work. I am perfectly happy to remain agnostic on all matters relating to the end except that it will be in the hands of God which, after all, is the only thing that matters.

This long perspective helps me not to be utterly cast down by the realisation that nearly all the great causes to which I have given my best endeavours remain dreams rather than goals attained: peace, justice, Christian unity, a society freed from racial and sexual prejudice, personal holiness. The shrinkage in church membership in this country which has gone on during the whole of my ministry leaves no room for complacency, but neither should it be cause for fussy anxiety as if everything depends on our efforts. The church has faced many crises in its history and has survived. It is required of us only that we be found faithful.

Some of my fellow-Christians dismiss talk of a long future on the grounds of the almost infinite capacity of human beings to make a mess of things. They point to a technology that has outstripped our moral ability to deal with it constructively and responsibly. If the human race does not commit global nuclear suicide, it is suggested, it will find some other way of hi-tech self-extermination.

It is at this point that I finger my other stone – a fragment of the Berlin Wall. It speaks to me of the moments when history springs one of its glorious surprises and humanity demonstrates a capacity for wisdom and an ability to bury old enmities.

Charles Wesley wrote:

> Yet when the work is done,
> The work is but begun.

That wonderful hymn is about the work of God in the human soul, but it can equally refer to the larger matter of his work in the world. It does sometimes appear as if, in opening up the Pandora's box of scientific inventiveness, we have let all kinds of evil run free, as in the original Greek myth. Yet now, as then, hope remains. There are those who believe that it is wrong to hope for a remade earth and a world order purified and redeemed. But I believe that such a hope is justified by the Christian faith. This planet which God has entrusted to us is precious in his sight. He has forever set his seal upon it by deigning to make it the scene of his incarnation. If its fate is of no concern to the One who made it, and the care of it and its peoples of no concern to the Christian, then what on earth has been the point of all the devoted labours of countless men and women who have spent their lives seeking justice, peace and the integrity of creation?

In the days when television was still very young it was customary to end the day's programmes with a religious epilogue. I remember going up to the centre of London late at night and sitting in a small studio facing a camera operated by remote control. It was a rather eerie sensation to see this little machine moving on its own. I was expected to deliver a few soothing words to those who might still be awake but who were presumably soon going to bed.

I shall attempt no such peaceful epilogue at the end of this brief account of one minister's life. In any case the tale is not yet ended. These ministerial meanderings end not with a full stop but with a semi-colon. The journey continues and I am still making new connections. I hope that this search for meaning still finds reflection in my preaching. I have tried not to dodge the difficult intellectual questions raised by the articles of the Christian faith. Since very often I can find no answer to these questions myself I have sometimes wondered about the wisdom of raising them. Yet I cannot escape the conviction that integrity demands such an approach. In some areas where in younger days I seemed confident I must now confess to being a Christian agnostic. The tragedies of life, especially the sufferings of others, have not robbed me of faith, but they have taken away any desire or ability to provide simplistic answers. Often I am unable to see the connection between things that happen and the love of God which I proclaim.

At the end of the day, however, it is not our own effort which is of greatest importance, but the hold of God upon us which matters. Towards the end of his life Jabez Bunting used to speak of his 'obstinate faith' – a faith that cannot be vanquished by doubt or failure. It is a gift which I covet and which God will not withhold.

APPENDIX

THE CONSTANTS AND THE
VARIABLES OF MINISTRY

(Pastoral Address to the Ministerial Session
of the Methodist Conference in Norwich, 1981)

As this year of fifty-three weeks draws peacefully towards its close I find myself with a considerable heap of ecclesiastical flotsam and jetsam. It lies on the study floor awaiting the compilation of a scrapbook. These rags and tatters of a Connexional odyssey contain service sheets, press cuttings and innumerable pictures of so many mayors that if all their chains were joined together, they would assuredly stretch six times round the dome of Westminster Central Hall.

The service sheets indicate that I have sung 'O for a Thousand Tongues' at least two hundred times: in great cathedrals and modest chapels, and occasionally in secular buildings of such surpassing ugliness that even a deathwatch beetle would give them the go-by. I sing it now with increased conviction, for one tongue is a singularly inadequate instrument to cope with the cataract of words required for a crowd-filled tour of the whole Connexion.

Now I am expected to utter yet more words. The first part of my task at any rate is easy. It is to express simple and heartfelt thanks to so many who have helped during the past swiftly-fleeting year. My colleagues on the platform, in the office and the Divisions, have performed duties as if they were delights. The District chairmen and their wives have opened their homes with the most gracious kindness. The Chairman's car has been a travelling class-meeting. My wife has shared in almost everything, for which I am profoundly grateful.

One of the things I have valued most has been the opportunity to meet and talk with the ministers. C. S. Lewis asserted that 'the proper study of shepherds is sheep, not (save accidentally) other shepherds'. Nevertheless what I now have to say mainly concerns the ministry. I am well aware that many of my predecessors have addressed this session on the subject of the ministry. I still recall with gratitude Colin Morris chasing the theme through a magic wood of words with incandescent glow-worms of godly insight hanging from every branch. My justification for walking over what some will regard as well-trodden ground is that many of the dilemmas and opportunities of the Church are mirrored in the changing face of the ministry.

My visit to Sark on Easter Monday will serve as a parable to illustrate the theme I wish briefly to explore. Our journey across the water in a force eight gale may not have been quite as hazardous as John Wesley's trans-Atlantic voyage, but we had no Moravians aboard to comfort us. On arrival we found ourselves in another world. We drove in a horse and trap to the Seigneur's house, where the chief representative of that friendly, feudal community bade us welcome. He talked much about 'the succession' and revealed a mind strongly affected by the tension between the changeless and the changing. The conversation sounded strangely ecclesiastical.

We are, I judge, about to enter upon an intensified debate about the ministry. In saying that I recognise that our own internal discussions continue unabated. I have been back through the Conference Agendas of the last twenty years. The exercise is a paper chase across acres of painstaking attempts to pin down the meaning of ministry. The chase will go on, but now the field is to be widened. The Covenanting Proposals require us once again to set our understandings alongside those of other Christian Communions. Temperature-raising terms like 'historic episcopate', 'apostolic succession', 'incorporation' and 'orders' will no doubt enliven our exchanges.

It is of the greatest importance to give full weight both to the fact of continuity and to the fact of discontinuity. A valid ministry depends upon a due recognition of both constants and variables.

Let us consider the variables first. The starting-point must be the recognition that Jesus laid down no specific pattern of ministry. Moreover the notion that any form of ministry in the modern world derives in unbroken succession from the first apostles is untenable. The first apostles were also the last, in that they and they alone were direct witnesses of what Jesus said and did; they and they alone were sent out by his earthly command. But by a long and complex process of historical development there came into being a diversity of ministries for the establishment and direction of the Church and its mission to the world. The New Testament provides no ground for the canonisation of any particular form of ministry, but gives freedom to the people of God to develop ministries suited to the changing tasks of a Church set in a changing world. The apostolic succession is that of the whole Church prosecuting the Christian mission in obedience to the faith once and for all delivered to those whom Christ sent out into all the world.

What, then, is the origin of the ordained ministry as distinct from the laity? The answer is to be found in the incontrovertible fact that in any community of people there must be some who are called or appointed to lead. In the preface to the Examination in the Methodist Ordinal it is stated that ministers are 'to lead God's people in worship and prayer'. Clause 30 of the Deed of Union declares that those ordained 'have a principal and directing' part in the life and mission of the Church. We may wriggle and squirm as we try to escape from the awesome challenge of all that is implied by that, but the minister is called to lead. We will return to this central concept in a moment.

But let us pursue further the element of variableness in ministry. Hans Küng in his essay entitled 'Why Priests?' sets out to do a fairly thorough demolition job on some of the established positions of his own Catholic tradition. I refer briefly to four of his assertions, two of which you will find it easy to accept, and two of which may run counter to your own experience.

1. The ministry, he asserts, is not necessarily celibate. Clerical celibacy is a mediaeval interpolation which must be abandoned in order that the Church may repossess the liberty which the New Testament allows. It is an argument that seems self-evident to us. Lest, however, we sound too complacent, we might give more weight than we customarily do to the value of ministerial celibacy undertaken by some as a special vocation. You will forgive me for observing that the Stationing Committee must often feel when faced with an intractable problem: 'If only our dear brother had remained celibate, how much easier life would be.'

2. Again, Küng argues that the ministry is not necessarily exclusively masculine. We need no convincing on the point, though there was a day when we did. It took thirty years for this Conference to make up its mind to admit women to the ministry, and only in the last of those years was the delay the result of the fear of damaging our relations with the Anglicans. That should perhaps enable us to look with sympathy at the continuing struggles of the Church of England with the same question. We may humbly hope that if

Covenanting brings the Churches closer together, a nearer view of women ministers serving God effectually and devotedly will accelerate progress towards inevitable change in the Church of England.

3. The next assertion is that the ministry need not be full-time, and in support of this Küng points out that St Paul was a part-time minister. As a statement about the way the ministry functions that is a useful reminder that we must beware of binding ourselves to stereotyped patterns of ministry. Within Methodism we are aware of the problem of breaking out of the self-imposed rigidities of a system which is the product of a purely functional theology of ministry. Surely, however, our own experimental theology asserts that a purely functional view of ministry is inadequate. If we send a minister to serve in some important educational post, we do not thereby turn him into a part-time minister, any more than when you put me into John Wesley's Chair you made me a part-time husband. It is true you separated me from my own bed and board for unconscionably long periods, but I have been a husband all the time.

4. It is Küng's fourth assertion which appears to conflict most sharply with my own experience and with the Methodist understanding of ministry, for he declares that it is not necessarily for life. Now I can find nothing in the ordination service or in CPD that insists that the vows taken are for life, though I note that our representatives on the Roman Catholic/Methodist Committee state that the person ordained is 'commissioned to a lifelong ministry'. I believe that to be true. Of course, ministers do resign. If one asks what then happens to their ministerial orders, the usual answer is that they are held in suspense but not destroyed: witness the fact that if they return they are not ordained again. It is a somewhat academic line of argument. It does perhaps more closely accord with the facts of life to say that ordination to the holy ministry is,

like marriage, for life; but God in his mercy does release those for whom the keeping of the vows has become impossible. Perhaps when a man is restored to the ministry we ought to ask him to engage again in that part of the ordination service which contains his response to what God, who never breaks his vows, does once and for all.

I turn from these brief reflections on the discontinuities and variables of ministry to the elements which remain constant. I refer to three:

The minister is . . . pre-eminently the servant

I do not apologise for returning briefly to the theme of my address to the Representative Session of the Sheffield Conference for it sums up so much of what I believe about the Church and its ministry.

In the secular world there are different patterns of leadership and concepts change with the changing years. When I visited the Navy I was privileged to hear an illustrated lecture about the establishment I was to tour. The young, well-educated officer said, 'Don't hesitate to interrupt me with a question, Sir.' At one point he began to talk about leadership. I broke in to say, 'That's a subject which interests me. I myself believe in a consultative style of leadership.' 'Beg to differ, Sir,' came the prompt rejoinder. 'In the Navy, issue a command; result – quick and unquestioning obedience. That's leadership, Sir.'

Maybe, but not the leadership which characterises the Christian ministry. Ministerial orders are not the orders which the minister gives, but which he receives. And incidentally let us not make heavy weather of the word 'order' as applied to ministry. We use it in connection with our Wesley deaconesses. I should see no inherent difficulty in referring to an order of superintendents or of chairmen. They are, after all, under orders, Standing Orders, and different orders appropriate to their particular responsibilities.

I need say little about the burdensome nature of this high calling to lowliness. The secular world will seek constantly to distort our ministry by placing more emphasis on our status than our sanctity. A Presidential year is not a bad test of the ministerial vocation. It is not easy to be a washer of feet when the kitchen staff insist on treating you like the head waiter. The safeguard is the confessional where our true self is seen stripped of transient trappings, and from which I emerge under the judgment of him who was a man of sorrows and acquainted with grief.

The minister is . . . the Church's representative

But is it not the business of the whole Church to represent Christ to the world; is not the Church indeed Christ's body? Yes, but how shall the members know what that involves and be trained to do it? The answer is that the ministers are chosen and appointed to be the trainers, the enablers, the exemplars. It is to this task that Christ calls, and he calls through the Church which itself tests and validates the call.

In an odd way the secular world, with a kind of unconscious discernment, will not allow us to explain away or escape from our representative role. Let the minister commit some sin that in a circuit steward would almost be regarded as establishing his normality, and the press will, given half a chance, hang the dirty linen from the clothes-line of a heartless headline. Down the centuries the minister has been the representative man.

The minister is . . . the custodian of the apostolic tradition

John Wesley's views on the apostolic succession underwent an interesting change. His diary for 1746 records that while riding on his horse to Bristol he read Lord King's 'Account of the Primitive Church'. He says, 'In spite of the vehement prejudice of my education, I was ready to believe that this was a fair and impartial draught.' He concluded that the claim of bishops to stand in an uninterrupted succession from the Apostles, secured by the imposition of hands, was a myth.

We have perhaps been so keen to quote our father in God on this point that we have failed to recognise the great importance of continuity in the faith. In fact within the comparatively narrow compass of our own Methodism we lay great stress on the tradition. Have we not recently raised a memorial in London to Wesley's conversion? Do we not always hand the Field Bible to the man who sits in Wesley's Chair?

Incidentally, my heart warmed to the dear layman I met in this District who told me he was at the Sheffield Conference. When we had all gone home on the first day, he crept back into the hall and sat in Wesley's Chair. 'It was still warm,' he said, which caused me no surprise. I hadn't the heart to tell him that Wesley never sat in this chair. The genuine article is in the house in City Road.

But Methodists believe in the succession and find ways of symbolising it. How much more then should we seek to stand consciously in the apostolic tradition as received by the whole Church of Christ. The necessity to do this is laid upon us by the fact that there is no Christ of experience without the Jesus of history. Without the past the present has no meaning. The more rapid and far-reaching the changes in the world, the more essential becomes the preservation of that vital continuity with the apostolic witness to the Jesus who cannot be known in the present unless he is comprehended in the past.

It is in the light of all this that we are asked in the Covenanting Proposals to recognise the value of the threefold order of ministry with its deep and long-established roots in the history of the Catholic Church. Just as the marriage of two believers both signifies 'the mystical union that is betwixt Christ and his Church' and helps to secure it; so also the acceptance of the historic order of ministry both signifies and helps to secure faithfulness in and to the apostolic tradition. But let us note that the threefold order is itself an evolving one. Methodism is free to create a form of episcopacy best suited to its ethos; and as for the diaconate, that seems to be a matter under discussion just now in all the Churches.

Lest all or any of this should sound somewhat removed from the world with its hungry-hearted hopes and apocalyptic fears, I end by reminding you that the apostolic tradition is a tradition of service to the world.

I believe with you that the message of the gospel is to the heart and soul of every man. It is the good news of salvation. But for what are we saved? It is for the service of the world in all the variety of its pressing needs. A Church that has nothing to say to the unemployed, to the Brixton community, to an appetite-ridden society and the politicians who legislate for it, is a Church which has nothing to say.

And a Church which has no clear word to say to the post-Hiroshima age which faces, for the first time in history, the threat of global annihilation, is a Church with about as much relevance as a water pistol has to a forest fire. It surely can be no accident of history that the emergence of the Church as a truly supranational community coincides with the age when division between the nations could mean ultimate disaster. I say it is no accident, and we must wrestle with the implications of that.

The service of the minister is set within a Church which is called to serve the world. To which the only fitting response that we can make is:

> Lord have mercy upon us.
> Christ have mercy upon us.
> Lord have mercy upon us.